In loving memory of
HENRY PAOLUCCI, Ph.D. (1922–1999)

Portrait by Constance Del Vecchio Maltese

For details on the life of Dr. Henry Paolucci, see pages 34–35

In loving memory of
COMM. ANNE ATTURA PAOLUCCI, Ph.D. (1926–2012)

Portrait by Constance Del Vecchio Maltese

For details on the life of Dr. Anne Paolucci, see pages 222–24

HENRY PAOLUCCI

A CONSERVATIVE VOICE FOR ALL SEASONS

NARRATED BY

ANNE PAOLUCCI

THE HENRY AND ANNE PAOLUCCI FUND

The Intercollegiate Studies Institute (ISI) is a nonprofit educational organization that works to inspire college students to discover, embrace, and advance the principles and virtues that make America free and prosperous. ISI is proud to preserve and advance the considerable scholarly, civic, and cultural achievements of Henry and Anne Paolucci.

Through the Henry and Anne Paolucci Fund, ISI continues the Paoluccis' most important projects, including:

The Henry Paolucci/Walter Bagehot Book Award
Each year, ISI honors an important book that embodies the spirit, range, and scholarly rigor of the award's namesakes. The winning author receives a cash prize of $5,000.

The Council on National Literatures
Founded by Dr. Anne Paolucci, the Council on National Literatures has long provided a forum for the comparative study of established, emergent, and neglected national literatures. ISI will continue this work by sponsoring lectures, conferences, and prizes for scholars working in this field.

Griffon House Publications and the Bagehot Council
ISI will continue to distribute and promote the publications of Griffon House and the Walter Bagehot Research Council on National Sovereignty to ensure that these important works remain available to students and scholars.

www.isi.org

CONTENTS

This book is dedicated to

TED DABROWSKI

AND

FRANK D. GRANDE *D.PHIL(OXON)*

both of whom took on the challenge with Henry, each in his own way.

PREFACE

Much remains to be written about the Conservative Party of New York State, founded in 1962 — especially about the cataclysmic events of the 60s and 70s, when the Conservatives challenged the state liberal establishment, headed by Nelson Rockefeller, and were the prime factor in derailing the political ambitions of John V. Lindsay, Kenneth Keating, Jacob Javits, and Rockefeller himself.

In writing about her husband's commitment to conservative principles and his multifaceted activities in promoting the conservative way of life, Anne Paolucci has accomplished a long awaited feat and has provided the conservative community, as well as the general public, with an accurate and important account of the stellar role Professor Henry Paolucci played within the Conservative Party in its formative stages, especially his dramatic decision to lead the Party ticket as their candidate for U.S. Senate in 1964.

She comes to the task eminently prepared. A seasoned writer (award-winning poet, playwright and literary critic), she is internationally known for her work in multicomparative literary studies, drama and dramatic theory, and for her two critical studies on the plays of Edward Albee — penetrating analyses that have been praised publicly by Mr. Albee himself.

Utilizing her unique advantage as Henry's life partner and professional colleague, Anne Paolucci has brought together in a creative and memorable mosaic, letters, Op Ed articles, exchanges with prominent colleagues and friends, talk show interviews, and other material not easily found anywhere else, a good deal of it from the Paoluccis' personal files.

She begins with the early efforts of Ted Dabrowski to give Henry the exposure he deserved as a leading intellectual conservative. After Dabrowski's untimely death in 1972, the job of promoting Henry was taken on by Frank D. Grande. a younger colleague. The work of these two men was all-important in introducing Henry Paolucci to the community at large by means of such publications as the monthly newsletter *State of the Nation* (1969-1980). The formation of Griffon House Publications provided the publishing medium for *SN* and other writings by Henry. A non-profit organization, The Walter Bagehot Research Council on National Sovereignty, was formed to invite donations to support this work. I was especially pleased to see Ted Dabrowski remembered in a separate chapter. He was my friend, mentor, and predecessor as Queens County Chairman and state Vice-Chairman. His death was a great personal loss for me.

Anne Paolucci has rightly focused on these beginnings in the early chapters that follow and has in fact dedicated the work to these two enterprising men, who were the first to promote Henry Paolucci and bring him to the attention of the general public. Her account is especially timely, since this year marks the 50th anniversary of the founding of the NYS Conservative Party.

The chapter on Bill Buckley speaks for itself. From her unique vantage point, Anne provides a rare insight into the relationship these two intellectual giants enjoyed.

As a political buff, I especially appreciate the pertinent clippings and letters included as archival material at the end of chapters. They are a welcome addition to the historical perspective and give the reader a "you are there" feeling.

I have long been among those who have urged Anne to gather her memories, notes, and papers to write this book about Henry — necessary not only for its historical and archival value but also to preserve his memory among his many friends and colleagues.

My wife Constance owes her portraits of the Renaissance navigators and her work during the Columbus quincentenary to Henry's prodding. He found books for her to consult, gave her brief "lectures" on subjects she asked about and followed her work with tremendous interest.

The four state chairmen who have headed the Conservative Party — Kieran O'Doherty, J. Daniel Mahoney, myself and Michael R. Long (who still serves in that capacity), all relied on Henry Paolucci for sage counsel and advice. But I know I speak for all conservatives when I say that we also owe a great debt of gratitude to Anne Paolucci for this excellent review of her husband's life as a conservative leader.

Serphin R. Maltese
Former Chairman, NYS Conservative Party
Former NYS Senator (1988-2008)

HENRY PAOLUCCI

A CONSERVATIVE VOICE FOR ALL SEASONS

1. *INTRODUCTION: THE CHILD, FATHER OF THE MAN*

Several decades have passed since the general election of 1964. New York State was in the limelight during the hectic months prior to the election, after the state Republican Party refused to allow the recently established Conservative Party of New York State to include on their ticket the Republican nominee for president, Senator Barry Goldwater.

Those were exciting and unpredictable days, especially when the Conservative Party responded to the decision of the Republican leaders by refusing, in turn, to back Kenneth Keating, the Republican incumbent who was seeking re-election, and chose instead Henry Paolucci as their senatorial candidate. What Henry brought to that campaign was a clear assessment of the political scenario, a willingness to be put forward as an effective speaker who drew kudos even from the opposition but had no illusions about the outcome, a man willing to sacrifice his time in order to make an impact for what he considered to be a worthy cause.

He took the opportunity also, as a thinker and an effective spokesman for the conservative cause, to articulate whenever possible his views on domestic and foreign policy.

Following that sudden thrust into notoriety, Henry returned to his teaching and writing, resuming the life he loved best, until his death on January 1st, 1999. He left behind dozens of unfinished manuscripts on the ideas and subjects he had pursued intellectually all his life, particularly, long detailed assessments of authors he particularly favored — Hegel, Dante, Polybius, Machiavelli, St. Augustine, Aristotle, James Thomson etc. — as well as portions of novels and plays, some typed and some handwritten on whatever scraps of paper were at hand. His imagination knew no bounds. Unfortunately, except for some lecture notes, none of those intriguing projects were brought to conclusion.

He did not enjoy social functions but always welcomed friends and colleagues who sought him out, especially members of the Conservative Party. Always accessible, he spent many hours on the phone listening to ideas, strategies, complaints: the magician who put things right. Bill Buckley — who knew him pretty well by the time Henry ran against Bobby Kennedy and Kenneth Keating and continued into the 1990s to pick his brain for information and articles for *National Review* — dubbed him "the conscience of the Party."

I was often urged to write something that would preserve those exciting days when my husband decided to take a public stand and make his voice heard on behalf of the conservative cause and the Conservative Party. For a long time, I resisted the urging, knowing that Henry would have said: *forget it.* He was a born teacher who enjoyed the role, an effective speaker who knew how to hold an audience; but by nature, he was a modest man. He made no conscious effort at self-aggrandizement and, although he had plenty to offer a wide audience, he never approached publishers. Others did it for him. His first full-length book on a political subject, *War, Peace, and the Presidency,* was published only because a friend, Robert Rosenbaum, who lived a few blocks away from us near Columbia University, knew some editors at McGraw Hill and showed them the manuscript. Over the years, other titles were brought to the attention of commercial and trade publishers and have appeared in print. I myself edited and Griffon House Publications has issued since his death over a dozen or more reprints or new titles from material in his files.

In Henry's eyes, his life was nothing extraordinary; he would have been embarrassed to have someone write about it or single him out as "special." Nor had he political ambitions or a need for the kind of fueling that would pump up his ego. He had the self-assuredness that came with having honed his talents and used them well. As a scholar and teacher, he had ample opportunity to follow his intellectual interests. It was all he had ever wanted. Had he been alive he surely would have discouraged my intention to pick up the challenge: What was there to write about? He was just doing his job. . . .

For I finally did come around — not to writing a biography (a task I'll never be ready to tackle) but to providing a brief review of Henry's contribution to the conservative cause. At first I had misgivings, knowing that Henry would have objected to my decision; but I felt there was enough historical and archival value in his activities, especially between 1960 and 1980 — a period when Henry joined forces with other conservatives as part of an historic movement — to warrant attention and worth preserving.

He assumed his public *persona* with the confidence that comes with a profound understanding of philosophy, literature, astronomy, history and law. He was perfectly "at home" in the life of thought (a phrase I did not really understand until I got to know him).

I had just graduated from Barnard College when I met him.

One of my college professors, to whom I had gone for advice about graduate school, had responded without a moment's hesitation: "You must take Professor Bigongiari's course!" I soon discovered that the man with that name was a legend on the Columbia campus. A graduate of what was then Columbia College (1904), Professor Dino Bigongiari had begun his career teaching Greek at the College, but over the years he had risen to the top of the profession, recognized for his proficiency in several ancient and modern languages and for his profound knowledge in a number of disciplines. He had, in fact, taught in several different departments within the University, recognized as Columbia's greatest scholar, the most learned man on campus. When I went for an interview, he was Chairman of the Italian Department, where his extensive knowledge of the ancient and medieval world was being offered in a graduate course: "Dante and Medieval Culture." My interview resulted in a generous grant (*manna* from heaven!), and I immediately signed up for the Dante course.

Henry had already taken the course for credit but had returned to "audit." He had, in fact, become a fixture in the classroom, the one to whom Bigongiari seemed to address his hardest questions, the one who knew all the answers.

I couldn't help noticing the intense young man who responded readily to whatever Bigongiari tossed out and who wasn't shy about adding his own comments. I realized with amazement during that first semester that he knew in fact more than the rest of us put together, and that Bigongiari deliberately prodded him to participate in order to nudge the rest of us into some kind of intelligent response.

He had been fortunate enough to have had others instill in him at an early age a love for knowledge and the written word. Louis Paolucci, the second oldest of the family's five children, a self-educated man, was Henry's first unofficial mentor and guide. A sensitive man with a poetic strain, an eclectic approach to reading, and dozens of books to fall back on for quotations to support his views, Louis had refused to submit to the regimen of college courses, the rules and regulations students have to follow; would not bend to others who thought they could direct his intellectual life. For him, getting a degree was a waste of time. His only compromise was a brief sojourn on the Columbia University campus as librarian of the Paterno Collection, housed in the Casa Italiana. The job gave him a great deal of spare time in which to read and write. He enjoyed the peace and quiet of the beautiful Renaissance *salon* on the main floor of a building that was a replica of a Florentine *palazzo*. He would no doubt have stayed on, except for an administrative decision to combine the Paterno holdings with the larger collections in the main library in Butler Hall and to turn the beautiful Italian *salon* into classrooms.

Ironically, Louis himself was a great teacher. He found a ready audience in his two sisters and two brothers, especially in Henry, the youngest of the family, eight years his junior. Later, the "student" surpassed the "mentor," but Henry retained a deep respect for his somewhat eccentric older brother, who, like their father was a self-educated man with an intrinsic sense of what was worth pursuing and what wasn't.

By example, Louis impressed upon Henry the power of words, the importance of logic and how to best present an argument; of being able to support what you had to say by citing others with similar views. He would read out loud to Henry passages from his favorite authors, especially his favorite poems, often reciting them from memory. Years later, Henry convinced him to collect a number of his poems in a slim volume. The only other works he ever published were a long poetic/analytical critique of current political events of the time, *Nixon and the Foxes of Watergate*, and some articles under the pseudonym Aldebaran — his interest in politics having been sparked by Henry's sudden appearance in the political arena.

Eager to share the things that animated and excited his brother, Henry was ready to listen to whatever Louis had to say. He was an excellent audience; but by the time he reached high school, he was his own master. His brother's unofficial mentoring had given him a clear edge on other students and some of his teachers as well. By then he could recite long passages from many of the English poets, as well as passages from the *Divine Comedy* and Leopardi; had read and assimilated the writings of Schopenhauer and Emmanuel Kant, empirical philosophers like Bertrand Russell and pragmatists like William James, in whose writings Henry found buttressing for his own views. Like James, he too was offended by Rousseau's easy optimism of "unalloyed happiness," especially after reading the excerpts James had quoted from the dark poem that echoed Henry's own deep-rooted pessimism, James Thomson's *City of Dreadful Night*, a Dantesque rendition of what St. Augustine called The City of Man, a godless modern Hell on earth. Only later did he recall that James had also written:

> Pessimism is essentially a religious disease. In the form of it to which you are most liable, it consists in nothing but a religious demand to which there comes no normal religious reply.

James' conclusion is either to give up the religious demand or accept a non-religious answer.

Henry understood those words only too well. His father, Donato Paolucci, came from a long line of stern men who professed to be atheists and agnostics and had instilled those beliefs in their sons and grandsons. Louis had launched Henry on his intellectual journey in life; but Donato instilled in him his stoic attitude, a sense of pride of honor and respect, and a rigorous commitment to family loyalty — the non-religious values that ruled his life.

Donato had left Colle Sannito, his native village in the hills near Benevento, at the age of twelve, and with his father had joined friends and others from that area who had settled in Newark, New Jersey. His first job was as "waterboy" on the Baltimore and Ohio Railroad; but before long he was apprenticed to a master carpenter, a trade that worked for him in good stead, especially during the Depression.

At some point, relatives and friends arranged for him to marry Annunciata (later, Americanized into "Nancy") Petriella, a pretty girl from Circello, the next village, walking distance from Colle Sannito. The young girl remembered the boy she used to play with back in the village but initially was reluctant to leave her people and sail to America. She finally agreed, won over by her uncles "Charlie" and "Louie," who were earning good money as sought-after stone masons, responsible for many of the beautiful carved facades of public buildings and churches like St. John the Divine. They spoke well of the Paoluccis, who were part of their community, and were hard workers.

Henry was the last and unexpected addition to the family. His name was chosen by the other children, all of whom had been christened with Italian names (which in due course had undergone translation and abbreviation). Why they chose that particular name, insisting on the English version (not the Italian "Enrico") has never been explained.

Henry left behind a long hand-written account of his family, in which he describes his "fierce-looking" grandfather, whom Donato resembled in many ways. His own father is described in a much kinder light.

> Not passions, but duty governed his behavior, as it had governed his father's existence. . . . "His father," my mother used to say, "was severe," and here she would raise her hand, palm facing us, to indicate that the old man's scowl called an immediate halt to things. . . . My father followed the same line. . . . My mother had to shield us, she always felt, from his justice, . . . temper it with mercy.

> But if duty governed [my father's] conduct . . . behind his brow and in his heart was a profoundly tender love of music. He had studied the violin for a brief time and then learned to play the mandolin. His educative influence was most strongly felt by us in the early years through his playing, usually in the twilight hours or at night with a dim light that gave the effect of twilight. Long before I had learned a Chopin nocturne, I had felt the beauty of a "little night music." When I first read those verses of the poet who was soon to take possession of me —

> > And then with the delicate tender fantastic dreamer of night
> > Whose splendour is starlight splendour and his light a mystic
> > moonlight,
> > Nocturn on nocturn dreaming while the mind floats far
> > in the haze
> > And the dusk and the shadow and gleaming of a realm that
> > has no days. . . .

> — I linked those verses emotionally with the mood of my father's mandolin playing. Sometimes he would close his eyes and play a dozen songs without opening them: operatic arias, Puccini,

Verdi, Leoncavallo, "Evening Star," "Tra sonno e veglia" (which still haunts me), and many Italian ballads. . . .

Later, I was to fill the house with another kind of music, "first with the colossal Beethoven, the gentlest spirit sublime," then Bach, Brahms, and Mozart, as well as Chopin. . . . In the years before he died, my father liked to hear especially the Beethoven piano sonata, "Les Adieux," and beyond all else, the middle part of the funeral march of Chopin's second piano sonata — the song-like melody which, he said, "was heaven enough."

Henry was about two years old when his father brought home from Krakauer Co., where he worked, an old discarded upright player-piano, the metal roller long gone. The piano was never thrown away or replaced; it was still around in their house in Yonkers, where I first saw it, and survived for many more years.

Donato tuned it periodically, as best he could, especially for Lucille, the oldest of the children, who would search out the notes to popular romantic songs she had memorized, and then (again from memory) would sing the lyrics, filling the house with her strong contralto voice. Louis' taste veered to the classical. Henry appreciated both. He wrote in his memoir about the still-vivid image of his leaning against the doorway of their living room, at the age of three, his ankles crossed, listening to Lucille playing and singing for her friends. When thirteen-year-old Lucille turned and saw her little brother standing there, enraptured by the music, she said something that made her friends laugh. It was Henry's first experience in what he later recognized as self-consciousness.

When I met him, Henry had collected a whole library of music books. They were to become an integral part of my life as well: the St. Matthew *Passion*, the major works of Beethoven and Mozart, the songs of Brahms and Schubert, and much else (including Scott Joplin) — music I had yet to discover.

What struck me about the old piano was that Louis and Lucille, the first two children who learned to play it, as well as Henry, who taught himself much later, seemed utterly oblivious to its tinny sound, unmindful of keys that often stuck and produced no sound at all. I was a much better pianist than any of them but lacked their ability to hear in the imperfect sounds that rose from their uneven self-taught playing the clear melodies, the powerful chords of a concert recital.

After Henry and I were married, we used to drive to Yonkers on Sundays, where the entire family came together for dinner. While my mother-in-law prepared the meal (refusing to let any of us "help"), I would settle at the old piano and start to play from the meager collection of music books Louis had somehow managed to assemble. Soon I discovered that my father-in-law followed me into the room when I started to play and would seat himself unobtrusively at a distance behind me in a straight-backed chair against the wall, as I went through a small repertory of his favorite arias and songs. He never commented on the mini-concert I performed for him, never asked for a particular selection. When I was through, he would disappear until it was time to eat. A mutual understanding had developed that needed no words.

Before moving from the big house in Yonkers to a small one out in Setauket, Long Island, Louis and his parents (the other children all married and gone by then) had rented for a brief time an apartment in Rego Park. Donato had retired . . . but not to watch more television or play cards or to indulge in trivial pursuits to fill his free hours. At the age of sixty-five, he gutted a small closet, built shelves, and brought in an old table on which he started what was to become his full-time passion: oil painting. He was an exceptionally good draughtsman, the buildings he painted were impressive by any standards. The lush greenery of a vaguely remembered Naples dominated his landscapes, as in his large painting of the churches of Assisi, in Umbria (copied from a picture he had found). A special gift for me and Henry was his painting of Columbia's Low Memorial Library, with the statue of Alma Mater on the stairs leading up to the imposing entrance. He also painted for us San Francisco's Bay Bridge against a flaming sunset.

I learned in due course that he was also a practical man of business. Soon after his marriage, he had managed to save enough to buy a small apartment building in the Bronx, where he had moved with his new bride. Later a cousin joined him, and the two men bought, independently, adjacent apartment buildings on Washington Avenue and 183rd Street — a much better neighborhood.

The area was heavily Jewish. His mother made friends

with some Jewish women who often took her with them to their synagogue. They communicated by sign language, for Donato's mother spoke only her Neapolitan dialect and her Jewish friends spoke only Yiddish.

Henry remembers being told by his mother that there might be some family connection with the Jews, for (the story goes) some of Nancy Paolucci's people had come from a suburb of Naples called Crispano, its residents mostly Jewish merchants and their families. Over the years, many had converted or married outside their faith. Henry's maternal grandmother had been a Bonomo — the English equivalent of Goodman. "And so you see, *figlio mio*," Henry mother would say to him occasionally, "you're probably part Jewish."

When the Depression hit, Donato moved his family to the top floor (the hardest to rent) and put up walls to create extra rooms in the other apartments, so that children could economize by moving back with their parents during those hard times. He had become a skilled draughtsman and amateur architect during World War I, working on barges and boats in the Brooklyn Navy Yard — an experience that enabled him to redesign and modernize his building. For this work, he had also mastered the art of setting up pulleys so that one man could maneuver very heavy things by himself. Occasionally, if they had time, the boys would help; but no workmen were ever called in to do a job.

When Krakauer Piano Co., where he had worked for several years as master cabinet-maker, had to shut down during the Depression, he found work on City Island, restoring or reshaping damaged yachts, sometimes on a scale that involved stripping away the entire outside paneling of the hull to strengthen the frame. He would come home with hull drawings, specifications of tensions, designs for steam-room bending of planks for the hull, specifications of lumber grain-lines, and original designs of his own for new interiors.

His longest sessions with Henry in those days were those in which he explained how, in a well-made hull, every plank has a specially twisted curvature. The problems of infinitesimals and differentials intrigued him and he became a master of geometric solutions. In his account of this period, Henry acknowledges that he owes a great deal to his father's example in learning new skills. Donato's enthusiasm was contagious as he shared with his son his experience rebuilding yachts. He later applied those new skills to the designing and building of pianos for Krakauer, when that company called back their former master-carpenter as the only man who could put a piano together from the raw materials to the roughly-tuned finished product. They served him again in World War II, when he returned to the Brooklyn Navy Yard, to build wooden assault-landing barges.

A self-educated man, Donato was an avid reader of such works and authors as Ralph Ingersol, Thomas Paine's *Common Sense*, Voltaire, Schopenhauer, and especially Machiavelli, whose writings he knew better than most professors. Like Machiavelli, he was a realist in his views about government and about human nature generally. I had been told about the Paolucci men and that Donato, like his father and grandfather, was an agnostic and atheist. If so, he knew discretion: I don't recall his ever voicing activist views or belittling religion in my presence.

The whole family was an intriguing discovery, but Donato in particular fed my imagination with his quiet intelligent concentration. Long after he died, I published in *Sepia Tones*, my first collection of short stories, a piece called "Buried Treasure," in which I draw on my impressions and what I learned about him from other family members. I was pleased when the book was reviewed in the *Times,* but even more pleased when that particular story was reprinted in an anthology (*The Voices We Carry*) and singled out by a reviewer as "a brilliant, haunting memoir of an unforgettable Italian-American man, narrated by his daughter-in-law."

It was a fictionalized account, of course; but Donato Paolucci was indeed an unforgettable man. Henry did not resemble him physically (he took after his mother), but — more than any of the other children — he had his father's temperament, his stoic attitude toward life, his strength of character; the same subtle wit and humor, the same stern exterior and kind heart within. From him, Henry learned the value of rigorous habits and how to nurture the innate desire for knowledge which is man's natural impulse. Indirectly, through the attraction they exerted on him, Donato also taught Henry to appreciate literature and music. I can't resist the notion that Henry was his father's "favorite," that Donato recognized in his youngest child the ideal self-image the older man had created for himself in some secret place in his soul.

Other factors had come into play before I met him that set Henry apart from anyone else I had ever known. At the beginning of World War II, he had just received his B.A. from the City College of New York, where he had also completed ROTC training, and immediately enlisted in the Air Force. His knowledge of astronomy determined his assignment as a navigator in the 15th Air Force. He was sent for training as a Bombardier-Navigator to the A.A.F. Pre-Flight School in Louisiana, where he remained until May 21, 1943. Active service as a 2nd Lieutenant began on October 10th of that same year, with assignment to Company B, 909th ABS Bn Unit of the 47th Wing Command crew that flew combat missions to the Naples-Foggia and Rome-Arno areas, as well as Southern France. He earned the American Theater Ribbon, the European, African, Middle Eastern Campaign Medal, four stars, and the World War II Victory medal.

When the war ended, he decided to stay on for a while and was reassigned as Intelligence and Education Officer, responsible for "organization, administration, and supervision of a school for training of instructors and instruction of the personnel enroute to port of embarkation in academic subjects . . . [and] for orientation of troops being redeployed to the Pacific and to U.S. from Italy." Eventually, he was assigned to an all-black unit, the first to integrate black and white officers. The group was part of a team that was given charge of maintenance and care of 100,000 German and Italian prisoners of war, as well as "turncoat Russians," all of whom were housed in pup tents until supplies arrived and adequate living quarters could be built.

The man who had bombed Italian and German-occupied French cities a short time earlier nonetheless treated the men who had fought against the American forces and were now his responsibility with the respect he felt they deserved. He did not hold them in contempt for having followed orders, for doing what he himself had done, bombing places that were in many ways part of his personal history, in the country where his parents were born and raised. They in turn reciprocated by building living quarters, an entire village in fact, on the muddy terrain where they'd been left to cope. They even managed to assemble a jeep for the man who had been assigned to care for them. One POW, Em Fiala, presented Henry as a Christmas gift in 1945 over a dozen original charcoal sketches he'd made of the camp and its surroundings.

Henry remained on that assignment until his official release on May 2, 1946. Back home, he immediately took advantage of the G. I. Bill and enrolled in the graduate school of Columbia University.

Although I wasn't aware of any of this background when I met him in the course we shared at Columbia in the late forties, Henry presented a dilemma from the outset. Here was a man working toward a Ph.D., who knew much more than most of his professors and made it known when he felt their arrogance deserved to be put down. Not exactly the best way to win friends and influence people; but he had lived through too many horrors to resort to petty compromises in a classroom of much younger people, where the professors themselves were no match for him.

Henry might have followed his older brother's example and abandoned the notion of a degree; but unlike Louis, he stuck it out, often indulging in bold criticism of his instructors. He probably would not have survived as a candidate for the Ph.D. except for Professor Bigongiari. who in his mild unassuming way managed to defuse many potentially disastrous situations.

He was by far the most articulate student in the Dante class, but aggressive and often cynical in his responses. Bigongiari never took offense. I, on the other hand, like the rest of the students who witnessed their exchanges, was not prepared for what often were presumptuous comments by a young man who had all the answers and was arrogant enough to challenge the learned professor. Eventually I found out about confrontations they'd had in the past, words on Henry's part which any other professor would have found offensive but which Bigongiari not only ignored but seemed to encourage.

On one occasion, reviewing the backgrounds of the *Divine Comedy*, Bigongiari had dramatized St. Augustine's response to the profound dilemma presented by man's free will and the omniscience of God, by placing a finger on his lips and repeating St. Augustine's admonition: "On this subject, 'silence'." To which Henry promptly had countered: "That may be good enough for St. Augustine, but it's not good enough for me." Everyone thought he would bolt from the room and not be seen again. Instead he kept showing up in class but no longer spoke out. Finally, some weeks later, at the end of the hour, as students were leaving, Bigongiari approached him and asked: "Why don't you ask questions any more?" Henry's reply was: "Because I *know* everything you know." To those within earshot, his arrogance was shocking, an inexcusable insult; but Henry's next words demolished that impression and took everyone by surprise. "I've known it upside down. You've turned it right side up for me."

It was the beginning of a long, profound friendship between the two men. There's no doubt in my mind that Bigongiari from the outset saw in Henry the student every professor longs for: someone who had read all the texts, digested them, and came out ready to do intellectual battle. I am sure Henry would have abandoned graduate studies had Bigongiari not been there to redirect his uncompromising intellectual honesty.

I learned in the years that followed that Henry had also absorbed from his mentor (by now my mentor as well, and a friend also) the scholarly certainty that enables you to answer any and all questions no matter how difficult, the enviable ease which encourages students to take part in the Socratic exchange that is the heart of the learning process. Eventually, when I too started to teach, I found myself emulating Bigongiari's method and trying to achieve Henry's patience in transforming the meanest, most elementary, even stupid questions into provocative ones, giving the student a quick boost from the trivial to a more serious level of awareness.

It was in Bigongiari's class that I experienced the first inkling of Henry's complicated but intriguing personality, one that I was irresistibly drawn to and meant to explore, given the chance. . . .

The opportunities came naturally, during the second half of Bigongiari's course, when we'd go for coffee after class. Casual conversation quickly turned into long monologues by Henry on subjects which I probably would never have explored on my own. He would arouse my interest by connecting the little I knew with things I'd never dreamed of, luring the fledgling poet in me with talk of poets and works I'd never heard of, like James Thomson, whose chief work, *The City of Dreadful Night,* was not only a modern equivalent of Dante's Hell on earth, but a more somber rendition of T.S. Eliot's *Wasteland,* which I knew well. He introduced me to Hegel's views on dramatic theory and tragedy through A.C. Bradley's Shakespearean criticism, which I had read. He would recite long passages from the major English poets I had grown to love. Perhaps it was a form of courtship; or maybe as an appreciative listener I encouraged him to express his deepest feelings through the authors and works he knew so well, as his brother Louis had done.

By the end of that year we had grown close in mind and heart; and although no formal commitment was made, we knew instinctively that our lives were now inextricably joined.

At the end of that year, Henry left for Florence as Eleanora Duse Traveling Fellow in Columbia University, a generous and coveted prize for which Bigongiari had submitted Henry's name. He was away for the next twelve months, during which time I continued my graduate studies in the late afternoon and evening and worked my full-time job during the day as Executive Assistant to the Head of the Columbia Libraries, Dr. Richard H. Logsdon — a job that kept me going until I landed my first teaching assignment in a private girls' school in Westchester County.

Henry and I were married when he returned from his year abroad. Two years later we went to Italy together as Fulbright Scholars at the University of Rome — an exciting time, which included making the rounds of relatives (I hadn't seen mine since I'd left Rome at the age of eight).

I think if we hadn't married, Henry would have spent several more years stretching the G. I. Bill as far as it could go to attend classes and harass professors he caught in error. As things turned out, marriage heightened his innate sense of duty. On our return to New York, he completed his work for the doctorate and, at the age of 28, took on his first civilian job: writing articles for an encyclopedia. When a temporary opening became available teaching English at Iona College in New Rochelle, he accepted. He continued on a full-time basis and in due course was given tenure and promoted; but his reputation as a charismatic teacher and serious scholar had already begun to spread, and in 1967 he was invited to join the

Department of Political Science at St. John's University in Queens NY, as full professor with tenure on appointment.

One of the first things he did was to convince his new colleagues to change the department name from "Political Science" to "Government and Politics," since so many of their graduates went into public service. He was also one of the principal designers of the department's new Doctor of Arts degree — an interdepartmental offering that drew many graduate students. He was honored by St. John's with the University's "Outstanding Faculty Achievement" medal in 1989. Other awards followed, including the American Patriot Award, the Conservative Party's Kieran O'Doherty Award, the Bella Dodd Memorial Award.

The classroom honed his skills as a speaker and gave him the opportunity to share his learning with others. Students sought him out; a number of them became friends and colleagues. Three in particular stand out for their long attachment to their teacher and mentor and their unwavering dedication to the conservative principles Henry upheld as a scholar and a political thinker: Herbert Stupp, Ronald F. Docksai, and Robert Searby. Predictably, they rose to important positions, having learned from their master not only the subject they had come to study but many useful skills, especially the art of writing and speaking effectively — for Henry not only commented on the content and arguments of their assignments but also "edited" them closely for proper and effective use of language.

Herb Stupp started out as a legislative assistant in the NYS Senate, spent six years as Editorial Director of WOR-TV — where his many awards include an Emmy for "Best Editorial" (1982) — moved back to government service as Regional Director of Federal ACTION, Region II (now known as "Corporation for National Service"), working closely with governors, US Senators, members of Congress and their staffs. In 1994 Mayor Rudolph Giuliani appointed him Commissioner of the New York City Department for the Aging. His initiatives in that job won him recognition in the media and in Congress. In 2009 he launched his own consulting firm, making good use of his wide experience in government affairs, communications, advocacy, and media relations. But, while moving ahead in the career goals he had set for himself, Herb also campaigned actively for conservative causes. While at St. John's, he joined the Buckley camp as a volunteer, distributing campaign literature in Queens, moving up quickly to become chairman of Youth for Buckley and an active member of the new group that had emerged, Young Americans for Freedom (YAF). where his leadership skills were put to good use in key executive positions, including NYS Chairman. Herb still has a vivid memory of his mixed feelings when, as an Adjunct Professor in the Department of Government and Politics at St. John's in 1985-1986, he shared an office with his former mentor.

> It was great to see a plaque that read "Professor Herbert W. Stupp" under the one that read "Professor Henry Paolucci," the man who meant so much to me. But (as I confided to a few of my colleagues) sharing a campus office with Henry Paolucci is like sharing a weight machine with Arnold Schwarzenegger. One would always feel inadequate!

Ron Docksai, currently Vice President of Federal Government Relations at Bayer Corporation and a member of its political action committee's board of directors, had gone to New York University for his Master's degree, where he wrote his thesis on "A Study of the Organization and Beliefs of the Young Conservative Movement." He continued for a Ph.D. at Georgetown University, choosing as his dissertation topic (no doubt with a nudge or two from Henry) Walter Bagehot, the British economist of the latter part of the 19th century, whose work Henry had introduced him to. Ron's interest in Bagehot brought him even closer to Henry, who by then had adopted Bagehot's name for the Research Council on National Sovereignty, the organization he had founded to promote Bagehot's historical views, especially his forceful arguments in favor of the nation-state system.

Ron's scholarly achievements were right in line with his long-standing political interests and did not distract him from actively pursuing those interests. As far back as 1964, the year Henry ran for the US Senate, he had helped launch — while still in high school — "Young American Conservatives." The group received a good deal of media coverage during their first year, which prompted the leaders of "Young Americans for Freedom" to invite Ron's group to join YAF. By 1971, Ron had become National Director of YAF but his energetic commitment to the conservative cause brought him quickly to the top as National Chairman, a position to which he was re-elected four times. He played a leading role in Jim Buckley's successful 1970 campaign for US Senator as the Conservative Party candidate and, later, was one of the most forceful voices in withdrawing support from Richard Nixon in the President's bid for re-election in 1972. Under Ron's leadership, YAF also played a major role in Reagan politics, especially the 1976 presidential campaign. Along the way, he served as Assistant Secretary for Legislation at the Department of Health and Human Services, staff director in the US Senate Committee on Labor and Human Resources, and Healthcare Legislative Counsel for Senator Orrin H Hatch.

In inviting Henry to serve on the Advisory Board of YAF's College Conservative Council and to speak at YAF's Mid-Atlantic Regional convention in April 1968, Ron Docksai paid tribute to Henry's role as a leader, whose wide-reaching message was nonetheless rooted in the classroom.

> In these days of wanting respect for college authority and American culture, it is vital that members of America's only conservative campus organization learn that there are still strongly nationalistic and eloquent national defenders of the conservative creed on campus. Your attendance at this convention would answer any questioning members of the press as to where YAF stands.

Bob Searby was to become Assistant Secretary of Labor for International Affairs and head of delegations to the International Labor Organizations with the personal rank of ambassador. After government service, he became Vice President of Pacific Trade and Investment Corporation and then Managing Director, Europe, for Hollister Incorporated, where he is currently Director of Government Affairs. A staunch conservative politically, culturally, and intellectually, Bob followed Henry's political career with enthusiastic support and enjoyed many conversations with him about political events and personalities, the nation's future, especially foreign policy. Their phone calls would often last over an hour and, while he still lived in Queens, Bob visited his former mentor frequently.

In a touching eulogy delivered at the memorial service held at St. John's in May, 1999, Bob remembered his former teacher and friend. His words echoed what many others who had known Henry, had thought and felt about him.

In paying tribute to Professor Henry Paolucci, we honor a man who has worked relentlessly over the years to preserve the essential values of conservatism within the structure of our national sovereignty. . . . In 1964, he gave the Conservative Party of New York State a dramatic boost when his candidacy for the United States Senate — running against Robert Kennedy and Kenneth Keating — attracted major newsmedia attention. The *New York Times* gave his nomination front-page coverage, featured him in its "Man in the News" column under the heading "A Scholarly Candidate," and assigned a major reporter to cover his campaign. . . .

Professor Paolucci . . . distinguished himself as what the *New York Post* called the "ultimate hardliner" on the right with respect to our national policies and foreign affairs. In 1968, on the eve of the national election, he published *War, Peace and the Presidency* (McGraw Hill) in which he warned that the anti-nationalist ideologues who had dumped a Democratic President for having tried to win in Vietnam were prepared to use a Republican, if need be, to get the kind of *detente* they wanted between the United States and the Communist powers.

In 1969, when it was apparent that many Republican conservatives meant to hold their tongue on vital issues while Mr. Nixon was President, he founded his monthly newsletter, *State of the Nation*, where he has, with incredible prescience, anticipated the events that brought us down to the status of a third-rate power. Many of his articles have appeared on the Op Ed page of the *New York Times,* where they serve, apparently, to confirm the conviction of the internationalist readers that dumping President Johnson to make way for a Republican compromiser was sound strategy. Professor Paolucci is founder also of the Walter Bagehot Research Council on National Sovereignty, dedicated to scholarly research, lecturing, and publishing to the end of securing our nation's sovereign values.

An intriguing lecturer, teacher, writer — author of hundreds of articles and books on ancient history, the history of science, philosophy, aesthetics, government, and current affairs — a self-effacing helper to all who called on him, Professor Paolucci serves as a constant model for all of us. . . .

Henry left a rich legacy; but many had come to

recognize and appreciate early on those qualities that made him special, drawn by his bold way of confronting problems, his historical approach to subjects — especially government and politics — his ease in handling the opposition.

Two individuals especially stand out as catalysts responsible for Henry's taking a public stand as a conservative thinker and writer: Ted Dabrowski, president of a printing company, who had recently been elected Chairman of the Conservative Party in Queens and was also on the governing board of the newly-formed Conservative Party; and Frank D. Grande, a young colleague of Henry's, who would be elected several times Chairman of the History Department at The City College of New York and would eventually earn a doctorate in the history of science from Oxford University.

I have dedicated this book to them, for they played a large role in prodding Henry to give public voice to his conservative views.

From the Archives

HENRY PAOLUCCI

Donato Paolucci

**On the wall: oil painting
of Low Memorial Hall,
Columbia University, NY,
by Donato Paolucci.**

**Collage of events in Henry Paolucci's life, prepared by the Board of
Trustees of City College, CUNY (1999)**

RESPICE, ADSPICE, PROSPICE
(A Song for the Last Days)

YES I came to City College
to acquire heaps of knowledge
And to spare myself the coarser kinds of labor;
For the many lores of learning
I had in me quite a yearning
And an idle life at college met my favor.

But I found on my arrival
That the struggle for survival
Was much keener there than I'd anticipated;
So instead of all the pleasures
That a college student treasures
I had to go on grinding unabated.

On the day of registration
I was filled with jubilation
Til I learned about the closing of the classes;
Every time I made selections
They would quickly close the sections
Til my hours were like those of toiling masses.

My indomitable spirit
Was still able then to bear it
So courageously I undertook my studies;
While the sun on high was riding
Til the moment of its hiding
I was busy grinding with my college buddies.

Oh I learned much self reliance
Taking first a course in science
Then across the hall to study mathematics;
From a class in foreign language
I'd go down to buy a "sanguage"
Then directly to the gym for acrobatics.

Song written by Henry Paolucci for a City College anthology
of writings by faculty and students (1983). Adapted to an old folk tune.

After sweating there an hour
I was pushed into a shower
Then descended to the subway feeling dizzy;
When a worker homeward hurries
He can leave behind his worries
But at home a City student must keep busy.

Still I'm really not complaining;
With few college days remaining
I look back upon those days that used to be;
With a kind of pleasant sadness
With some tears and yet with gladness
For with age, tis now a mellow memory!

Columbia University
in the City of New York
[NEW YORK 27, N. Y.]
SECRETARY OF THE UNIVERSITY

October 5, 1948

Mr. Henry Paolucci
2254 Washington Avenue
New York 57, N. Y.

Dear Mr. Paolucci

    I beg to advise you that you have been appointed Eleonora Duse Traveling Fellow in Columbia University for the year 1948-1949. The stipend is $2500., which is normally paid in two installments. Please notify the Bursar in writing at what address and in what form you wish payments made. The first half is available July 1, or earlier by special arrangement.

    Please send your acceptance to this office. If we can be of assistance to you in making your plans, do not hesitate to let me know.

    With congratulations upon this award, I remain

Very truly yours

Philip M. Hayden

Secretary of the University

**Letter from the Secretary of Columbia University
informing Henry that he had been awarded the
Eleonora Duse Traveling Fellowship.**

CHRISTMAS IN NEW YORK

Christmas in New York,
Manhattan's lights are all aglow,
The crowds downtown are moving slow,
All hearts are gay tonight.

Christmas in New York,
We'll watch the skaters on the square,
Bump into friends from everywhere,
Their faces beaming bright.

Though we can't go dashing
Through the snow
In a one-horse open sleigh,
We can hear New York's church bells
Ring out,
'A happy, holy holiday!'

Christmas in New York,
Come out and join the friendly fun,
Eight million hearts will beat as one
In happiness tonight!

"Christmas in New York": one of several songs for which Henry
wrote music and lyrics. Jimmy Durante planned to record it, but his
agents decided against it and provided him with something called
"Knickerbocker Christmas" for him to use instead.

Three sketches by Em Fiala, German POW (1945).

Henry Paolucci receiving the "Outstanding Faculty Achievement" Medal of St. John's University. On the right: Father Joseph Cahill, President of the University.

The New York Times

OBITUARIES *WEDNESDAY, JANUARY 6, 1999*

Henry Paolucci, 77, Scholar and a Leader in Conservative Party

By WOLFGANG SAXON

Dr. Henry Paolucci, a prolific scholar of classical politics and literature, professor emeritus of government and politics at St. John's University and vice chairman of the New York Conservative Party for the last 20 years, died Friday at New York Hospital Medical Center of Queens. He was 77 and a resident of Beechhurst, Queens.

The cause was complications from prostate cancer, said John Hamill, a spokesman for the City University, where his wife, Dr. Anne Attura Paolucci, heads the board of trustees.

Dr. Henry Paolucci taught comparative literature as well as ancient Greek and Roman history at Iona College, Brooklyn College and City College before he joined the St. John's faculty in 1967. He was American correspondent for Il Borghese of Italy and contributed to the Encyclopedia Americana and to national magazines and dailies, including the Op-Ed page of The New York Times.

He was the founding president of the Walter Bagehot Council on National Sovereignty. Its affiliate, the Council of National Literatures, published his studies on subjects from Aristotle and Dante to Southern political history and Dr. Henry A. Kissinger's persona and policies. Many of them remain in print.

With his wife as collaborator, he did a translation of Machiavelli's "Mandragola" (Macmillan, 1957), which is in its 32d printing. He also wrote the introduction to his translation of "Beccaria: On Crimes and Punishment" (Bobbs-Merrill, 1963).

Dr. Paolucci, a Bronx native, graduated from City College in 1942. In World War II, he was a navigator in the Army Air Forces in Africa and Italy, where he spent a year as a prisoner of war. He completed his education at Columbia University with an M.A. degree in 1948 and a Ph.D. in 1961 and also studied at the University of Florence and the University of Rome.

In 1964, Dr. Paolucci was persuaded to run as the Conservative candidate for Senate against Senator Kenneth B. Keating, a Republican, and Robert F. Kennedy, who won the seat for the Democrats. Dr. Paolucci was named vice chairman of the Conservative Party two years later.

He retired from St. John's in 1991.

Besides his wife, he is survived by two sisters, Lucille Gorton of Stamford, Conn., and Phyllis Albano of Queens.

Political Science & Politics

Volume XXXII   Number 2   June 1999

Henry Paolucci

Henry Paolucci, professor emeritus of government and politics at St. John's University and vice chairman of the Conservative Party of New York State, died Friday, January 1, 1999, at New York Hospital Queens Medical Center from complications caused by prostate cancer. He was 77.

After graduating from the City College of New York with a B.S., he joined the Air Force as a navigator and flew numerous missions over Africa and Italy. Later, he resumed his education, earning an M.A. and Ph.D. from Columbia University.

Professor Paolucci's wide range of intellectual interests was reflected in the variety of subjects he taught, including ancient Greek and Roman history at Iona College, Brooklyn College, and City College; a graduate course on Dante and medieval culture at Columbia University; and, since 1968, courses on U.S. foreign policy and political theory, Aristotle and Hegel, and others in the department of government and politics at St. John's University. He is especially known for his studies of the political thought of Aristotle, St. Augustine, Machiavelli, and Hegel.

A frequent contributor to the Op Ed page of *The New York Times* and magazines like *National Review* and *Il Borghese* (Rome), Dr. Paolucci wrote a number of articles for the Columbus quincentenary and helped to prepare three volumes drawn from the massive work of Justin

Winsor, the great historian of early America. He translated Cesare Beccaria's *On Crimes and Punishments* and Machiavelli's *Mandragola* (in its 32nd printing) and edited Maitland's *Justice and Police*, as well as a notable collection of *The Political Writings of St. Augustine*. His books on political affairs and foreign policy analysis include *War, Peace and the Presidency* (1968), *A Brief History of Political Thought and Statecraft* (1979), *Kissinger's War* (1980), *Zionism, the Superpowers, and the PLO* (1964), and *Iran, Israel, and the United States* (1991). In 1948 Professor Paolucci was chosen Eleanora Duse Traveling Fellow in Columbia University and spent a year studying in Florence, Italy. In 1951 he revisited Italy as a Fulbright Scholar at the University of Rome.

In 1964 he was asked by William F. Buckley Jr. to accept the New York State Conservative Party nomination for the U.S. Senate and he ran against Kenneth Keating and Robert F. Kennedy. His stimulating campaign drew considerable interest and he was written up in *The New York Times* as the "Scholarly Candidate." In 1995 the party honored him with its prestigious Kieran O'Doherty Award.

Founder and president of the **Walter Bagehot Research Council on National Sovereignty (a nonprofit educational foundation), Paolucci** was for many years chief editor of its newsletter, *State of the Nation*, and organizer of its annual discussion panels at meetings of the American Political Science Association. He also contributed to the international publication *Review of National Literatures* as research coordinator and feature writer. He leaves his wife, Anne Paolucci.

Henry's obituary as carried in *APSA*, the American Political Science Association journal.

Excerpts from letters from colleagues, state and government officials, former students, friends, that arrived after Professor Paolucci's death. Each records characteristic traits or a particular incident.

"a gentleman, a scholar, and a patriot. . . ." *Lewis E. Lehrman (conservative leader).*

"My favorite memory of Old New York was my first summer nights at Columbia, encountering Henry at 111th and Broadway discoursing on Dante, Augustine, St. Thomas, et al. I thought I was in Athens — or at least Hyde Park. Broadway has not been so elevated since — a little touch of Henry in the night. . . ." *Robert Rosenbaum (friend and colleague).*

"What a remarkable life he led! What contributions he made! — a patriot who flew combat missions for his country, a scholar whose written works ranged over the spectrum of ancient and modern history and philosophy, a political leader and a public man who stepped into the political arena and engaged in thoughtful debate." *John Marchi (former NYS Senator).*

"Henry's achievements are varied and impressive. He served his nation during times of war. He contributed to academics as a respected scholar, a writer and an educator. Perhaps most notably, Henry left an indelible mark on the political landscape for the state and the nation as a candidate for the U.S. Senate and as the Vice Chairman of the New York State Conservative Party for the past 20 years. . . ." *Bradford J. Race, Jr., (Secretary to NYS Governor George Pataki).*

"I had the privilege of being one of Dr. Paolucci's students at Iona College in 1964. Throughout the years I have never forgotten his unique insight and zeal. . . .I last sat in his class 36 years ago, but I can recall as if it happened yesterday Dr. Paolucci inimitably parodying some rich industrialist, replete with feet up on the desk and cigar in mouth voicing contempt for the underprivileged. Long before Stephen E. Ambrose won fame for his book *Citizen Soldiers* in 1997, Dr. Paolucci conveyed to us the responsibilities incumbent upon members of the 'polis' and shared with us the thoughts and feelings of a young man as he peered through his Norden bombsight and observed the lights of the city below appear as the plane made its bomb run. I particularly recall his love of St. Augustine and how, in a flash, he could intertwine the experience of Augustine and Thomas Merton and his own experience to produce a memorable lecture. . . . He was an Orator who could hold a class enthralled. He also had a sense of humor, which made him all the more believable. He remains a part of me." *Frederic Eder, former student).*

"I long admired Henry Paolucci as a scholar and political and social thinker. He was a very special man." *Matthew Goldstein (Chancellor, City University of New York).*

"Dr. Paolucci remained, to the end of his life, committed to the cause of educating our nation's young people. . . . His studies on Aristotle, Machiavelli, St. Augustine, and Hegel remain exemplary works of scholarship. In an age where knowledge of our political heritage is not integral to the success of a politician, his political actions were grounded in a solid understanding and respect for classical ideals. A scholar as well as a politician, Dr. Paolucci was clearly what used to be called "a renaissance man" — a man of thought as well as action." *Leon M. Goldstein (Kingsborough CC of CUNY).*

"Each day's news brings reminders of Henry's sage counsel. This ongoing travesty with nuclear secrets being stolen by the Chinese, for example, underscored the need for vigilance on national security. Henry was the pre-eminent authority on this subject. . . . He was a renaissance giant in an age of materialist pygmies." *Anthony R. Spinelli (Investment Broker).*

"Dr. Paolucci taught me European History and the History of Rome at Iona College in the mid 60s. To this day I remember his telling us, 'Look at the tallest structure, that will tell you what people value,' as he tried, with some success, to transform himself into the cathedral of Chartres. He was an inspirational teacher and was one of the reasons I chose an academic career. . . ." *Terence F. Martell (The Weismann Center, Baruch College of CUNY).*

"Henry's fascinating ideas and clarity of vision were unique. The difficulty, if any, of living with such a mind I'll wait to read about in [Anne Paolucci's] autobiography. . . ." *William A, Bocchino, Ph.D.*

"Henry's combination of integrity and courage was a powerful example to me as to so many others. And he was fun to be around. Some of my fondest memories of the conservative wars in New York were the times I was fortunate to share a platform with him, including the time in the Bronx when he invited a heckler outside. The guy wisely did not take Henry up on it." *Charles E. Rice (Professor of Law, Notre dame University).*

"I mourn the loss of a loyal and dependable friend. St. John's has lost a star in the firmament." *Tom Vincitorio (Friend and Colleague).*

"Time to remember those words of Samuel Beckett, I can't go on, I'll go on." *Eric Bentley (Drama and Theater critic, writer, playwright).*

"His astute, logical analysis of political affairs — not to mention wry humor — made a great impression on me." *Edmund A. Bator (US Former Service Officer, retired).*

"I will always remember him as a vibrant teacher, as well as a supportive mentor. His lectures were always provocative, and I can say with confidence on behalf of myself and my fellow graduate students, that they will not soon be forgotten. Dr. Paolucci's recommendation helped me to get into law school, and I attribute much of my career success to his encouragement." *Nancy Tracy (former graduate student).*

"You have lost a life-partner and the academic world has lost that rare combination of scholar-activist who tried to put his ideals into practice. That loss cannot be replaced." *Saul Cohen (Ch. Higher Education Committee, NYS Board of Regents).*

"My first memory of Henry was on the Columbia campus. We stood outside the eastern stairway of Butler Hall arguing vigorously about Hegel. The sound of his voice rising in excitement remains with me. . . . Why we were arguing about philosophy, I'm not sure; politics would have been a more natural area for disagreement. I liked and admired Henry. He was a vital and interesting personality. His career and achievements were certainly distinguished." *Edmond L. Volpe (President Emeritus, Staten Island College, CUNY).*

"What a wonderful influence he had on everyone!. . . . I remember particularly his fine critique of some of the muckraking about perhaps the greatest person of the millennium, Christopher Columbus. What fine insights he gave." *Henry Middendorf (conservative colleague).*

"Henry will be remembered not only as a scholar (his preface to the Beccaria translation was my guide), but also as one who was willing to articulate his principles in the public arena. His legacy is large." *Dominic R. Massaro (Justice of the Supreme Court, New York State).*

"Because at my seldom best, I remain as he called me "a jewel-in-the-rough," I will put it succinctly and unadorned. I first met Henry in Roman History class as a freshman at Iona. I was spellbound. His words, gestures, and beliefs had a cathartic effect on me. In a moment, I realized that it was OK to feel the way I did. He gave an intellectual fig-leaf to my passions. He gave me the self-confidence, critical to every man, to successfully complete the journey from adolescence into manhood. . . . I have taught all of our sons the "Band of Brothers" speech [*Henry V*] as I remember, like yesterday, the very first time I heard it." *Larry Franklin (former student).*

2. STATE OF THE NATION *AND* *THE WALTER BAGEHOT RESEARCH COUNCIL ON NATIONAL SOVEREIGNTY*

In the early sixties Henry, who was one of the first to contribute toward the formation of the Conservative Party of New York State, was also one of the first to recognize the great asset the Party had in Ted Dabrowski, President of Dachs Printing Co. in College Point, Queens NY. Dabrowski, an ardent supporter of the conservative cause, was not a stranger to the political scene. He had served on the Staff of NYS Assembly Speaker Perry B Duryea, Jr. and had been active in promoting conservative causes before becoming a member of the new Party's Executive Committee and Chairman of the Conservative Party of Queens County. His keen perceptions and practical approach to politics were welcome in a political environment full of empty rhetoric. He drew into the conservative community many new members who were looking for a platform that took the liberals and self-serving factional interests to task and, most important, who insisted unambiguously — as he did — on a commitment to preserve our national sovereignty.

Dabrowski saw in Henry a compelling crusader, ready to do battle, a voice that could carry the conservative message to a wide audience. Henry, in turn, saw in his new friend and fellow-conservative, not only an idealist who knew how to survive in a hostile political environment but also a practical man who knew how to deal with people and run a business — and, as fate would have it, not just *any* business, but one that had the outlets needed to spread the conservative message.

Predictably, irrepressible instinct found its irresistible opportunity. Once the business of helping to get the newly-formed Party under way, the many tasks connected with the 1964 campaign behind him; on the eve of his taking on responsibility for liaison and communications connected with Jim Buckley's upcoming bid for the U.S. Senate, Dabrowski approached Henry to offer his printing services if Henry was prepared to issue a political newsletter on a regular basis. They quickly came to an agreement and *State of the Nation* was officially launched in October 1969.

With *SN*, Dabrowski provided Henry with the perfect outlet as a spokesman for conservative ideas, especially his unwavering commitment to the nation-state system. Henry welcomed the opportunity to articulate those ideas to a wide audience; through *SN* he could speak out without the reservations or restrictions imposed by liberal-oriented publishers, on those rare occasions when they expressed interest in his work.

Because of limited funds, early mailing lists focused on senators, congressmen, political personalities, government agencies — where Henry's views could have some impact, or at least be given a hearing.

Having been prodded into this new activity — one he would not have generated on his own but which he quickly took on when offered — Henry produced between 1969 and 1980, incisive monthly critiques on major issues, especially on American foreign policy; but he also focused on political personalities ("The National Ideal of William E. Hocking" *SN*, 7, 12, December 1975); events that had a national impact ("The Postal Strike and Moynihan's Mob," *SN*, 2, 4, April 1970); domestic issues that carried a wide message ("New York City: On the Edge of Social Chaos," *SN*, 2, 9, September 1970).

There were also newsletters that brought current events into an intriguing historical perspective, such as the one on "Moynihan, Solzhenitsyn, and St. Augustine," which carried the subtitle, "How Much Does Freedom Matter?" (*SN*, 7, 9, September, 1975).

A number of issues were dedicated to what he believed to be the cunning, hidden political agenda of Henry Kissinger: "Carter's Kissinger: Z. Brzezinski" (*SN*, 8, 6, June 1978); "Kissinger's War" (*SN*, 10, 2, February 1978); "Two American Embassy Seizures" (*SN*, 12, 9, September 1980); nine issues with the subtitle "The Kissinger-Carter Iran Crisis" — all of which were incorporated later into a pamphlet and still later into a book with the title *Kissinger's War*. More about Kissinger appeared in three newsletters by Louis Paolucci (under the pseudonym Aldebaran).

Charles Burton Marshall, chief adviser to former Secretary of State Dean Acheson, was invited to contribute a two-part "Bicentenary Interview" entitled "The Common Defense": Part I, "Sovereignty and Responsible Government"

(*SN*, 8, 7&8, July-August 1976); Part II, "'The Top of Sovereignty'" (*SN*, 8, 9, September 1976).

Subscriptions quickly increased. Letters began to arrive on a steady basis. Mario Tedeschi, editor of *Il Borghese* (Rome, Milan), not only sent for copies of the newsletters but translated and published them as they appeared and soon began to commission Henry to write original pieces on the current American political scene. A lively correspondence developed between the two men. In one letter, Henry brings him up to-date about Henry Kissinger:

> As you know, Henry Kissinger has now agreed 1) to become a topic director of David Rockefeller's Chase Manhattan bank-empire, 2) to take the post vacated by Zbigniew Brzezinski in the Government Department of Columbia University, and 3) to supervise, at a salary of several million, NBC-TV's coverage of foreign-affairs news.

> Kissinger was the sole survivor of the Watergate Presidency because he was part of the successor-regime even before poor Nixon was aware that there would be any need for a successor-regime. Kissinger's government, with Ford as the figurehead, quickly summoned his old patron, Nelson Rockefeller, to the Vice-Presidency — and the palace coup d'ètat was complete. Everyone knows that a coup d'état took place under the cover of Watergate — Oriana Falaci said so on American TV — but Kissinger's obvious triumph in that coup has been smiled at rather than discussed. . . .

Il Veltro (Milan) also translated and published some newsletters. A French magazine quoted extensively from the piece on Brzezinski and President Jimmy Carter. Several American journals and magazines picked up one or more of the issues. *The Birmingham News* printed the one on Brzezinski and President Jimmy Carter, providing a cartoon for the piece. *The New York Times* published between 1971 and 1973 more than a dozen Op Ed articles by Henry, based on or reproducing *SN* newsletters, often with striking illustrations to go with the text.

One new reader wrote: "It is encouraging to know that you are in there working hard when so many of us are getting discouraged!" Lester Waterbury, who had written "his bit on the no-win war," wrote that he had been subscribing to the newsletter from the beginning and that he "treasured it."

Robert E. Lane, Chairman of the Department of Political Science at Yale University, wrote in for more issues. James Cagney wrote twice, the first time in 1975 from Beverly Hills:

> I have given [the newsletters] to friends of mine who I think are sympathetic to our view of the Nixon situation. I have yet to have one of them make a statement regarding them. Caution seems to be the reason. That they are cautious in this area is understandable. Careers have been ended for less.

Almost two decades later (1994), Cagney acknowledged from his farm in Stanfordville, New York, the newsletter he had just received. "It is an inspired piece. . . . I'm sending it to people in California who I'm sure will be properly appreciative. . . ."

Zbigniew Brzezinski himself, at the time with the Center for Strategic & International Studies at Georgetown University, wrote Henry about the newsletters on the Iran crisis: "I certainly agree with you regarding Sullivan, and it reminds me of a truly regrettable period in U.S. foreign policy making."

In the late seventies the newsletters carried an "exclusive." While in Kuwait, where he had been invited to lecture and to study the political situation in that country, Henry had interviewed PLO spokesman Khalid Al-Hasan. Embassy officials had approached Al-Hasan with the suggestion that he meet with Professor Paolucci, who — they assured him — was not a journalist out for controversial quotes he could use to pepper up his day-to-day stories but a serious historian and a keen observer of political events in the middle East.

After "researching" Henry's credentials. the PLO leader agreed to the meeting (a rare concession). Henry did not shy away from discussing "The 'Palestinian-Arab' Question" (*SN*, 11, 2, February 1979). or asking: "An American-Jewish Exodus?" (*SN*, 11, 4, April, 1979). These and other newsletters came out of that interview; they were later expanded into a book, *Zionism, the Superpowers, and the PLO*, subtitled, "A Background Study of the Mid-East Political Crisis and the Dilemma of Diplomatic Recognition, Including an Exclusive Interview with Khalid Al-Hasan, Policy Planner and Top Political Strategist of the PLO."

In the 1982 Foreword to the book, Ambassador Robert Searby wrote:

This book deals with a very important and timely subject: the paradigm of the stages of diplomatic recognition which must constantly guide the conduct of our foreign relations, in both war and peace, if that conduct is ever to measure up fully to our responsibilities as a major power. . . .

In the Preface to the 2002 edition, Edmund A. Bator — at the time of Henry's visit to Kuwait, Counselor of Public Affairs in the Embassy — summed up the book in these words:

The issues discussed in this book have not only withstood the test of time but are surprisingly relevant today. The "middle east" crisis has not been resolved in the twenty years since Henry Paolucci wrote his appraisal of it; nor has his careful assessment of it lost any of its force. It is still a powerful statement and can still serve as a guide to our political leaders, who have for so many years been trying desperately to help negotiate an effective and binding settlement. His arguments, based on the hard lessons of history, are especially powerful in the context of Israel's place in the family of world nations and Palestinian demands for a homeland of their own.

Having assumed his public role boldly and with *SN* firmly established under Dabrowski's skillful handling of distribution, Henry was now eager to find ways and means to shake up the liberals on the college campuses. The time was right for challenging their empty message of abstract "rights" and peace at any cost. Soon after the launching of *SN* and with the cooperation of friends and colleagues, he formed a non-profit educational foundation (1) to serve as the "umbrella" for the monthly newsletter, (2) to attract non-taxable contributions, and (3) to help implement other projects he had in mind. He named his new organization The Walter Bagehot Research Council on National Sovereignty.

Although friends, wife, and collaborators urged him on, Henry didn't need much prodding to approach the American Political Science Association — the major academic group of its kind in the nation, representing faculty and advanced students in the field of government and politics — to request listing for The Bagehot Council as an "affiliated" association of APSA. If granted, it meant The Bagehot Council could hold meetings at APSA's annual convention, attended every year by thousands of members.

The newsletter was undoubtedly a tremendous plus in

getting APSA approval; but with or without it, the people running that liberal-oriented group must have been pleased to be able to prove their impartiality by accepting an independent organization headed by a conservative like Henry. Or they may have assumed that Bagehot (1826-1877), a member of the British Liberal Party was — like the modern American breed — a vitriolic activist for liberal causes, when in fact he was an articulate spokesman for traditional values and the nation-state system. Whatever the reason, APSA granted the request.

The listing with APSA was a critical move that gave young conservative academics an opportunity to gain points toward tenure or promotion for delivering a paper and, eventually, getting it published — for Henry made sure that the conference presentations were made available to Griffon House Publications, the small press that Dabrowski had set up to serve as official publisher for *SN* and for other writings Henry was turning out.

From the outset, GHP was linked with The Bagehot Council in order to take advantage of the latter's tax-exempt status, which encouraged contributions that made printing and distribution costs feasible not only for the newsletter (issued monthly, except for February and August, as a single sheet initially) but also for "occasional papers, booklets, and books on the subject of national sovereignty and on its national cultural-political foundations."

Henry, in fact, had begun to write pamphlets that expanded on the newsletter's major theme, "to provide in-depth analyses . . . of events that have a bearing on questions relating to the concept of national sovereignty and its actual exercise in contemporary international relations." At the same time, Dabrowski began to search out "remainder" copies of important books that dealt with the kind of topics covered by the newsletter and offering them at discounted prices to subscribers of *SN*. One such book was *The Exercise of Sovereignty* (John Hopkins University Press, 1965) by Charles Burton Marshall, whose interview with Henry had been published in *SN* and who had often met with him since then. Another was Henry's first full-length political book, *War, Peace, and the Presidency,* put out in 1968 by McGraw Hill, for which Henry had acquired the rights from the publisher.

When it first appeared, the book drew immediate

attention. Perhaps the most provocative assessment was a long, thoughtful article by Jeffrey Hart, which appeared in *National Review* (February 25, 1969):

> It's not often that you come across a book that really makes a change, something not quantitative but qualitative. Many of the books you read are *good* books, you have a nose for the bad ones, and you avoid them; and so you almost always learn something from your own book of the day or the week. But Henry Paolucci's book is something else. It did not merely provide me with this or that insight, or with one or another bit of information. It provides *qualitative* news — a perspective, a way of seeing the relations among seemingly disparate events, and of perceiving their larger meaning and tendency. The result, for me at least, was an increase in understanding.
>
> It is not an easy or predictable book. And this is one of the formal characteristics of its originality. . . . I expected another discourse on the powers of the Presidency. . . .
>
> But this book is nothing of the sort. Rather, it is a compelling historical and theoretical re-examination of the idea of the nation . . . and [Paolucci] conducts his argument against those — very much more numerous and authoritative than I had ever supposed — who regard the nation as an anachronism, and look forward to an imminent parliament or directorate of Mankind, to world government. . . . But, as Paolucci argues, and, in my opinion, convincingly argues, any viable world government would necessarily be a tyranny.

Hart continues at some length, expanding on points that especially interest him, in many places adding examples of his own to those Henry put forward. In the last portion of the review, he focuses on the author's illuminating discussion about the political meaning of anti-nationalist manifestations here and elsewhere. World government may be "nonsense" but, Hart points out, it has "powerful advocates,"

> and the disturbing part of Paolucci's book is this demonstration. W.W. Rostow, for example, envisages the withering away of the nation; so did Adlai Stevenson; so, for example, do James P. Warburg, James MacGregor Burns, William C. Foster. Some of Fulbright's utterances, apparently not very widely known, are startling.
>
> I think that Henry Paolucci has called attention to an enormously interesting theoretical and practical issue. Is the nation the optimal unit for the preservation of civilized values?

And to what extent does the negative answer to that question influence American policy-making?

The immediate interest generated by *War, Peace, and the Presidency* made Dabrowski double his efforts in making "remainder" copies of the book available, taking every opportunity to promote it.

In a letter dated July 2, 1971 he contacted Barry Gray, whose radio talk show had gained an impressive following.

> I understand that on a recent show of yours, Professor Van der Haag cited Henry Paolucci's book, *War, Peace, and the Presidency*, with high praise, especially illuminating as background for understanding the Pentagon Papers Affair.

> Inasmuch as Paolucci's book is now available once again, through The Walter Bagehot Research Council on National Sovereignty, . . . you might be interested in having the Professor as your guest to talk about it, as also about his newsletter, *State of the Nation*, which updates its arguments to the present.

The suggestion was quickly picked up: Henry soon after appeared as a guest on the Barry Gray show.

Years later, people were still ordering the book, often eager to share personal memories of the author. Writing for a copy in the late 70s, Professor C.P. van der Walt of the Center for International Politics at Potchefstroom University, in the Republic of South Africa, took occasion to recall the indelible impression made on him by Henry, whom he had heard speak at the Center for African Studies in New York, two years earlier. "With the eloquence of a Demosthenes and citations from Shakespeare he advocated South Africa's case. . . . I was disappointed when he had to leave for a lecture."

In a letter occasioned by the publicity Henry had generated with his book and as a candidate for public office, Mario E. Smith, Lt. Col. U.S. Army with the US Medical Field Service School in Fort Sam Houston, Texas, recalls sharing a room in a BOQ in 1945, in a staging area outside of Bagnoli (near Naples),

> with an extremely interesting ex-bombardier in the Air Corps who was named Henry Paolucci. He made quite an impression on me and I still happily recall the hours of conversation dealing with music appreciation, history, philosophy and everything else that his amazing spectrum of interests and intelligence encompassed. . . . When I returned to the USA I made a

considerable effort to locate him . . . . His name caught my eye in the San Antonio *Light*, where reading about "an obscure professor of history and political science . . . who is extremely individualistic . . . who left to his own personal inclinations would prefer to spend his leisure time composing music" convinced me that this was my friend.

Dabrowski promoted Henry's writings in other ways also. Whenever he could, he encouraged bulk orders for newsletters, pamphlets, or books, with a keen business sense that often produced surprising results. On one occasion, the editor of a weekly in Oklahoma had called in an order for 10,000 copies of *Who is Kissinger?* or, as a second possibility, had asked what it would cost to reprint the 40-page booklet at their end. Dabrowski quickly wrote back to "clarify" in writing what was said on the phone — in reality, to offer an irresistible option that would clinch the deal.

> An accurate assessment of our printing, overhead, author costs comes to 35 cents per booklet for 10,000. Your printing and overhead costs may be less than ours. In view of the urgency of the matter, we are anxious to have the Kissinger story reach your readers. We would be agreeable to a contract of 10 cents per booklet if your organization undertakes to reprint it (with our format intact), pricing the booklet at $1.00 with its back cover material (inside and out) as it stands.

His offer freed GHP from having to produce 10,000 new copies of the booklet yet insured some profit. More important, he saw his chance to gain 10,000 new readers in one stroke and made sure his price was too good to refuse.

Dabrowski spent most of his spare time "marketing" Henry, making the fullest use of his business skills to expand publications within a limited budget; but he found time also to defend conservative ideas in his own voice and did not hesitate on occasion to speak out directly. His style was forthright and unadorned, as in his answer to an editorial in the *Long Island Press* (December 16, 1970):

> Your editorial on the dilemma of cross-endorsements facing the Democratic and Republican leaders throughout the state, and in other states as well, was entitled "A Danger to the Two Party System," — but it ought to have been entitled "A Danger to the Tweedle-dee Tweedle-dum Two Party System."

When the Republicans put up a Goodell and the Democrats match him with an Ottinger for senator, you don't have a two party system; and the election of James L. Buckley, who campaigned against both of them as if they represented a single political ideology, is proof of that.

The Conservative Party was formed in 1962 because many of us feared that the two party system was going down the drain. . . .

The two-column piece goes on to assess Rockefeller's position and to review the impact of recent events on the question of cross-endorsements — an excellent analysis that reflects a strong grasp of political strategies while keeping conservative principles up front.

Although he always found time to answer misleading and controversial statements by the opposition, the top priority item in Dabrowski's agenda remained, to the very end, promoting Henry's conservative views. He had shown Henry to be a provocative intellectual speaker and writer; but he also realized that they could not afford ongoing large-scale advertising that could reach a wide audience. A small press, GHP depended largely on tax-exempt contributions to The Bagehot Council. Its readership was still an "elite" group. And although the connection between the publishing operation and The Bagehot Council had proved effective, financial support remained limited. The long hours Dabrowski gave to the project he had so eagerly taken on were not enough. New initiatives were needed, especially new funding sources. There was also a major hitch of another kind, for people kept asking, "Who is Walter Bagehot?"

He is not exactly a forgotten man. Articles about him and his works still appear from time to time, a reminder of the controversies he often provoked: a long piece by Alan Ryan occasioned by the publication in England of several volumes of Bagehot's collected writings, part of an ambitious project undertaken by Norman St. John-Stevas to make available Bagehot's complete works (*Times Literary Supplement* [London] December 21, 1971); a scathing assessment by C. H. Sisson (*The Case of Water Bagehot*) reviewed in "No word for Bagehot" (*TLS* August 18, 1972); "Bagehot: Economist for All Seasons" by Frank C. Genovese (*New York Times*, August 21, 1977); a long and intriguing article by R. T. Shannon entitled "The Greatest Victorian?" (*TLS*, August 29, 1986), which appeared as a review of the final volumes of the collected works, which had recently been published.

Perhaps the best article on Bagehot appeared some months earlier than Shannon's, at the very time the massive 21-year project of the collected works, edited by Stevas, came to completion. It appeared in the April 12, 1986 issue of the very periodical Bagehot founded, *The Economist*, and opens with a striking assessment of the man, including high praise by Woodrow Wilson, writing while he was still President of the United States:

> Walter Bagehot (1826-77), banker, economist, political thinker and commentator, critic, journalist and man of letters, was Victorian England's most versatile genius. G. M. Young called him the "greatest" in the sense of the "truest" Victorian, and Woodrow Wilson referred to him as his master. "Had I command of the culture of men," wrote President Wilson, "I should wish to raise up for the instruction and stimulation of my nation more than one sane, sagacious, penetrative critic of men and affairs like Walter Bagehot. . . . It would be a most agreeable good fortune to introduce Bagehot to men who have not read him. . . .

Bagehot keeps turning up in books and articles. In a recent piece by Professor Elizabeth Corey of Baylor College on the conservatism of Michael Oakeshott ("A Disposition of Delight," *First Things*, February 12, 2112), the author turns to Bagehot who, writing about Macaulay, speaks of the same disposition to delight Professor Corey finds in conservative Oakshott, who did not indulge in the pessimism or somber manner many people attribute to that breed but enjoyed such ordinary everyday pleasures as fishing, conversation, liberal arts and learning. friendship, poetry. The passage she quotes carries something of Bagehot's ironic humor:

> Talk of ways of spreading a wholesome Conservatism through-out this country: give painful lectures, distribute weary tracts (and perhaps this is as well — you may be able to give an argumentative answer to a few objections, you may diffuse a distinct notion of the dignified notion of politics), but as far as communicating and establishing your creed are concerned — try a little pleasure. The way to keep up old customs is, to enjoy old customs; the way to be satisfied with the present state of things is, to enjoy that state of things.

In spite of the controversies still surrounding him, Bagehot was unquestionably among the most famous writers of mid-19th century England, author of many books and articles on a variety of subjects, best known as the founder of *The Economist* and author of *Lombard Street* (London's financial district, comparable to our Wall Street). Henry's description in the announcement he prepared for The Bagehot Council's annual meetings at the APSA convention is perhaps the most meaningful reply (allowing for humor at the same time) to the persistent question, "Who is Walter Bagehot?"

Although he "has been conceded genius often and willingly enough," Jacques Barzun has written, "yet he remains a shadowy figure in that part of the public mind where reputations are considered settled." For the uncertainty of his fame — Barzun suggests lightly — Bagehot is himself, of course, in part responsible, for it appears that he made "two capital mistakes: one, the mistake of bearing a name puzzling to pronounce; the other, the mistake of dying at 51, before the variety and superiority of his mind could force themselves on public opinion by the necessary repetition of tenets and attitudes."

The work in which Bagehot most concisely summed up his thought on the meaning of sovereign nationhood is his *Physics and Politics*. There he confronts the same hard facts of the rapidly developing industrial society of the West that his contemporary Karl Marx confronted. But whereas Marx brought to the study of those facts a spirit of alien hostility, bent on subversion and revolutionary destruction of the nation in which he happened to live, Bagehot's concern, as a Westerner and Englishman, was invariably to protect the national unity of his own people, and to strengthen the nation-state system of which England is a responsible member.

Our Research Council on National Sovereignty takes up the name of Walter Bagehot as best suited to characterize its educational mission.

That mission consists in recalling the attention of Americans from all walks of life to the ideal of nationhood — of enforceable, deeply felt national unity, culminating in government by discussion — for which Bagehot has been the most enlightened advocate in the English-speaking world.

To the extent that it succeeds in its aim, our Council on National Sovereignty will fill an obvious educational vacuum. Specifically, it will complement the activities of several other educational organizations, such as the Center for the Study of Democratic Institutions, the Council on Foreign Relations, and World Law Fund, which have had a very different emphasis, virtually ignoring or rejecting the traditional ideal of nationhood.

Here, as in all his writings, as in his talks as well, Henry focuses on essentials, or (as Jeffrey Hart characterized *War, Peace, and the Presidency*) on the *qualitative* rather than the *quantitative*. He also conveys the unmistakable impression that he shares Bagehot's views about national sovereignty unconditionally; and, although it is not mentioned, we know that he prided himself in sharing Bagehot's many other interests as well, especially literature and literary criticism. Both were men of many facets, who thought clearly and wrote with flair. What Henry admired most, however, was Bagehot's keen historical vision, especially his firm stand on the importance of the nation-state system.

In introducing each year the Henry Paolucci/Walter Bagehot Book Award, I feel compelled to explain why Bagehot's name appears with Henry's. The first step, however, was to explain the linking of the two names to the sponsor chosen to administer the annual award, the Intercollegiate Studies Institute. An education-oriented organization, with national headquarters in Wilmington Delaware and 66,000 members throughout the country, ISI publishes books and journals, hosts lectures and discussion groups on subjects that promote conservative views. It is especially active in restoring traditional teaching values in the classroom — incentives very much in line with Henry's views, especially the idea that the academy should be the curator of history, not a soap-box for promoting factional interests. current enthusiasms, or partisan ideologies.

The logic behind my choice was reinforced when I discovered in the listing of executives and committee heads on ISI stationery familiar names, friends and colleagues of Henry's like William F. Buckley, Jr., the group's first President, who referred to Henry as his "mentor" and had published several of his articles in *National Review*; Henry Salvatori, the California businessman who visited with Henry when he came to New York and was candid enough to acknowledge his mistake in trusting Richard Nixon; the publisher Henry Regnery, who had issued Henry's two books on St. Augustine (carried by ISI at discounted prices for student members); others like M. Stanton Evans and Russell Kirk, who knew Henry well because of his connection with *National Review.* . . .

My contacts at ISI must have wondered (like so many others) who Walter Bagehot was and why his name and bio were·to appear with Henry's in publicizing the award. When the importance of the connection was explained, they quickly put the information to good use in the pamphlets and letters that went out: Henry Paolucci not only had tremendous admiration for the man who held political views similar to his own but also recognized in Walter Bagehot many of his own intellectual preferences, especially Bagehot's love of literature. He was especially appreciative of Bagehot's literary essays. His own literary writings included a Master's Essay at Columbia on the British 19th-century poet James Thomson, the author of *The City of Dreadful Night.* Later it was expanded into a doctoral dissertation — a provocative comparison with the earthly City of St. Augustine, the doomed City of Man.

There was another reason for my wanting the two names together in the description of the award. Mindful of objections Henry would have raised had he known such an award was being contemplated in his name, I felt I could ease my conscience by adding Bagehot's name — convinced that Henry would have accepted a compromise that gave new visibility to the man with whom he identified so closely.

By then, the man who had worked so diligently to promote The Bagehot Council, who gained a wide audience for *SN*, and who had been instrumental in setting up GHP — bolstering through its publications the morale and political commitment of many young conservatives who were just finding their stride — was regrettably long gone. Ted Dabrowski died suddenly on March 15, 1972 at the age of 57, while attending a Conservative Party meeting in Albany.

With his death, the Party lost one of its most effective strategists. Henry lost a loyal friend, a man who put in extra hours after a long business day to get the conservative message out. He was ready to do whatever it took to help the cause to which he had dedicated his life but especially to find ways to bring Henry the respect and honor he felt he deserved as a man who fought hard for the values they both cherished. No one could have done more.

His wife and five young children lost a beloved husband and father and their only source of income. The family suddenly found themselves in dire straits also because Dabrowski, generous to a fault, had never turned away anyone who approached him for help. The oldest son, still a teenager, was left to carry on his father's printing business. He had worked closely with his Dad and now took on the heavy responsibility that had come to rest on his shoulders without complaint. Nonetheless, difficulties loomed large. Henry approached the Party leaders eliciting their cooperation in finding ways to help the family, tapping contacts in Albany and elsewhere to insure, first and foremost, much-needed business for the printing operation. The result was gratifying.

Speaking at the first presentation of the scholarship set up by the Party to honor Ted Dabrowski's memory, Henry recalled the man who in a short span of time had won his respect and admiration as well as his friendship:

> At the time of his death, Ted Dabrowski, whom we remember and honor, was busy with a thousand things for God and Country and our Conservative Party. Not the least part of his tireless concern was to do all he could to relieve the most pressing needs of hundreds of persons whose paths crossed his, whom he helped substantially. . . .

> He combined toughness with gentleness, just severity with merciful compassion, political astuteness with unwavering patriotism. His service to our country was worthy of the exemplary sacrifice of our best policemen and soldiers in the line of duty.

> His death has infused many of us with new strength in our efforts to promote the conservative cause. . . .

Dabrowski will long be remembered for his political acumen and his strategic decisions. He should also be remembered as the man who worked assiduously to bring about what most political pundits thought impossible: the election in 1970 of Jim Buckley to the U.S. Senate on the Conservative Party line. At a political dinner in March, 1971, the newly-elected senator had occasion to pay tribute publicly to the man who had worked indefatigably to get him elected. His remarks were recalled in *The Queens Conservative* (X, 5

April 1972) at the time of Dabrowski's death.

Ted Dabrowski held the infinitely important job of liaison through thousands of individual communities and committees and groups throughout the state using his tact and knowledge of the state to make what was a citizens' effort succeed.

📂 *From the Archives*

THADDEUS ("TED") DABROWSK

WALTER BAGEHOT

NORMAN ST. JOHN-STEVAS
(ED., BAGEHOT'S COLLECTED WORKS)

THE CONSERVATIVE PARTY OF QUEENS COUNTY

STATE of the NATION
Newsletter

ublisher and Editor . . . . .Henry Paolucci

,ssociate Editor . . . . Thaddeus S. Dabrowski

ubscription Manager . . . . Barbara Carle

:irculation Manager . . . . William A. Hostek

*"Your newsletter is saying more than any othe
publication. It's great."* —Arnold McCullougl
Conservative American.

*"I just thought I'd write to tell you how much I ar
enjoying State of the Nation. It provides the kind c
"conservative" insight National Review seems i
almost consciously avoid (except for hints froi
James Burnham) . . . . Please continue. The newslett.
is one of its kind."* —James Fitzpatrick

*I am impressed by your anlaysis of the appeal th
the politics of stability has to the working class*
—William F. Buckley, Jr.

See for yourself — Subscribe now:

State of the Nation
40-02 150th Street
Flushing, N.Y. 11354
$2.00 per year

A GRIFFON-HOUSE PUBLICATION

WASHINGTON'S BIRTHDAY — 8th DINNER-DANCE

**Early flyer announcing the launching
of *State of the Nation***

THE WALTER BAGEHOT RESEARCH COUNCIL ON NATIONAL SOVEREIGNT

1983 ANNUAL MEETING
in conjunction with the
AMERICAN POLITICAL SCIENCE ASSOCIATION

Palmer House, Chicago, Illinois
Thursday, September 1 through Sunday, September 4, 1983

PANEL

FRIDAY, September 2, 1983   8:30 A.M.   PARLOR A

TOPIC:

NUCLEAR DETERRENCE STRATEGIES
and the CHRISTIAN "JUST WAR" TRADITION

CHAIR: Thomas Mangieri, *Christendom College*

PAPERS: " 'What in God's Name' is Strategic Nuclear Sufficiency? "
Henry Paolucci, *Bagehot Research Council*

"Peace, Pacifism, and the Bishops"
Thomas Molnar, *Yale University*

DISCUSSANTS:

Arthur A. Belonzi, *Academy of Aeronautics*
Frank P. Le Veness, *St. John's University*
Frank M. Sorrentino, *St. Francis College*
Joseph C. Bertolini, *St. John's University*

THE WALTER BAGEHOT RESEARCH COUNCIL ON NATIONAL SOVEREIGNTY, founded in 1972, is
an educational foundation made up of scholars whose primary concern is the study of the past, present, and
possibly future atatus of the nation-state ideal of political organization, and more particularly of the nation-
state system of international relations. Its chief educational activities include publication of STATE OF THE
NATION (Quarterly) and occasional papers, pamphlets, and books; participation in interdisciplinary programs that focus on the cultural and historical aspects of the development of the nation-state ideal, par-.
ticularly on national literatures as expressions of national identity and as a medium of international communication and understanding; and study of the writings of Walter Bagehot, with special emphasis on his
contribution to the understanding of the characteristically American form of Presidential "Government by
Discussion."

Address all correspondence to:

SECRETARY
THE BAGEHOT COUNCIL
P.O. Box 81, Whitestone, New York 11357

**Program for the 1983 annual APSA meeting
of The Bagehot Council**

Brzezinski: Carter's Mentor

One of the most frequently mentioned names among Democratic presidential nominee Jimmy Carter's advisers is that of Zbigniew Brzezinski.

Brzezinski, a Polish immigrant, is a professor at Columbia University and a close associate of David Rockefeller. In cooperation with Rockefeller, Brzezinski founded the Trilateral Commission, a group of influential individuals drawn from North America, Europe and Japan working to promote the interests of the industrialized capitalist nations.

Brzezinski has been mentioned frequently in recent months as a possible secretary of state if Carter is elected.

In an article by Robert Scheer in *Playboy* magazine, the author said he asked Pat Anderson, Carter's speech writer a question on foreign policy. Scheer said Anderson at the time was working on a speech which Carter was to deliver before the Foreign Policy Association in New York. Anderson said, "Later. I have to check this speech out with Brzezinski."

The relationship between Carter and Brzezinski, according to Scheer, goes back to 1973 when David Rockefeller asked Carter to join the Trilateral Commission. An aide of Carter said the selection to the commission was "one of the most fortunate accidents of the early campaign and critical to (Carter's) building support where it counted."

Obviously, Brzezinski has immense influence over Carter's views.

And, according to an article in *The Washington Post* (May 8) by Laurence Stern, Brzezinski and Rockefeller sought out Carter early as a possible presidential aspirant: "When Rockefeller, Brzezinski and other recruiters were looking for a Southerner to round out the ranks of the commission in 1973, they were also considering Florida Gov. Rubin Askew. But they settled on Carter."

Henry Paolucci, writing in *National Review* magazine, contends that Carter was selected because he "had revealed himself to be a politician of 'educable' ambition—and with a Wallace-type Southern appeal to boot!"

But what does Brzezinski stand for? Where would he, through Carter, guide the nation?

* * *

PAOLUCCI describes Brzezinski as

espousing a "Marxist-humanist-technetronic philosophy of history."

In this view, according to Paolucci, "The Western peoples, since their identifiable beginnings in the feudal era, advanced through three great stages and are now entering a fourth and culminating stage."

The first stage has to do with religion, the second nationalism, and the third Marxism—which Brzezinski says "represents a further vital and creative stage in the maturing of man's universal vision."

But Brzezinski envisions a fourth stage. "Beyond religion, nationalism and Marxism," writes Paolucci, "we now have, he tells us, his emerging technectronic-age ideal of *rational humanism* on a global scale."

In his book, *Between Two Ages: America's Role in the Technetronic Era* (1970), Brzezinski himself writes. "A new pattern of international politics is emerging. The world is ceasing to be an arena in which relatively self-sustained, 'sovereign,' and homogeneous nations interact, collaborate, clash or make war... Transnational ties are gaining in importance, while the claims of nationalism, though still intense, are nevertheless diluted. This change, naturally, has gone furthest in the most advanced countries, but no country is immune to it. The consequence is a new era—an era of the global political process."

Brzezinski sees the world in the future as "that of the 'global city'—a nervous, agitated, tense, and fragmented web of interdependent relations."

And, Paolucci gathers from his works, Brzezinski believes "the burden of advancing the era of global politics

must fall most heavily, if not exclusively, on the American people."

"Realism," writes Brzezinski however, forces us to recognize that the necessary political innovation will not come from direct constitutional reform, desirable as that would be. The needed change is more likely to develop incrementally and less overtly in keeping with the American tradition of blurring distinctions between public and private institutions."

So, to Brzezinski, American sovereignty is a dead letter. The American people will resist being merged with the rest of the world in some supranationalist scheme, but they can be duped by gradual and covert actions of their leaders.

And, as Paolucci put it. "To get where Brzezinski would like to lead them, free people would have to undermine their national governments which still have the force and authority to quell domestic disorders. Once such 'relatively watertight' national units are cumulatively undermined, the global city of the technetronic age will being to take clearer shape; after which, all that will remain to be done will be to create, in a higher dimension an ultimate *pacifier*, whose pleasure must have the force of law everywhere."

Do Americans want to elect a candidate indoctrinated in this "global city" ideology?

Reprint of *State of the Nation* newsletter on Brzezinski and Carter, *Birmingham News*, October 3, 1976.

HENRY PAOLUCCI

CARTER'S

Zbigniew Brzezinski:
*Lying in Wait for an Ambitious and
therefore 'Educable' Politician*

KISSINGER

In the shadows—

**Cartoon for *State of the Nation* reprint on Brzezinski and Carter,
Birmingham News, October 3, 1976.**

4 *Gennaio 1970*   Il BORGHESE

LE »ATROCITÀ«
del marzo 1968

di HENRY PAOLUCCI

**Cartoons for *State of the Nation* reprints in the Italian political
journal, *Il Borghese* (Milan, Rome).**

Dust jacket for *War, Peace, and the Presidency* (1968)

NEWS photo by Ed Giordino

Conservative candidate James Buckley is greeted by Ted Dombrowski in Bayside. Queens, on campaign swing yesterday.

Jim Buckley and Ted Dabrowski, 1970.

3. GRIFFON HOUSE PUBLICATIONS

The man chosen to replace Ted Dabrowski as the President of Griffon House Publications was Frank D. Grande, a younger colleague of Henry's, who taught history at The City College of New York, where Henry himself was often asked to teach Greek and Roman History as a special guest lecturer. Grande had known Henry for over a decade and had served on the Board of Directors óf GHP for several years.

A quiet man, with a wry sense of humor, Grande was a confirmed conservative but very different from his predecessor in that, like Henry, he was an academic. It was only natural for him to bring his scholarly interests — and Henry's — to bear on the publishing list he developed over more than thirty years as head of the small press founded by Ted Dabrowski. Henry remained his major author, but the emphasis now was not exclusively on political subjects. Areas in the humanities began to be explored, especially those in which Henry had a vital interest. GHP was about to enter a new phase.

What was to become a long, productive relationship and a rewarding friendship developed slowly. In 1959, Grande — a graduate student — had applied for an adjunct position at Brooklyn College. Called in for an interview with the man who was then in charge of the evening division, Professor Harry Bernstein, Grande presented his brief resumè. As Bernstein scanned it, he asked casually if Grande knew anyone on their faculty. "I told him," Grande later wrote,

> that I had once briefly met Henry Paolucci. The name was like a *zauberwort*. Bernstein launched into a panegyric, telling me that Henry was one of the greatest teachers he had ever encountered.

While he was speaking, Bernstein was interrupted and called outside. He had risen to leave when he suddenly whirled around, pointed at me and said: "You know Henry Paolucci — you're hired!"

Grande didn't miss the opportunity to search out the man who elicited such praise. His classes ended just before Henry's on ancient Roman history began, but instead of leaving for home, Grande would rush to Henry's lectures. On his first visit, he was amazed to see the room "overflowing with students." After a while, he began to hang back to ask questions or "just listen to the Professor answer other questions." Grande was a good listener, eager at all times to hear more about subjects "the Professor might have merely touched on." What he heard made him aware of the rich base of knowledge that lay beneath the most casual remarks and he wanted to hear more. Whenever he could, he would even drive to St. John's University, to sit in on whatever graduate course or seminar Henry was teaching — political theory, Hegel, foreign policy — and afterwards would linger, as long as he could, to talk with him informally.

By 1972, the year of Dabrowski's death, Grande's unobtrusive, undemanding presence had made him part of that inner circle whom Henry accepted as loyal friends and whose intellectual curiosity matched his own. It was no surprise when he was chosen to succeed Dabrowski.

In spite of heavy academic demands — he was now Chairman of the History Department at City College and would be re-elected to that office several times — Grande quickly picked up where Dabrowski had left off, encouraging Henry to produce longer newsletters (four to six pages), and more pamphlets and booklets. Three pamphlets appeared in 1978: *A Separate and Equal Station, The South and the Presidency,* and *The Political Thought of G.F.W. Hegel.*

Without losing sight of Henry's writings as the major focus, Grande also began to enlarge the GHP list to include an eclectic assortment of plays, poetry, literary criticism and translations. Among the new titles was a long-overdue English version of Alfred de Vigny's *Chatterton* that turned out to be a "best-seller" on many college and university reading requirements in English and French literature, drama and theater; Armenian plays (like *Chatterton,* never translated before); two short plays by Mario Fratti (co-author of the award-winning play that became the hit musical *Nine*); and scientific subjects like *The Achievement of Galileo* (Paolucci and James Brophy).

The history of science was of special interest to him. Long sessions with Henry during the 1960s resulted in a personal decision to shift gears: instead of getting his Ph.D. at Columbia, he decided to try for a degree in the history of science at Oxford University. It took years of rigorous scheduling, several summers in England and quick trips between semesters and whenever else possible to complete the work for the doctorate. All that time, Henry served as Grande's "unofficial" mentor, suggesting books, pointing out the crucial ideas that should be mastered, reading the pages of the dissertation as Grande produced them.

Henry's death was a devastating blow, but in the months that followed it, Grande put out three new books: a collection of Henry's essays, *Selected Writings on Literature and the Arts; Science and Astronomy; Law, Government, and Political Philosophy*; Matthew Pauley's *Criminal Law: It's Nature and Sources*; and the proceedings of the 1998 Bagehot Council meeting at APSA, with the title *Morale in the Military in War and Peace.* This last was edited by Jack Ryan, whom we met in the mid 60s in Naples, where I had gone as a Fulbright Lecturer to teach American Drama at the University.

Ryan, a hard-line conservative, had been with NATO for several years when we first met him. When he retired and returned to the States in the 80s, he came back full of new energy and lots of free time. With a Master's degree in Business Administration and a wide experience as a European sales representative for Josten while still in Italy, eager to join fellow conservatives in "marketing" their views, he was more than ready to use his skills in whatever way was called for, when Grande invited him to join GHP as General Manager. Among other things, it gave him an opportunity to work closely with Henry, whose friendship, especially the many hours of solid good talk on foreign policy — he had come to treasure.

It also gave him the opportunity to develop a growing interest in publishing. Before long, he began to contribute to the processing and distribution of books, proving himself knowledgeable and creative in those jobs. He used his contacts both here and abroad to enlarge the GHP mailing lists and, on occasion (with Henry's help and Grande's approval), prepared programs and special events, such as the panel at APSA on morale in the armed forces (in which Henry took part), which he quickly turned into the book already mentioned. He learned to edit manuscripts and helped in that area as well. Most important, his managerial skills kept things running smoothly.

In 2003, several years after Henry's death, I turned to both Ryan and Grande to determine whether a manuscript I'd found in Henry's files was his writing or the work of two older students who (I'd been told) had taken extensive notes one year, in his course on Roman history. I was almost certain I recognized Henry's terse style, the spontaneity of a delivery rooted in an ordered sequence of ideas, the frequent interjections with references to current events, the rich comparisons that brought the past into the present — all the earmarks of Henry's writing — but I wanted to be sure.

Both agreed that is was very likely Henry's work; but it was Grande who ultimately resolved the issue, with his excellent memory and meticulous habits as a researcher. He quickly came up with the names of the two students who had taken "verbatim" notes in the course — one which Henry had taught several times at City College and Brooklyn College, as well as at St. John's, one that Grande himself had audited more than once — and volunteered to call one of the students, with whom he had kept in touch. He agreed that the manuscript was indeed a "finished product," either an edited version of the notes taken by the two students or a version Henry himself had fleshed out for publication and may have set aside after Dabrowski's death.

After tracking down and talking with one of the two students, Grande was able to confirm that Henry had been given a collated readable version of the notes the two students had taken. Was that the manuscript we were looking at? The question was finally answered, as luck would have it, when a copy of the students' manuscript turned up as I continued clearing Henry's files. It was fluent and accurate, but totally different in style from the "finished product" Grande, Ryan, and I had — correctly as it turned out — ascribed to Henry.

The question of authorship now resolved, Grande proceeded to read Henry's manuscript for publication with his usual care, noting things that had to be double-checked, researching sources, rewording passages here or there — in short, reading every page with a fine-tooth comb and providing (as only someone with a substantive knowledge of the subject could) whatever was necessary. Having read the manuscript closely myself, I was especially pleased with Grande's comments in the Foreword about Henry's easy, often "chatty" style, and the enlightening passages "in which the *Pax Romana* is compared to the political realities of our day, especially the role of the United States in our updated global scenario. . . ."

Lectures on Roman History went to hundreds of libraries here and abroad as part of a project Grande had taken on some years prior to Henry's death.

The plan was to promote Henry's writings on a wide scale and at the same time attract new readers to Grande's growing humanities list, thereby drawing new donors as well — although the primary purpose was not to increase revenues but to increase GHP visibility on an international level.

Dabrowski's main purpose had been to disseminate Henry's political writings and the conservative agenda with the money that came in as tax-exempt contributions to The Bagehot Council. He had worked hard to keep within that budget. Grande's plan was to publicize Henry's conservative thinking in other areas besides politics, expanding at the same time a humanities list which included books by other authors who reflected the same values. It was an ambitious plan that could only be implemented by rearranging priorities and by a careful monitoring of funds, so that money would not be filtered away from ongoing projects. After initially consulting with Henry, Grande had decided to move ahead but slowly.

Jack Ryan and I volunteered our services in preparing manuscripts and taking on other editorial tasks. Most important, a sponsor (essential for the project to succeed) had already been found. Council on National Literatures — a non-profit foundation set up to promote neglected and emergent literatures as part of the traditional, European-centered mainstream (a conservative approach to global literary studies) — had agreed to take part. A strong point in favor of the plan was that GHP costs would not escalate: anyone in publishing knows that adding a few hundred copies to a "run" doesn't amount to much: the more copies printed, the less the cost per copy. With a few adjustments and some minor cuts, GHP would not exceed its limited printing budget.

Briefly: CNL would cover the costs of packaging and mailing newly-published GHP books to several hundred academic libraries drawn from the CNL list of 1200 subscibers to CNL's *Review of National Literatures* for over thirty years, if GHP would donate books for the purpose.

The arrangement would insure thousands of new readers with every mailing and bring high-level visibility to

GHP. It might also bring in new contributors to The Bagehot Council from among those new readers.

Grande took the plan to the Board of Trustees and got them to accept it.

Since then — and still an ongoing project — six hundred CNL member libraries in Norway, Japan, Israel, Russia, Italy, Australia, Germany, England, Scotland, Wales, Holland, China, France, Canada, Mexico, etc., and the United States, have been receiving free books as gifts from GHP.

The partial listing below shows the unusual nature of the publications that have reached the shelves of the CNL libraries selected for this project, most of which are on subjects and reflect views not easily found anywhere else.

Henry Paolucci. *Selected Writings on Literature and the Arts; Science and Astronomy; Law, Government, and Political Philosophy* (1999).

Matthew Pauley. *Criminal Law: It's Nature and Sources* (1999).

Jack Ryan, ed. and contributor. *Morale in the Military in War and Peace* (1999).

Henry Paolucci. *James Thomson's City of Dreadful Night* (2000).

Constance Del Vecchio Maltese. *An Artist's Journey of Discovery.* In large-format, this art book contains reproductions of the artist's award-winning series for the Columbus quincentenary, "Age of Discovery Navigators" and includes photos, sketches, and anecdotes that record the artist's conception and execution of her subject in each case. Highlights of the individual's life are featured in the background of each portrait (2000).

Dino Bigongiari. *Essays on Dante and Medieval Culture* (Biblioteca dell'Archivum Romanicum), originally published by Leo S. Olschki, Florence, 1964. Edited with a Preface by Henry Paolucci. Contains the few essays written by the eminent Dantist and Da Ponte Professor at Columbia University (2000).

Anne Paolucci and Henry Paolucci. *Hegel on Tragedy.* First published by Doubleday, then Harper & Row, later by Greenwood Press, currently with GHP. A unique anthology of excerpts from the many works of G.W. F. Hegel, prepared by the two leading Hegelians in America. Contains A.C. Bradley's essay on Hegel and an excellent and detailed index (2001).

Henry Paolucci and James Brophy, eds and contributors. *The Achievement of Galileo.* An invaluable collection of materials about Galileo's controversy with the Church, including an excerpt from Pierre Duhem's massive work, *Le Système du Monde* (translated for the first time by Anne Paolucci) (2001).

Vincenzo R. Latella, *Dante's Gallery of Rogues.* An unusual collection of 34 paintings (one for each canto of the *Inferno*) with a 44-page Introduction ("The Strident Voices of Hell") by Anne Paolucci. Excellent feedback (2001).

Henry Paolucci. *Public Image, Private Interest. Kissinger's Foreign Policy.* Includes *Who Is Kissinger?* and *Kissinger's War* (2002).

Anne Paolucci and Henry Paolucci. *Hegelian Literary Perspectives.* A unique collection of essays on literary subjects by two of the leading Hegelians of our time (2002).

Henry Paolucci. *Zionism, the Superpowers, and the P.L.O.* (2002).

Henry Paolucci, Richard C. Clark. *Presidential Power and Crisis Government in the Age of Terrorism* (2003).

Azar Attura. *The Nobel Prize Winners of Italy* (1906-2002) (2003).

Potpourri Magazine. Carries the winning short fiction and poetry of several annual contests sponsored by CNL (2004).

Anne Paolucci. *Beyond the Commedia.* An important book containing the long essay from the India volume of *Review of National Literatures,* "Dante and the Quest for Eloquence in the Vernaculars of India" (singled out for praise in the India *Times*); presentations at the MLA Bicentennial meeting of the Dante Society of America in 1976, "Dante's Influence on American Writers"; and a little-known work attributed by many to Dante, *A Question of the Water and the Land,* translated into English in 1897 by Charles Hamilton Bromby (2004).

Henry Paolucci. *A Brief History of Political Thought and Statecraft.* Originally prepared as a series of graduate lectures at St. John's University. Original edition 1979; 2nd edition 2002. New edition (2004).

Dino Bigongiari. *Backgrounds of the Divine Comedy.* The first half of Professor Bigongiari's prestigious graduate course at Columbia University, "Dante and Medieval Culture." His impeccable credentials give it an important place in Dante scholarship. The volume was prepared from verbatim lecture notes taken over a period of three years by Anne Paolucci and Henry Paolucci, both students of Bigongiari. The notes were collated and edited by Anne Paolucci between 2002-2004 (2005).

Anne Paolucci. *The Women in Dante's "Divine Comedy" and Spenser's "Faerie Queene."* Winner of the First Woodbridge Honorary Fellowship in the Department of English and Comparative Literature, Columbia University, 1963. A detailed analysis of the important role of the women in the two great epics of the Renaissance (2005).

Dino Bigongiari. *Readings in the Divine Comedy.* The second half of Professor Bigongiari's prestigious graduate course at Columbia University, "Dante and Medieval Culture." His impeccable credentials give it an important place in Dante scholarship. The volume was prepared from verbatim lecture notes taken over a period of three years by Anne Paolucci and Henry Paolucci, both students of Bigongiari. The notes were collated and edited by Anne Paolucci between 2002-2004 (2006).

Ann Merlino and Anne Paolucci. *Italian-American Perspectives.* Preface by Paul J. Patané. Two unusual essays: "Preserving the Future Through the Past" (A.P.) and "The Legacy of Elena Cornaro" (A.M.), the first woman ever to receive a Ph.D. (University of Padua, 1678) (2007).

Anne Paolucci. *Dante Revisited.* A collection of new essays and reprints brought together in a single volume. Included, as the Introduction, is "The Man and the Poet," an essay by the eminent Columbia University scholar and medievalist, Dino Bigongiari, written in 1965 at the request of the commission in Florence, to serve as the opening speech in the long ceremonies commemorating the 700th anniversary of Dante's birth (2008).

Herbert W. Schneider (translator). *On World Government (Dante's De Monarchia).* A new edition, with a Preface by Dino Bigongiari (2008).

Some of the titles listed are reprints of books Henry published elsewhere, for which Grande acquired the rights. It was a genial move that gave his growing humanities offerings a solid base, but his first efforts were disappointing.

In 1957, the Liberal Arts Press, a small but well known publisher of classic works, carried a new translation of Machiavelli's dramatic masterpiece, *Mandragola,* in which Henry had collaborated and for which he had written an Introduction. It sold well and has been used often for stage productions, one reason being that it was the first new version in English since Stark Young's rather formal version, back in the twenties. It also attracted both teachers and students of political science, who found in Henry's Introduction an incisive review of Machiavelli's major political theme in *The Prince* and the resolution of that major theme as expressed in a powerful minor key, in *Mandragola*. The play is shown to be a dramatic illustration of how a state is reduced to moral and political chaos when there is no leader strong enough to prevent individuals from indulging in personal self-gratification, where there is no guiding force to promote common interests and direct a society toward a common goal.

Henry's introductory essay was a welcome departure from the prevailing view of the play as a kind of Boccaccian romp, verging on pornography.

To-date *Mandragola* has gone through several major publishers and is close to a 50th printing. For a time, it was required reading in the School of International and Public Affairs of Columbia University. Still an active title with the current publisher, it could not be released to GHP.

Also inaccessible to GHP (for the same reason) are Henry's two books on St. Augustine, published and still being sold by Henry Regnery Co.: *The Enchiridion* (1961), one of the lesser-known writings of the great theologian of the Church, which Henry edited and for which he wrote a long Introduction, adding at the end an analysis and historical appraisal of the work by the great German-Lutheran historian of Catholic dogma, Adolph von Harnack; and (long-overdue) *The Political Writings of St. Augustine* (1962), edited with an Introduction and, once again, a welcome bonus at the end, "The Political Ideas of St. Augustine," by the best scholar on the subject, Dino Bigongiari.

In 1963, Henry published with Bobbs-Merrill, a new translation of Cesare Beccaria's famous argument against laws and precedents on punishments and execution of criminals, *On Crimes and Their Punishment* (1764), another book for which Grande was not able to secure the rights.

Still unavailable also is the 1974 edition of *Justice and Police* by Frederic Maitland (1850-1906), the greatest historian of English law, which Henry edited with an Introduction.

Grande's efforts paid off with what was perhaps the most important work Henry produced during these years: a selection of excerpts on drama and dramatic theory, tragedy in particular, from the works of the German philosopher G.F.W. Hegel. Passages were culled from existing English translations of the major works (corrected here and there) and brought together into a "seamless" organic whole — the kind of book only an accomplished Hegelian could produce. The final result, *Hegel on Tragedy*, is a unique anthology of passages from *The Phenomenology of Mind, Lectures on the Philosophy of Religion, Lectures on the History of Philosophy,* and *The Philosophy of Fine Art,* which has the continuity of an original study. Included as an "appendix" is the essay on Hegel (originally in *Oxford Lectures on Poetry*) by the great Shakespearean critic, A.C. Bradley, one of the Oxford "Idealists" and a thoroughgoing Hegelian, whose work still remains to be scrutinized in the light of Hegel's discussion.

First published as an Anchor Book by Doubleday Co. (1962), the book was picked up as a Torchbook paperback by Harper & Row (1974), and later brought out in hard cover by Greenwood Press (now part of a conglomerate, with new logo and new name) (1978 --).

It is an invaluable book, the only one of its kind. Its importance for theater and drama scholars is reflected in the book's publishing history. Indirectly, the book points readers to Hegel's other writings, especially his political philosophy, where Hegel goes well beyond the limited and misleading interpretations of biased critics, many of whom credit him solely for having influenced Karl Marx.

Grande was able to get the rights to the paperback edition from Harper & Row and reissued the book in 2001. (Although my name is on the cover, with Henry's, my contribution was minimal — preparation of an Index, proof-reading, and some suggestions.)

Hegel on the Arts (1979) for Frederick Ungar Publishing Co. was a much smaller volume, but no less important. This time Henry produced his own English version, a fluent translation of selected passages from the *Philosophy of Fine Art* — Hegel's provocative and detailed discussion on architecture, sculpture, music, painting, and literature.

The far-reaching influence of Hegel's incisive analysis, particularly of literature and literary genres, need not be labored. Students of those subjects are familiar with its impact on writers and literary theorists who followed, especially in the twentieth century — the New Critics in America; the Italian philosopher and literary critic Benedetto Croce; the Italian literary historian Francesco De Sanctis; and (worth adding, although not many literary critics have bothered to study the matter) the British poet and literary critic T.S. Eliot who, late in life, admitted in *The Criterion* having read some Hegel and regretted not having read more. (One of the most obvious example of Hegel's influence on Eliot is his essay "Three Voices of Poetry," where Eliot cites as his source the famous German Expressionist poet-critic Gottfried Benn, an acknowledged Hegelian.) The best example of Hegel's direct influence on English literary studies is to be found in A.C. Bradley's Shakespearean studies, mentioned earlier.

Grande managed to get the "rights" to this book also, and reissued it in both paperback and hard cover in 2001.

Henry's appreciative reading of Hegel's many pages on ancient and modern tragedy and dramatic theory was not arbitrary or casual. He had come to recognize and admire Hegel's ability to hold together the many areas he explored in an organic whole, a structured universe that gave solid meaning to the parts. Henry saw in that rare talent his own innate impulse to relate knowledge into a unified intellectual whole. It explained his habit of answering questions indirectly, giving a sweeping overall view of how the answer should be interpreted, where it fit in the larger picture. He too came to master what he considered to be Hegel's greatest contribution: an intellectual world that held fast under the most severe scrutiny. Like Hegel, he saw drama, like all other human activities, as part of a larger picture.

My interest in the arts and particularly drama and theater may also have had something to do with Henry's choosing to produce these two Hegelian texts, for they carried constant reminders of the philosophical base on which ancient and modern drama came to rest and broadened the horizons for those of us who were not philosophers. I was already converted to the Hegelian views on these subjects, and Henry's books proved enormously useful to me personally; but other readers must have found something compelling in them because, except for the hard bound edition of *Hegel on Tragedy*, which is still carried by Greenwood Press, the sold out

out in a short time. Grande's re-issuing of these two books resulted in bulk orders.

Whatever his motivation in producing *Hegel on Tragedy,* Henry gave readers easy access to what is certainly the most thorough discussion on the subject of drama and dramatic theory. In *Hegel on the Arts*, he introduced English readers to what is perhaps the most cohesive argument found anywhere on the intrinsic interrelationship of the fine arts, where the distinctive characteristic feature of each form of artistic expression is isolated and presented in a translation that is fluent and accurate.

The third book for which Grande succeeded securing the rights and added to GHP's growing humanities list was *The Achievement of Galileo,* first issued by Twayne Publishers Inc. in 1962 and reissued by GHP in 2001. The book (prepared with James Brophy) examines the documents and letters connected with the well-known controversy and reviews the Copernican theory in historical perspective. (I was surprised and gratified to receive a letter from the Cultural Counselor of the Italian Embassy in Washington, soon after the book was reissued, telling me how important it was.)

Grande exploited other opportunities to give Henry wider visibility. *A Brief History of Political Thought and Statecraft* was an original GHP book, first published in 1979 — the substance of three graduate courses Henry gave at St. John's University in prior years and that had been made available in 1978 as a series of programs on CBS-TV. The television series elicited praise from all quarters. Fred Olsen, archeologist and author of *Indian Creek* and *On the Trail of the Arawaks*, summed up Henry's talks as "by far the most intellectual discussions on the subject," calling attention also to his "intriguing humor." George Dessart, at the time Vice-President of CBS TV, wrote Henry that he "became absolutely enraptured." Wilmot Robertson, author of *The Dispossessed Majority*, wrote, when he read the published lectures:

> I don't think I have come across a more lucid or intelligent and more balanced summary of the development of Western politics. The first lecture was more than a work of history. It was a work of art. . . .

The book was reissued by GHP in 2004. It is described in the Preface to that edition as "a wide-sweeping account of major political thinkers and statesmen, from Aristotle to Abba Eban, and of the historical realities they helped shape. . . . [It] remains a tour-de-force."

At the time of his sudden and untimely death in 2006, Grande's bold initiative enjoyed prominent status and had attracted a number of new sponsors.

It was Grande who encouraged me to take on this account of Henry's dedication to conservative principles. For two years prior to his death, he drove into Queens once a week with the sole purpose of sorting out Henry's files about the 1964 election and its major players; articles he wrote between 1971 and 1973 for the Op Ed page of the *New York Times*, essays for *National Review*, for the Italian journals *Il Borghese* and *Il Veltro*, as well as French publications; correspondence relating to his political activities; transcripts of his interviews on major talk shows during the 1964 senatorial campaign (interviews that always produced a flood of letters from people who had not expected to hear such lucid arguments on that side of the fence!) — piles of folders that soon took over my dining room table.

Grande set himself the heavy task of examining each folder, weeding out casual or unimportant notes and letters, suggesting what might be discarded and what might be kept for future use. He produced a long annotated list of what he reassembled, made detailed notes about what he thought should have priority and in what context such material might be used, and made detailed inventories of what the new folders contained. Most of what he had set out to do was done when he collapsed while visiting his sister on Thanksgiving Day, 2006. Jack Ryan had died the previous November. With the sudden loss of its President and General Manager, GHP came to a temporary halt. I personally found it difficult to get my bearings under those circumstances and pushed aside the idea of writing a book about Henry's conservative views and activities. Even after a most efficient, creative, and totally supportive replacement for Grande had been found in Dr. Clara Sarrocco, I still was daunted by the piles of material waiting to be put to use in my projected book.

Sporadic forays into the neatly stacked folders Grande

had assembled convinced me that the material they contained had become an insurmountable barrier. There was so much to sift through, all seemingly indispensable. It was overwhelming. Where to begin?

It wasn't until November of 2011 that I found my way to resolving the difficulties that had plagued me and kept me from writing this book. A phone conversation with my good friend, former NYS Senator Serphin R. Maltese, around the middle of November, started me thinking again about the project. He knew about the book and thought I might want to say something at the Conservative Party's 50th anniversary celebration in June 2012 about Henry's contribution. I readily agreed, but didn't disillusion him by admitting I hadn't even started to write the book he was looking forward to reading.

The conversation stuck in my mind long after I'd put down the phone. I followed my scattered thoughts into all kinds of possibilities, considering and dismissing them, realizing finally that the initial plan to talk about Henry and the Conservative Party seemed inadequate and at the same time too broad a topic. It didn't give the whole picture of Henry as a conservative who was also a rigorous academician trying to stem the tide of liberal ideas in the classroom by flawless credentials as a scholar and researcher. Nor was I equipped to do justice to any discussion of the Party itself.

I decided I was looking at things from the wrong end. What I needed to do was start writing about events and people connected with Henry's political odyssey, as I remembered them. News stories and other supportive material would be added later but only as "archival footnotes" to each chapter. I decided my goal should be to give an account of Henry's contributions to the conservative cause, not limiting myself to either the senatorial campaign of 1964 or his other activities in the Conservative Party, but to focus on his conservatism as a writer, teacher, historian, and philosopher who preserved traditional values in every aspect of life, giving his conservative premise a solid intellectual base.

I came to terms with the idea. Amazingly, the book began to take shape. A workable outline emerged.

What resulted is not a history of the Conservative

Party. Dan Mahoney, founder and long-time Chairman of the Party, had covered that ground in his excellent book *Actions Speak Louder* (Arlington House); George Marlin had also produced an important archival history, *Fighting the Good Fight* (St. Augustine Press). Both comment on Henry's astounding role in the 1964 campaign, Mahoney's account perhaps somewhat more detailed. In it, Mahoney recalls Henry's warning in an earlier speech:

> The great danger to our nation today lies in the fact that the hierarchy of intermediary groups in our society — I mean neighborhood groups, citizens joined in local school boards, churches, business and labor associations, municipal and state governments — is caught in a vise-like squeeze, with street violence applied menacingly from below and with the might of the federal executive pressing down inexorably from above.

He also reproduces the story carried by the *New York Times* the day after Henry's nomination about the Conservative Party's unusual senatorial candidate. It begins:

> There may have been at some time a politician with odder qualifications and ideas about campaigning than the Conservative Party's candidate for the United States Senate for New York. But diligent research fails to find one who can compare with Henry Paolucci. . , .

My goal in writing the present book was a much more modest yet important one: to contribute to the archives by tracing Henry's conservative activities as a scholar and writer as well as a political figure, highlighting but not limiting my.01self to his 1964 senatorial campaign.

Frank Grande deserves to be remembered, with Ted Dabrowski, for never having missed an opportunity to promote Henry and his writings. He also saw in his friend and colleague the ideal Socratic teacher, the scholar par excellence, a man worthy of the greatest honor and respect.

Grande's death marked the end of the most productive period in GHP history. His commitment to Henry and what he stood for gave direction and meaning to all his efforts. In an era of shifting values and compromises, he maintained both in politics and in the academy those values that made our nation great. In the academy, he was an uncompromising conservative stood for gave direction and meaning to all his efforts. In an era of shifting values and compromises, he maintained both in politics and in the academy those values that made our nation great. In the academy, he was an uncompromising conservative in an environment that was essentially liberal, never backed away from expressing his views of what he considered to be the conservative lessons of history. As President of GHP he registered his political convictions as well as his traditional values as a humanist in new ways, all of which he explored without hesitation. In many respects, he was Henry's most effective spokesman.

Conservatives owe him a great deal for having preserved for future generations Henry's contributions as a political historian and philosopher, especially his articulate support of Western culture. Were he alive, he would have greeted the publication of this book in his quiet way, pleased to have his friend and mentor remembered as an important figure in the expanding conservative agenda he had defined and implemented as President of Griffon House Publications.

From the Archives

Frank Grande   Jack Ryan

HENRY PAOLUCCI

LECTURES ON
ROMAN HISTORY

Foreword by ANNE PAOLUCCI
Preface by FRANK D. GRANDE

CRIMINAL LAW:

ITS NATURE AND SOURCES

MATTHEW A. PAULEY

Covers of some of the books put out by Frank Grande
for Griffon House Publications.

Alternative Futures and the
History of Political Thought

A BRIEF HISTORY of
POLITICAL THOUGHT
and STATECRAFT

FROM SOCRATES TO ROUSSEAU

HEGEL AND MARX

TOMORROW'S WORLD OF FREE NATIONS

THE POLITICAL THOUGHT OF
G.W.F. HEGEL

WITH AN INTRODUCTION
AND ILLUSTRATIONS

HENRY PAOLUCCI

Preface by ANNE PAOLUCCI
Foreword by JACK RYAN

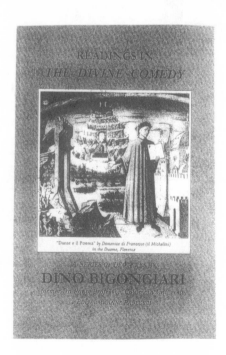

READINGS IN
THE DIVINE COMEDY

"Dante e il Poema" by Domenico di Francesco (il Michelini)
in the Duomo, Florence

A SERIES OF LECTURES BY

DINO BIGONGIARI

Former Da Ponte Professor, Columbia University

EDITED BY ANNE PAOLUCCI

The New York Times

On the Waging Of Peace

The Danger Is Not From the Military but From Peace-Mongers

By HENRY PAOLUCCI

To the historically trained ear, the most ominous drums of war have always been those pounded in the name of peace.

Those drums are rolling today with a mounting intensity unparalleled in American history. They are telling us (in the rhythms of Adlai Stevenson's eloquence): "We must abolish war to save our collective skins. For so long as this nuclear death-dance continues, tens of millions—perhaps hundreds of millions—are living on borrowed time." Or in the accents of Norman Cousins's frenzied appeal for a world federation of peace-lovers: "At a time when the fingertip of a desperate man can activate a whole switchboard of annihilation, and when defense is represented by retaliatory holocaust, the historical social contract between man and the state has ceased to exist."

The intention of such talk is peace; but its emotional intensity is unquestionably such stuff as wars are made of. When peace is proclaimed as a sovereign value, when its lovers declare themselves disposed to sacrifice all things else for its attainment—even their pledged national allegiance—we can be sure that ignorant armies, terrible with self-righteous banners, are about to clash. For it is not at college teach-ins or on the Op-Ed page of The Times, but in the arena of war that the supreme national sacrifices for peace are ultimately made.

Peace is, like liberty, one of those Janus-faced ideals that look two ways. The Road to Peace remains a peaceful road only so long as no serious obstacles are encountered. According to some wise men, the fiercest wars have been fought to remove man-made obstacles to peace. Hitler was such an obstacle. While the rest of us were plodding down a depressed stretch of the Road to Peace, he mobilized an entire people for war. Yet, what he was ultimately after with his talk of a "New Order" was surely an arrangement of enforceable peace—under which the entire world would indeed be living now, had our physicists not outstripped his in that first great arms race of the nuclear age. Those who finally crushed him in war openly acknowledged that his goal was peace in their branding as "appeasers" all who sought to prevent our military intervention against him.

Wars result from the desire to impose one's will upon others and to resist being imposed upon. Peace is the condition of having one's willful

---

Between 1971 and 1973, the *New York Times* published over a dozen of Henry's articles on its Op Ed page. Above: "On the Waging of Peace," June 1, 1971.

way, whether actively or passively. Even a bawling infant knows the difference between being resisted and being pacified.

The maturity of the Western nations has consisted in their mutual recognition that the desire to establish a regime of enforceable peace over a vast multitude is itself the greatest provocation of war. That fact first impressed itself on Western statesmen during the three decades of war that preceded the so-called Peace of Westphalia, in 1648—which was peaceful only in the sense that, by its arrangements, the age-old longing for an enforceable world peace, such as animates so many educated people today, was at least temporarily laid to rest.

Napoleon resurrected that longing. He marched his armies back and forth across the Continent to remove the many national obstacles to its attainment. Later it was the turn of Imperial Germany, whose Kaiser, like Russia's Czar, celebrated in his very name the august aspiration of Imperial Rome to impose its peace everywhere, by uplifting the lowly and putting down the proud.

Vying to establish an enforceable world peace today are the Marxist-Leninists, who are as tough as the toughest old Romans, and that motley band of American social scientists, English teachers, journalists, Sanskrit-reading physicists, existentialist philosophers, playwrights, film-makers, etc., aptly characterized by Joseph Schumpeter as "ethical imperialists." The Marxist-Leninists have an obvious advantage, for they are realists. They can be deterred by a nuclear policy of assured destruction, strictly adhered to by the United States. But, if American policy insists on an enforceable world peace, the tough men of Moscow are not about to let themselves be "Pugwashed" into accepting the petulant rule of a Western intelligentsia that thinks it can gain the world by a "great act of persuasion" conducted on the pattern of a Harvard seminar on international affairs.

The irony is that, with all their drumbeating for "peace now," the men, women and children who lead today's peace crusade are making it impossible for serious counsels to be heard in the halls of government. Even the Commander in Chief of our armed forces has been reduced to gibbering that he's a "devoted pacifist."

Our great danger today comes not from American military arrogance, which is nonexistent, but from the arrogance of our peace-mongering, which intoxicates and must eventually paralyze the will to act prudently.

The New York Times

Sovereignty and SALT

By HENRY PAOLUCCI

If Henry Kissinger and the President he advises were committed to guarding the sovereign independence of this nation at all costs, nothing could be more conducive to the stabilizing of international relations at this time than Strategic Arms Limitations Talks with the Soviet Union.

On the other hand, if Henry Kissinger and the President he advises are committed to eliminating the possibility of a general war at all costs, then nothing could be more dangerous, nothing could be more disloyal than to veil in absolute secrecy, as the SALT meetings are indeed veiled, the negotiations

Above: "On the Waging of Peace," June 1, 1971 (cont.) and "Sovereignty and SALT," October 8, 1971.

whereby our sovereign independence of almost 200 years' standing may be bargained away.

Although the Soviet Union is not constituted as a nation state—although it legally and ideologically rejects the notion of occupying a "separate and equal station" among the powers of the earth—it has consistently exercised the prerogatives of sovereignty in its relations with the United States. It was not in the least tempted to make a sacrifice of its sovereign independence to purchase peace even when the United States enjoyed an absolute monopoly of atomic weapons. Certainly it is not prepared to do so now. Our atomic monopoly was reduced to a preponderance before it faded into parity. And now parity has been reduced to sufficiency, which, by definition, cannot suffice to do what preponderance or parity could do. Sufficiency is a move downward.

What are the Soviets disposed to sacrifice in the SALT negotiations to spare mankind the risks of a nuclear holocaust? We can be certain of this: they will not sacrifice their sovereign independence with all the prerogatives of their major power status.

One way the Government of the United States could purchase a "secure peace" with the Soviets would be by a sacrifice of the prerogatives of sovereign nationhood. Is it conceivable that Henry Kissinger and the President he advises might, for reasons best known to the great brain-trust of civilian war strategists who have advised our Presidents since 1961, contemplate such a sacrifice? Today, because of the shift of focus in our war-peace debate — a shift brought to unexplored frontiers by the Pentagon Papers affair — Walt Rostow can now be represented as some sort of hard-line traditionalist, whereas, when he came to Washington in 1961, he was clearly a revolutionary in his concept of "security" in the nuclear age. He wrote in 1960:

"It is a legitimate American national objective to see removed from all nations — including the United States — the right to use substantial military force to pursue their own interests. Since this residual right is the root of national sovereignty and the basis for the existence of an international arena of power, it is therefore an American interest to see an end to nationhood as it has been historically defined."

Despite its academic articulation, that is a highly revolutionary doctrine. The legitimacy claimed for it is certainly not an American constitutional legitimacy.

McGeorge Bundy shared Rostow's view of the matter. And Henry Kissinger, too, expressed as recently as 1965 the conviction that the time was at hand for a surrender of nationhood because "institutions based on present concepts of national sovereignty are not enough."

Bundy, Rostow and Kissinger have put their theory into practice in their increasingly powerful service as chief Presidential advisers for national security affairs under Presidents Kennedy, Johnson and Nixon.

Is the time now ripe for negotiation to put an end to our nationhood, for taking the step beyond the nation-state? If it is done in secrecy, while The Times and its powerful allies are celebrating an end to secrecy, it will have to be registered in the annals of history as the greatest betrayal of public trust ever perpetrated in a civilized nation.

That is the great danger of the secret SALT negotiations. The "temptations" not to lose the Vietnam war experienced by Presidents Kennedy and Johnson have been extravagantly publicized. Now we ought to have comparable publicity on "temptations" of Henry Kissinger, and the "devoted pacifist" he advises, to put an end to our nationhood as it has been historically defined.

Above: "Sovereignty and SALT," October 8, 1971 (cont.)

If the Soviets are assured, through secret SALT negotiations, that our posture of nuclear deterrence is indeed what the Nixon - Kissinger messages say it is, then that "American interest," of which Rostow wrote, "to see an end to our nationhood as it has been historically defined" will have been realized.

If we have not the will to do what McNamara defined as the essence of deterrence then we have no deterrence. We invite the ultimate form of nuclear blackmail.

Needless to say, if the secret papers on this subject are published, and, by some act of military boldness, our armed forces prevent an American surrender to blackmail, there are bound to be recriminations.

The New York Times

FRIDAY, JUNE 30, 1972

The Thin Line: Settlement or Surrender

By HENRY PAOLUCCI

How far to the left has President Nixon moved in his quest for "peace" in Vietnam? He has himself said that if he took a single step further to the left, he would be in the camp of the enemy whose combat-fire has already killed over 45,000 American soldiers.

President Nixon is deluded if he thinks history will not charge him with having lost a war and humiliating this nation in the eyes of the world. His latest peace plan closely parallels the peace plan offered to the Allied powers by Italy's little King in 1943, after he broke with Mussolini. The Italian King offered to give the Allies all they wanted compatible with "Italian honor." But the Allies insisted on unconditional surrender; they insisted that, in addition to giving up, the King would have to declare war on his German allies. To her disgrace, petty-monarchic Italy did just that.

How close to being America's little leftist monarch has Nixon become? Characterizing his latest "peace" offer, the President has said: "The only thing this plan does not do is join the enemy to overthrow our ally, which the United States of America will never do. If the enemy wants peace, it will have to recognize the important difference between settlement and surrender."

The fine professional hand of Henry Kissinger is discernible in that distinction between settlement and surrender. Surrender, here, obviously means "unconditional surrender," while settlement is used as a euphemism for "conditional surrender."

In his first "on the record" news conference, Secret Agent Henry Kissinger explained why the Nixon Administration refused to submit to the nine-point North Vietnamese peace plan of June 26, 1971. "One of the nine points," he said, "is a demand for

Above: "Sovereignty and SALT," October 8, 1971 (cont.)
"The Thin Line: Settlement or Surrender," June 20, 1972.

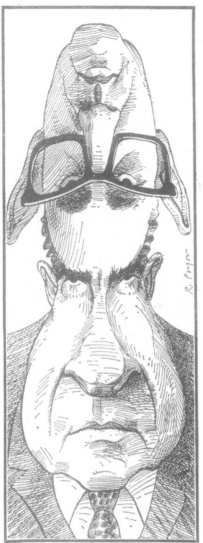

Robert Pryor

gram for all of Indochina in which North Vietnam could share to the extent of several billion dollars." In other words, the Nixon Administration is prepared to pay reparations, like a defeated country, provided they are not called reparations and included as such in the "settlement."

Kissinger defined the limits of America's willingness to surrender (just short of unconditionally) in the following terms: "They are asking us to align ourselves with them, to overthrow the people that have been counting on us in South Vietnam. They are asking us to accomplish [their ends] for them. If we will not do it for them, then the longer the war continues the worse that situation gets which they are trying to avoid, and they may settle for a political process which gives them less than 100 per cent guarantee but a fair crack at the political issue."

In other words, short of unconditional American surrender, the North Vietnamese Communists cannot hope to get more for themselves than the Nixon peace plan offers. We repeat: a single step to the left of where Nixon stands today would take him, like the little King of Italy in 1943, into the camp of the enemy as a cobelligerent.

How low have the mighty fallen! Nixon has had a Metternichian adviser constantly at his ear. He has therefore been reduced to thinking and acting like the head of a third-rate power—like a 19th-century Austrian "emperor" —trying to eke out an existence in the crevices of *realpolitik*. Or, as the tough-minded French critic André Malraux recently summed it up: "President Nixon maneuvers as if he were the President of Luxembourg."

reparations. We told them that while we would not include reparations as part of a settlement, we would give a voluntary massive reconstruction pro-

Above: "The Thin Line: Settlement or Surrender" (cont.) and cartoon, June 20, 1972.

The New York Times

NEW YORK, THURSDAY, OCTOBER 12, 1972

Acheson Remembered

By HENRY PAOLUCCI

Tragic nemesis is apparently catching up with Richard M. Nixon. He is being forced, as President, to pursue the same temptations of naive statesmanship that once led Alger Hiss, on a much lower level, to collaborate secretly with Communist officials and to lie about it when caught.

In 1950, Dean Acheson had to decide with great public embarrassment how to treat a friend charged with espionage and convicted of perjury. Now it is the turn of some of Mr. Nixon's supporters to be similarly embarrassed. The editors of National Review, for instance, have already followed Acheson's example to the point of refusing to turn their backs on their friend in the White House, even though he is charged in their own pages with having compromised the nation's safety.

Apart from his crimes, Alger Hiss was, after all, essentially an Ivy-League New Dealer who professed to believe in the late forties what Mr. Nixon (belatedly tutored by Harvard's Henry Kissinger) professes to believe in the early seventies. The Hiss view back then—which is now the Nixon Doctrine—was that America shouldn't try to be an armed custodian of the world's freedom, that it should instead pursue peace as an end in itself, and that collaboration with Communist regimes, rather than anti-Communist militancy, is the only risk-free way for Americans to pursue peace in the atomic era.

That was, of course, the pre-Truman legacy of World War II. Winston Churchill had rejected it with his Iron Curtain speech of 1946. President Truman's rejection followed in 1947, The occasion had been the crises of Greece and Turkey, where the British acknowledged that they could no longer afford to guarantee the independence of small nations threatened by the expansive might of world Communism. Guided by Dean Acheson, Mr. Truman took up the challenge.

When first announced, the Acheson policy aroused a storm of protests from the left. Walter Lippmann led the attack. The policy would oblige us, he complained, to play policeman and, worse, involve us in the "repression of legitimate nationalistic or revolutionary movements."

But there were attacks also from the right, and, before long, Mr. Nixon was leading them. As General Eisenhower's running mate in 1952, he ranted fiercely against what he called "Dean Acheson's College of Cowardly Communist Containment." Mere containment was not enough for that old Nixon. He talked of freeing captive nations and, occasionally, of rooting out Communist imperialism in its Peking and Moscow capitals as well.

Now, twenty years later, the tables are turned. The leftist critics of the Acheson-Truman doctrine are having their way, and Mr. Nixon, having suffered a sea-change, has been the means. Is there not a sense of tragic nemesis in this turn-about? As Walter

Above: "Acheson Remembered," October 12, 1972.

Lippmann said when Henry Kissinger's secret mission to Peking was first disclosed, "only Nixon, among the available public men, could have made such a reversal . . . because he had been such a violent and unscrupulous anti-Communist."

For Dean Acheson, the new Nixon Doctrine was the same old pre-Truman doctrine he had rejected as Secretary of State. It was wrong then; it was doubly wrong now.

The New York Times

THE NEW YORK TIMES, SUNDAY, SEPTEMBER 30, 1973

The Shabbiness of It All

By Henry Paolucci

Mr. Nixon cannot serve as a valid test of ultimate Presidential prerogatives. In his heart, as in his peace and disarmament deals, he has long since abandoned the source of his prerogatives, which is the principle that the nation's safety is its highest law. He survives now only as a crippled captive of his old enemies.

On the back wall of the Lincoln Memorial in Washington, we read these words inscribed in stone: "In this temple, as in the hearts of the people for whom he saved the Union, the memory of Abraham Lincoln is enshrined forever."

Lincoln's temple is the crown of a mighty cross in our nation's capital— a cross that has Capitol Hill at its base and the White House and Jefferson Memorial at the ends of its cross beam. Washington's Monument, rising near the point where the long and short beams intersect, is like a spear in the side of an invisible savior of our body politic, for whose ultimate agony Lincoln Memorial, with all its solemn words, will one day serve as a fitting crown of glory.

Washington, Jefferson, Lincoln— each of them confirmed in word and deed that profoundest truth of our Western political tradition, which is that coercive government is at best a necessary evil, and that when free men deny either its evil or its necessity they must soon cease to be free.

The Watergate affair recalls our attention to that painful truth, but unfortunately with misplaced emphasis and miscast spokesmen. Surly John Mitchell, to the delight of the Ervins and Weickers, has put the brand of "White House horrors" on what officious John Ehrlichman has professed to defend as Presidential prerogatives in national security affairs.

Hoping to save himself with his old boss, Mr. Ehrlichman has made a cynically ruthless appeal to the old principle of *raison d'état*: a principle of statecraft that Winston Churchill summed up accurately when, to justify the Anglo-Soviet alliance against Hitler, he snarled: "Madam, I would make a friend of the devil himself if it would save England."

But the principle of *raison d'état* is ill applied in Mr. Nixon's case. Guided by Henry Kissinger, our President has committed his Administration to pur-

Above: "Acheson Remembered," October 12, 1972 (cont.) and "The Shabbiness of It All," September 30, 1973.

sue peace as an end in itself, thereby invalidating the traditional grounds on which Presidential prerogatives ultimately rest.

What about the Nixon Administration's prosecution of Daniel Ellsberg? Was it a "national security" prosecution in the traditional sense? Senator Sam Ervin, a stanch defender of our nation's sovereignty against the supranational pretensions of the so-called Genocide Convention, correctly rejects the Ehrlichman-Haldeman-Nixon claim that it was. Ellsberg was charged, he notes, not with giving treacherous aid and comfort to Communist powers but merely with "stealing some papers that belonged to the Government."

On this same point, Presidential spokesman John T. Lofton has tried to set the record straight, arguing in the August issue of First Monday that Mr. Nixon had little motive for political vindictiveness against Ellsberg, "since the Kennedy and Johnson Administrations were hurt by the disclosures." Revealing that President Kennedy, hardly less than Lyndon Johnson, had been tempted to try to win a military victory in Vietnam, the stolen papers validated, in effect, President Nixon's claim that he, rather than Kennedy, deserves to be honored by the liberal establishment's conscience élite as the first American President of the Atomic Age to be thoroughly committed to peace.

But why then did so many presumably anti-Nixon liberal academicians and journalists collaborate to get the pro-Nixon Pentagon Papers published? Mr. Lofton's explanation reads: "It is evident that the liberal media had, by 1971, written off the Kennedy-Johnson Vietnam policy as a disaster. If, in order to save high-priority liberal fantasies about Vietnam, they had to destroy some liberal myths about Kennedy and Johnson, the liberal media were ready." And that statement helps to explain also why the cases against The Times and Ells-

berg were so ineptly argued. The Nixon Administration was not about to go to court to injure itself!

Where does Mr. Nixon really stand on the question of ultimate Presidential prerogatives? Is he prepared to defend even so shabby a version of *raison d'état* as Mr. Ehrlichman has advanced? Hardly. With Watergate, as with Kissinger's peace strategy and Moynihan's welfare reforms, the President apparently intends to pursue a Disraelian course, hoping to "dish" his opposition by claiming its positions as his own.

Emerson must have had a prescient vision of the post-Watergate, crippled Nixon Presidency in mind when he wrote in "Compensation": "The President has paid dear for his White House. . . . To preserve for a short time so conspicuous an appearance before the world, he is content to eat dust before the real powers behind the throne."

"The Shabbiness of It All," September 30, 1973 (cont.)

Cartoon for "The Shabbiness of It All," September 30, 1973

4. *BILL BUCKLEY*, NATIONAL REVIEW, *AND THE KISSINGER CONTROVERSY*

How and when Henry met Bill Buckley is not clear; but in 1958 they were already on easy terms. In a brief letter in November of that year, acknowledging Henry's presence at a debate he had taken part in, Buckley had written:

> A belated word to tell you how pleased I was to see you at my debate with John Cogley. You asked the most intelligent question of all and the answer did not do it justice.

By then, a firm relationship was in place; Buckley could send Henry a submission he'd received on "post-mechanistic philosophy" and ask him to write an article in answer to it. Similar requests continued into the 80s and 90s.

Buckley had quickly come to rely on his articulate, well-read conservative colleague as a ready source of information; and Henry, in turn, was from the outset responsive, more than happy to share what he knew, especially when the person was such a willing and appreciative listener as Bill Buckley. For Henry, Buckley's requests were often intellectual forays into areas he would not have chosen to explore on his own but which he was more than happy to investigate for his friend. The two often had lunch; at times, with the editorial staff of *National Review*, where Henry took part in lively exchanges on subjects of current interest.

Their growing friendship allowed Buckley to turn to Henry as a reliable source for replies to some of the more awkward or difficult letters that crossed his desk. Henry was always ready with answers, giving (as he gave his students) elaborate replies that went beyond what was expected.

Some of those letters were hardly compelling or worth answering; but if Buckley felt they should be acknowledged with more than a cursory line or two and reached out to him, Henry never hesitated to help. On one occasion Buckley got an 18-page article, suggesting certain actions conservatives should consider. It had been written by a thoughtful reader of *NR*, and Buckley felt it deserved a thoughtful answer. He asked Henry for his opinion. In reply, he received a three-page single-spaced letter in which Henry extracts and summarizes eight major points and rates their validity. Buckley may not have expected that kind of thoroughness but made good use of it.

On many occasions, the subject was controversial, such as the still-open question as to whether or not Sacco and Vanzetti were really guilty of treason. Buckley wrote to Henry on October 12, 1960:

> The thought had passed through my suspicious head that Sacco and Vanzetti's famous last testaments were ghosted.

He went on to explain his reasoning and asked Henry if he would examine the materials he was sending him

> and explore by hard textual analysis the possibility that . . . Sacco and Vanzetti used a ghost (heaven knows, there were enough of them around — every litterateur in the country danced in attendance on them).

Henry's tight three page reply began,

> The project you suggest . . . is certainly interesting. But after reading the two articles you sent me and . . . the several hundred pages of Sacco-Vanzetti writings and reported statements (as well as Montgomery's book) I am afraid that I must conclude that one utterance will do as well as examination of a thousand for making up one's mind on the subject.

He explained his conclusion, with a brief excursion into St. Augustine at the end. Was it relevant? Apparently it was, for Henry, who had become a confirmed Augustinian and cited him constantly. For Buckley, it was an unexpected but welcome personal "bonus," or more precisely, another genial insight from the man he had come to regard as his "mentor." Still, as editor of *NR*, he was in for a challenge. In spite of Henry's reply, Buckley asked him to write an article on Sacco and Vanzetti, which he published soon after.

They had grown easily into an intellectual relationship that Buckley enjoyed immensely and that gave Henry the opportunity to express his views to a mind as sharp as his and just as ready to do battle against the liberal academy as well as the liberal media. If he differed with opinions expressed in the pages of *NR*, he did not hesitate to let Buckley know. But he was also capable of generous praise, even when dressed in ambiguous terms. In a long letter to Buckley on June 22, 1960, he begins with this backhanded compliment for what Buckley had written about Nelson Rockefeller.

> The cover editorial of the June 25 *Bulletin* . . . despite the

exposé tone of some paragraphs and the self-righteous, dogmatic libertarianism throughout — was refreshing to read, as evidence that the reigning spirit of *National Review* is capable of getting off the treadmill on which it is currently exhausting too much of its precious intellectual energy.

The criticism was not lost on Buckley, who answered in an equally long letter, defending what he had published. Reading that exchange is like hearing a sharp witty debate.

Henry's response to Buckley's personal request — "Do you know a good readable book on Catiline?" (December 12, 1960) — rewords the question before going on:

> Assuming you mean a book on Catiline readable for you, I suggest the very readable, chief historical source, Sallust's *War Against Catiline,* in the Loeb Classics volume of Sallust, trans. by J.C. Rolfe, pp. 1-129. . . .

> The best "modern account is Theodor Mommsen's (*History of Rome,* Vol. IV, pp. 461-491, beginning with the marginal note: "Worthlessness of the democratic successes"). The W.P. Dickson translation has been re-issued recently, without date or translator's name, by The Free Press, Glencoe, Illinois.

He could have stopped there, having given Buckley what he had asked for. Instead, he launches, in his usual fashion, into (in this case) a two-page account of Sallust's history, citing Mommsen (the greatest classical historian of the 19th century and 1902 Nobel Prize Winner in Literature):

> a literary masterpiece that veils the part of Julius Caesar (even as Cicero cautiously veiled it in his four orations on the subject, which are a primary documentary source). Mommsen's account emphasizes the efforts of the democratic leaders (Caesar and Crassus) to use the anarchistic force of Catiline to destroy the oligarchy (led by Cato) and to check their too-powerful colleague, Pompey, who was abandoning his oligarchic supporters to become a popular leader. Mommsen's account is especially interesting in view of his high estimate of the "later" Julius Caesar, who abandoned demagogic intrigue, or rather, subordinated it to the higher aims of true statesmanship. Mommsen puts the Catiline conspiracy in perspective with a phrase in this brilliant estimate of Caesar. . . .

A long quotation from Mommsen follows. The letter ends with an unexpected comparison, which Henry knew Buckley would especially appreciate.

There are other works one might read: E. G. Hardy's *The Catilinarian Conspiracy* — a re-study of the evidence (115 pages, 1924) which is good but scarce and entirely academic; and William Bolitho's *Twelve Against the Gods*, which I, as an economic reader, have not read.

Sallust, by the way, was St. Augustine's favorite as a witness to what ailed the Greco-Roman world on the eve of the "Fullness of Time."

Later that same month, Henry shared with Buckley his experience as a participant in a City College symposium in which President Gallagher also took part. He sent Buckley the proceedings, which had been published in a City College anthology, with a note:

You might want to glance at this CCNY symposium on "Communism, Democracy and Academic Freedom." I was asked to contribute something to keep it from being altogether leftish — I suppose. . . . A review in the college paper assessed my serpent's cunning: "Professor Paolucci advocates complete withdrawal of the College from the outside life of society. His argument for the restriction of academic freedom is based on an unrealistic, highly personalized emotional concept of the College as a place for theoretic knowledge only." I owe the courtesy to my citations of Einstein.

While vacationing in Switzerland, in January 1965, Buckley received one of Henry's long documented letters on a subject that had gained his attention. Buckley wrote back:

I was so impressed by your letters and the enclosures, that I am promptly returning them! with the request that you write them into a 2/3,000 word article for publication in *National Review.* Okay?

I am, as always, proud to be your friend and student.

When he decided to run for the mayoralty in New York in 1965, Buckley informed Henry of his decision, adding that he was the first person to whom he had relayed the news. Henry replied:

Thank you for your note. Your candidacy honors me, as you realize.

I can speak more eloquently about you, Mr. Conservative! than I could speak for myself! Since last November I have on the average spoken publicly twice a week in the Conservative cause. Count on me to redouble my efforts. . . .

> Don't hesitate to direct my energies as you see fit. It's a risky campaign, but it can be a catalyst for a national recovery of will.

In spite of growing unease on Buckley's part, with regard to Henry's unrelenting and harsh criticism of Henry Kissinger, Buckley continued to rely on him not only for contributions to *NR* but also as a steady and accurate source of knowledge in matters he himself was unprepared to deal with. Always the gentleman and always grateful for Henry's replies to his inquiries, Buckley never failed to thank him, in his inimitable way, for the effort and time that went into those replies. Characteristic is the "thank you note" he wrote, after Henry had provided a long answer to a letter Buckley had received (November 30, 1972) from a supporter who had seen and enjoyed much of his witty interview with Johnny Carson some days earlier but had been greatly disturbed by comments Buckley had made that revealed (in the writer's opinion) a "misunderstanding of science" deriving no doubt from a "mistrust of it based not entirely on reason."

Buckley had sent a copy of the letter to Henry, with a handwritten note: "I'd appreciate your assistance in answering this!" Henry had seen the show and knew more than most people about the topic that had provoked the criticism Buckley had received. In his reply, he produced the major arguments Buckley could use in answering his critic, beginning with a comment about the contention that Buckley had been misled by an irrational mistrust of modern science.

> That's a nasty thought — unless he is prepared to admit that his trust of science might also have a not-quite-rational base.

He compares the letter-writer's "dogmatic confidence in the teaching of the schools" to "Galileo's colleagues, who refused to look through his telescope" then gives a summary of the prevailing and misleading notions that are still taught on that subject. Buckley wrote back:

> How greatly you rewarded my simple inquiry. You are dealing with a field of knowledge in which I am altogether ignorant, but I was much struck years ago by what you said about Galileo, so as you see I remembered it, however mindlessly. You are super-kind to your old friend to take such pains with him. . . .

Buckley was still contacting Henry for help in dealing with difficult correspondence in November 1980, when he asked for Henry's "reading" of a letter from a Jerome Downes (connected with the Minneapolis Institute of Arts), attacking Ralph de Toledano's comments about *National Review*'s use of classical sources. Buckley asked for suggestions in answering Downes' criticism. Henry drafted a letter and told Buckley he could send it out under his own signature if he so wished.

"You are a saint," Buckley replied. "But I'd feel like an awful phony reproducing your letter over my own signature, so I'll simply lean heavily on you, with a few editorial thises and thats."

In acknowledging the published response, which he enjoyed — "your 'yukked up' treatment, as you characterized, is certainly correct, which is to say, fair (with your infallibly courteous good spirit) to everyone, especially Downes!" — Henry showed his own "fair" and "courteous good spirit" in expressing reservations about de Toledano's position, which Buckley had felt obliged to uphold:

> I'm glad you let the implied defense of de Toledano stand without adding his name, for Downes was more right than wrong in his criticism. Your friend Ralph deserved a semblance of support only for having borne the brunt of the generalized attack on *NR*'s classical learning. Your handling of the exchange in Greek was a pleasure to read. It gives Downes his due, and he will sense its fairness, even if he doesn't search out the meaning.

Although he had already written to thank Henry, Buckley sent a Mailgram in addition:

> Did I thank you sufficiently for wonderful help in handling Mr. Downes? Do they commit hari kari in Minneapolis? Come on now, tell me, because you know everything.

When Buckley asked Henry if there was anything he could do in return for Henry's help, Henry had taken the occasion to remind Buckley of what he considered to be Kissinger's false posture as a conservative, hoping Buckley would finally come around to his way of reasoning. It was a constant prodding which Buckley constantly resisted.

Buckley's reaction was predictable and brief. Clearly, the subject had become one he preferred to avoid. They had already gone through the worst in this matter.

> As for your thesis, what is there to say that I have not already said? We fight from the same foxhole, and recognize at least the

same external enemy. With your great erudition you are wonderfully resourceful . . . You taught me more in three paragraphs about Bagehot than I had previously known. . . . I feel I can add little to the reconciliation of our understanding of HK and the general decline. Remember that as an early follower of Whittaker Chambers I drank deeply of that terrible Weltschmerz that makes our reversals so awfully predictable. Bless you.

Although the friendship had cooled, Buckley knew he owed Henry a great deal when he wrote from Switzerland (perhaps with a touch of guilt) with the excuse that he had actually lost sleep because of "a horrible feeling I didn't thank you adequately for your kindness of last fall. . . ." Henry waited for Buckley to get back to New York, before writing:

> I hesitated to answer your note of March 24 while you were still in Switzerland for fear that additional loss of sleep might make you unsteady on your skis!

> Not only have you thanked me much much more than enough for my part in answering the Downes letter of last fall, but it is rather I who owe you for what was then an unexpected delight — to share in a labor of yours that hadn't to do with politics.

In spite of their undiminished respect and admiration for one another, their fundamental disagreement about Henry Kissinger and what he stood for had taken its toll. For Buckley, the relationship had become awkward because of Henry's unremitting criticism; for Henry, Buckley's unwillingness to recognize what Henry was convinced was the true Kissinger — a dove masking as a hawk — had become a frustrating insurmountable barrier.

What was to become an irreconcilable difference began as far back as 1968-1969. The early issues of *State of the Nation* were written, it seems, to express Henry's growing concern about *NR*'s backing of Kissinger and, in particular, Buckley's acknowledged part in arranging a meeting between Kissinger and Nixon.

In his Preface to *Who is Kissinger?* — one of Henry's early booklets published by Ted Dabrowski, in which the early anti-Kissinger arguments of *SN* are brought together and reinforced — Henry cited James Burnham's *Suicide of the West*, where *NR*'s senior contributor (and "the number one intellectual influence on *National Review* since the day of its founding"[Buckley]) reminds his readers that "if America were to suffer the agonies of suicidal death, it could only happen with a Democratic liberal in the White House." Henry corrects what had seemed a transparent truth, when he first read the book:

> How pathetically mistaken that conservative notion was! Bad as things were under the Democrats, they have gone from bad to worse under the Nixon administration.

He argues that Kissinger was running the White House and that *Who is Kissinger?* was written primarily in the hopes that the editors of *NR*, would

> see through the Straussian ambiguities of Kissinger's long-range designs for America. But in fact it had the opposite effect. There was a troubled instant of doubt, but that immediately gave way to a re-affirmation of the earlier confident endorsement. Indeed, one *National Review* editor spelled it out for me quite plainly, saying: "You have greatly troubled my conscience. . . . But I am at this moment especially convinced that Henry Kissinger is a great patriot, and that you will one day come to agree. . . . Either that or he is the greatest hypocrite in the history of the world, and I cannot think so."

What Henry quoted was taken directly from Buckley's response to his little book on Kissinger, although tactfully, the "*National Review* editor" is not identified.

In spite of their basic disagreement, Buckley never failed to read what Henry wrote about the Harvard Professor who had eased his way into the Nixon camp. He might under different circumstances have gone along with Henry, who was as lucid on this subject as he had proved to be on any of the others he had shared with Buckley in the past. Buckley knew that Henry had read with tremendous care everything Kissinger had ever published and was ready to back his statements with Kissinger's own words, as in fact, he had done in exposing Kissinger's arguments in favor of limited war, detente with Russia, delaying the peace talks in Vietnam, and on other policies that, as national security advisor, Kissinger had proposed and Nixon had accepted.

Buckley's response was always the same: that Henry was attributing to Kissinger much more influence than he actually had; that he offered the President suggestions only. The final decisions were Nixon's.

Unfortunately, in this case Buckley was caught in a bind: not only had Kissinger been sponsored by him politically; he had also become a personal friend. It was Buckley who had introduced Kissinger to Richard Nixon and insured his appointment to succeed Walt Rostow as chief presidential advisor for national security affairs. For Buckley, Kissinger was a patriot, not the devious self-serving anti-nationalist Henry made him out to be . . . and a good friend. Their relationship went back to Kissinger's teaching days at Harvard, when Kissinger had invited him to give a lecture and, on another occasion, to write an article for a journal he edited.

At the time, Kissinger was clearly in the Rockefeller camp. In 1960, as Henry writes in "Nixon's Supreme Strategist: Henry A. Kissinger" (echoing in the title for his article the phrase used in a feature story by *Time* magazine about Kissinger) the Harvard professor was a vigorous exponent on the other side of the political fence.

> As Vice-President and candidate for the Presidency in 1960, Nixon had forcefully defended the Eisenhower-Dulles strategy of "massive retaliation"; whereas Kissinger, as spokesman for the internationalist Council on Foreign Relations, had literally led the attack on it, providing John F. Kennedy with the chief arguments he was to use against Nixon in the fateful television debate of 1966. And in 1968, when Nixon contended for the Republican presidential nomination, supported by the nationalist Goldwater wing of the party, again Kissinger was ranged against him, serving as chief foreign policy advisor for the party's leading internationalist, Nelson Rockefeller.

Kissinger claimed that the call from Nixon to replace Walt Rostow "came as a surprise." It may indeed have been a surprise, as the *New York Times* reported, to the "political scientists and law professors, many of them liberal Democrats and former members of the Kennedy administration," who "hailed [the appointment] almost unanimously." Arthur Schlesinger, Jr., long-time advisor and family historian of the Kennedys boasted to a *New York Times* reporter: "Kissinger asked my advice about it . . . and I urged him to accept. . . ."

There was really no need to ask anyone's advice; but Kissinger no doubt felt it was prudent to let his liberal friends know that he hadn't abandoned them. For Henry, Nixon's "most astute appointment" was clearly on the side of the internationalists. He could not understand how Buckley could claim Kissinger was a true "patriot" when the man clearly had supra-national goals in mind, as when he wrote in *The Troubled Partnership*,

> institutions based on present concepts of national sovereignty are not enough. The West requires a larger goal: the constitution of an Atlantic Commonwealth in which all the peoples bordering the North Atlantic can fulfill all their aspirations. Clearly, it will not come quickly; many intermediate stages must be traversed before it can be reached. It is not too early, however, to prepare ourselves now for the step beyond the nation-state.

Henry sums up Kissinger's ambiguities —

> To get the complete picture we have only to juxtapose its mosaic elements. Limited war is no substitute for constructive policy; but a constructive policy can be built upon it. Limited war will not provide national security in the traditional sense; but it will in Kissinger's new sense, which authorizes us to choose between survival and the realizing of our aspirations internationally. When we have fought our limited wars and have settled in each case for something less than the traditional meaning of security, the next step will be, as Kissinger says, the difficult one of perfecting ourselves in the art of "living in dignity when impotent."

In the office that Arthur Schlesinger Jr. had urged him to accept, Kissinger, in Henry's view, had served the international idealists well, teaching us, as Schlesinger had tried to do, how to live "in dignity when impotent."

In 1969, Buckley finally decided to approach Kissinger directly for the answers Henry wanted. Kissinger replied:

> I appreciate Professor Paolucci's suggestion that I submit my ideas on national security for publication in *National Review*, but I am sure he will understand why I feel it would be inappropriate for me to write such an article for publication at this time.

In a handwritten postscript, he added: "As to your friend, you may assure him that I have never had a desire to give up national sovereignty."

Having read all of Kissinger's writings and having followed all his actions as Nixon's closest advisor, Henry could not accept that answer. Buckley was not convinced; he maintained his position even though it was not always shared by other conservatives or conservative publications, or many Nixon backers. Someone close to Buckley had written to Henry confirming what was obvious, that "at the bottom of *National Review*'s strange behavior" was Kissinger's "very large influence" on Buckley.

Henry's persistent criticism had triggered a certain interest abroad as well. *Il Borghese*, the leading Italian political journal was quick to request Henry's newsletters, which appeared in translation on a regular basis in the pages of that publication. It often commissioned articles as well, which Henry provided and which appeared exclusively in that journal. *Il Veltro* took on some of Henry's pieces as well. The *Daily American* reprinted portions of his newsletters. A French publication featured excerpts from his articles. Here, they were reissued or requested in bulk orders by several journals and magazines. The *New York Times* ran his newsletters on the Op Ed page for over a year. In a column — "Master Spy Kissinger?" — *National Spotlight* juxtaposed Buckley's praise of Kissinger, where he is described as "brilliant, learned, intellectually bold, and a virtuoso of the public media," with Henry's estimate:

> The record of the Nixon-Kissinger years is now plain enough for all to read. Abroad the world communist leaders have piled one spectacular victory upon another and at home the liberals are jumping for joy.

"Henry Kissinger," the columns ends, "is a very expensive Secretary of State."

In *The Review of the News*, the editor of *National Review* is taken to task for being "woefully out of step with responsible Conservatives in his maudlin admiration of Kissinger. . . ."

Walter Darnell Jacobs, Professor of Government and Politics at the University of Maryland, praised *Who is Kissinger?* as "a much needed effort to describe just what our friend Henry Kissinger is doing."

U.S. Senator Mark O Hatfield wrote "what a pleasure [it was] to receive copies of Henry Paolucci's books on Henry Kissinger."

Anthony Harrigan, Executive Vice President of United States Industrial Council, drew attention in a news release to Henry's argument that "gradualism in surrendering American lives, honor, and sovereignty is the great American scandal of our time, for which the Watergate cover-up is itself but a cover-up. Dr. Paolucci is a rare figure in the academic world,"

a nationalist intellectual. He believes strongly in the concept of national sovereignty and its basis in a people with a common set of recollections from the past and expectations for the future. Sovereignty, in other words, is the essence of nationhood. It is what character and purpose are in an individual. Yet in our time and country, there is a studied effort to phase-out sovereignty and to substitute supranational authority. The effort to weaken the concept of national sovereignty is paralleled by a foreign policy leading to a submissive detente with the Soviet Union.

In a long letter to Henry (February 23, 1981). retired U.S. Army General A.C. Wedemeyer wrote that he was in "complete accord" with the views expressed in *Who is Kissinger?* and *Kissinger's War: 1957-1975,* having reached his own conclusions "through careful analysis and study of Mr. Kissinger's policies and actions." He expressed his deep-rooted concern:

Many of the individuals whom you mention in your books are friends of mine — people who have supported policies and actions that I recommended when in government service. I have been a friend of Bill Buckley's since he graduated from Yale, and his endorsement of Kissinger was a real disappointment to me. . . . I was deeply concerned about our country when this individual, who "modestly" claimed to be a modern Metternich and who was the darling of the liberal press and of certain selfishly motivated groups in our country, acquired so much power.

Wedemeyer expressed hope that the new administration would have "enough courage and the wisdom"

to restore sanity not only on the domestic front . . . but also in the international arena. The conditions that permitted a man of Kissinger's character to be foisted upon the American people must be changed, and drastically, otherwise the "Eastern Establishment" will have representatives exercising their sinister and destructive influence in all echelons of government. The Republican convention sounded a clarion call to all good Americans that people like Kissinger are determined to ferret their way into positions of responsibility.

"Both books," General Wedemeyer wrote, referring to

Henry's two books on Kissinger, "should be widely read in our universities and colleges."

Henry never stopped urging Buckley to reverse his support of Kissinger and continued sending him what he wrote on the subject. In the early days, Buckley had accepted articles like "Are Nations Washed Up?," where the main target was Walt Rostow (to become Kissinger's predecessor in The White House), whom Henry identifies as "the State Department's house ideologue," and whose book — *The Stages of Economic Growth* (subtitled, "A Non-Communist Manifesto") —

> urges the United States to facilitate the development of all other countries, especially the Soviet Union, to full economic maturity, so that the spirit of nationhood, which makes men willing to fight for their countries, may die in them as it has died in American Liberals. (*NR*, October 5, 1965)

Nor did Buckley turn down Henry's "Carter's Kissinger" (October 1, 1976), where the target was Zbigniew Brzezinski. Kissinger, on the other hand, had to be protected.

In his efforts to get Buckley to renounce Kissinger, Henry cites passages from *Persecution and the Art of Writing* by Leo Strauss (1952), in which the noted academic describes the oblique way in which things are said when true motives have to be hidden from the general public. Emphasizing Strauss' argument, Henry reminded Buckley that "it took us a long time to catch on to Hans Morgenthau's 'national interest' rhetoric — which James Burnham punctures in your May 6th issue." For Henry,

> Kissinger tops Morgenthau in the same rhetoric. If you want to know what you're up against in the Morgenthaus and Kissingers, the book to glance at is Leo Strauss's *Persecution and the Art of Writing*. Persecution gives rise to a peculiar kind of writing . . . in which the truth about all crucial things is presented exclusively between the lines. That literature is addressed, not to all readers, but to trustworthy and intelligent readers only. It has all the advantage of private communication without having its greatest disadvantage — that it reaches only the writer's acquaintances.

After citing a long passage from the Strauss book, Henry pressed home the point:

> Our anti-nationalists feel particularly persecuted in our age and, as the *Time* magazine statement about Kissinger suggests, they are working at the art of writing under persecution. *Time* wrote,

you remember: "a superficial reading of some of Kissinger's works make him seem like a hawk, but many intellectual doves regard him as Richard Nixon's most astute appointment."

"Are we ready for these fellows, Bill?" Henry asks.

But Bill had crossed his Rubicon, and there was no turning back. He had explained his opposition to Henry's unyielding criticism of Kissinger as early as 1969, when Henry had sent him his first article attacking Kissinger:

> I return your piece having given it the gravest consideration. I also enclose (in confidence) a memo on it from James Burnham, which suggests the reasoning why we think it unwise to publish it. I have only to add to this my own personal feelings based on several conversations with Kissinger and several other people who know him well, that he is the best thing we have in that part of the world. I really do mean this and trust that under the circumstances he will permit me to register both my admiration for you and your analysis, and my rejection of it as off the mark.

Henry's answer was blunt:

> Don't hope for the impossible from Kissinger. The piece I sent you is, right now, a thorough answer to the long article on Kissinger by Patrick Anderson that appeared in the *New York Times* yesterday.

> I boil inwardly to think how long we must wait for the ideologically obvious to become politically obvious.

Henry was persistent; Buckley was just as resistant, confirmed in his faith in Kissinger. He invited Henry's articles and read them with interest but asserted unambiguously, whenever Henry brought up Kissinger, that he could not be swayed.

> I'm always happy to hear from you. I still think in the matter of Kissinger that you are dead wrong. Either that or he is the greatest hypocrite in the history of the world and I don't think that. [August 1969]

Not even a long hand-written letter which Henry transcribed and sent to Buckley from the eminent Harvard Professor William Yandall Elliot, retired from his position at Harvard, where Kissinger had been his "cosmopolitan academic protegé," was enough to bring Buckley around. Elliot's seven pages, Henry had written,

> were evidently scrawled as rapidly as the thoughts and feelings came to his heart and mind. He agrees passionately with the

severest criticism I have ever directed against Kissinger, including the charge that Kissinger has used men like you and Elliott to advance himself with false credentials.

Kissinger, you should know took most of his diplomatic rhetoric from Elliott; but he took it literally, where it was not meant literally, and deviously where it was meant literally.

No argument registered. Buckley's replies to Henry's many letters reveal how their differences with respect to Kissinger were drawing them further and further apart.

It always pains me to disagree with you. But for one thing I do not believe that we can move in any direction so melodramatic quite thus surreptitiously. And anyway, if the metamorphosis is gradual and inevitable, what can we do about it? I am at this moment especially convinced that Henry Kissinger is a great patriot, and that you will one day come to agree about that. [January 2, 1970]

Inasmuch as you are going to hold me morally accountable for the demise of the Republic three months hence, please, tell me quite concretely what it is that I have failed to do. I am quite serious. [October 23, 1970]

You know . . . that I continue to disagree with you, though I recognize the danger. My point is that Nixon and Kissinger recognize the danger also. We do however need more public clamor on the point and I intend to do just that, to the extent that I can. Your letter is as always graceful, generous, and affectionate. [December 15, 1970]

Even the events of 1971 failed to persuade Buckley. In his informative book, *A Generation Awakes* (2010), Wayne Thorburn records the historic anti-Nixon surge of that year, when a group of conservative leaders (the "Manhattan Twelve") announced that they were suspending support of Nixon. A statement released by the group focused on Nixon's foreign policies, especially "his overtures to Red China, his failure to stop the Soviet advance in the Mediterranean, and the perceived deterioration of the nation's military position." Among those signing the statement were Anthony Harrigan of the Southern States Industrial Council, Neil McCaffrey of the Conservative Book Club, and J. Daniel Mahoney, Chairman of the NYS Conservative Party; but "the most significant name"

was Bill Buckley, not only because of his public recognition but also due to the efforts of those in the administration, especially

Henry Kissinger, to appeal for his continued support of Nixon. As one Washington newspaper noted, "The anti-Nixon movement . . . took a great leap forward . . . with the announcement that William F. Buckley, Jr., editor-in-chief of the *National Review*, had joined with 10 other conservative editors, authors and organizers to announce they planned to 'suspend' their support of Nixon."

Buckley could withdraw support of Nixon without hesitating or hedging in any way and still refuse to credit Kissinger for having convinced the President to accept his policies and follow his agenda. In his eyes there was no contradiction in his continued acceptance of the one and his dumping of the other.

I wish I could convince you about [Kissinger]. It is worse than you suppose — I introduced him to Nixon during the '68 campaign. The only thing that sustains me is that if you are surprised, it will be pleasantly. Anyway, I intend to look precisely into the points you mentioned, and precisely in the way you instructed me. [January 4, 1972]

What can I say? I have read your analysis. There is nothing in it particularly new. It is primarily asseverative: i.e., you make a series of deductions. You simply do not know what is the role of Kissinger in White House counsels. I think I do know. I speak with a heavy heart because I am dismayed by the events at Peking. You triumphantly conclude that they are the doing of Henry Kissinger. I conclude it would be worse except for Henry Kissinger. How will we come to know which one of us is correct? There is an easy answer to it. Meanwhile I do not doubt your own devotion to the truth, or the constancy of your friendship. [March 13, 1972]

The trouble with your piece is that is proceeds on the basis of a whole series of assumptions which we simply haven't shared, and for that reason cuts across a whole series of membranes carefully and I think fastidiously analyzed. Kissinger has not succeeded. But you are saying he has tried not to succeed. There's the difference. [June 10, 1975]

Kissinger remained a controversial figure. In his article of November 1980, James Reston, Executive Editor and Washington correspondent for the *New York Times*, sums it up nicely while making a strong pitch for Kissinger in Ronald Reagan's cabinet:

I believe that there is a strong case to be made for Henry Kissinger as Secretary of State but that the only way to make the case to Reagan's most conservative advisers is to oppose him. . . . Everybody in the Republican Party who was opposed to his policy of détente with the Soviets, his recognition of Communist China at the expense of Taiwan, his support of the U.S. treaty with Panama, or his refusal to accept the demands of Israel is against him. . . . And that's not all. Kissinger was Nixon's surrogate in the protracted tragedy of the Vietnam war, in the bombing and destruction of Cambodia. For this he will never be forgiven by [those] who question his judgment and oppose his return to power under Reagan. . . .

As Reston reports, the new President had "some leanings in certain directions [but was} still willing to hear cases . . . for others." Whether Buckley accepted that "interesting invitation" and put forward Kissinger's name, as he had with Nixon, or brought Kissinger to meet with Reagan, is not clear. In the end, Kissinger was not Reagan's choice.

Amazingly, Kissinger survived the harshest criticisms; abroad, his reputation never suffered.

Nor did it ever suffer with Bill Buckley.

As time went by, communication between Buckley and Henry grew more hesitant. Still, always the gentleman and honest enough in his feelings — Buckley took a few steps back from the unpleasant drama he and Henry had played out over Kissinger, and from the wings, as it were, remembered his old friend and mentor in the obituary published in *National Review* on January 25, 1999, three weeks after Henry's death.

> ■ Dr. Henry Paolucci belonged to the band-of-brothers phase of the conservative movement. In 1964, the fledgling Conservative Party of New York enlisted him to run against Sen. Kenneth Keating and Robert, then the regnant Kennedy. Dr. Paolucci had a day job, as a professor, nominally of political science, but also of any other subject that caught his avid attention (the translation of Machiavelli's "Mandragola" he and his wife produced 40 years ago is still in print). Nevertheless, he made the gallant, losing run..For the remainder of his life, he advanced his opinions, with their heavy component of nationalism, in the medium of feisty and scholarly articles. R I P.

⌂ *From the Archives*

X K Henry Paolucci   10/5

THE WHITE HOUSE
WASHINGTON

October 2, 1969

Dear Bill:

Please excuse this tardy reply to your letter of
September 11. I appreciate Professor Paolucci's
suggestion that I submit my ideas on national
security for publication in National Review, but
I am sure he will understand why I feel it would
be inappropriate for me to write such an article
for publication at this time.

I read your column on voluntary military service
in Vietnam with great interest and have no argument on the political desirability of such a move.
Whether it is feasible I cannot say, at least for
the moment. The idea is so intricately connected
with the studies now underway on general force
levels, draft reform and an all-volunteer army that
we will have to wait and see how these studies shake
out before we can start making any informed judge-
ments on the feasibility of your proposal. I will
keep you posted.

Warm regards,

Henry A. Kissinger

Mr. William F. Buckley, Jr.
National Review
150 East 35th Street
New York, New York 10016

As to your friend, you may assure him
I did not last idea to give up national
sovereignty.

Kissinger's reply to Bill Buckley about Henry's concerns.

HENRY PAOLUCCI

KISSINGER'S

A STEP-BY-STEP, BLOW-BY-BLOW ANALYSIS
OF THE STRATEGY OF DEFEATIST INTER-
VENTIONISM WITH WHICH AN AMBITIOUS
HARVARD PROFESSOR REVERSED 25 YEARS
OF AMERICAN COLD-WAR FOREIGN POLICY
IN A WAY THAT, AS WILLIAM F. BUCKLEY
HAS SAID, FINALLY "BROKE THE AMERICAN
SPIRIT."

WAR: 1957-1975

GHGP706/$5.95

HENRY PAOLUCCI

KISSINGER'S

★ A STEP-BY-STEP, BLOW-BY-BLOW ANALYSIS
OF THE STRATEGY OF DEFEATIST INTER-
VENTIONISM WITH WHICH AN AMBITIOUS
HARVARD PROFESSOR REVERSED 25 YEARS
OF AMERICAN COLD-WAR FOREIGN POLICY
IN A WAY THAT, AS WILLIAM F. BUCKLEY
HAS SAID, FINALLY "BROKE THE AMERICAN
SPIRIT."

WAR: 1957-1975

GHGP706/$5.95

Who is Kissinger? (1972, 1980). *Kissinger's War: 1957-1975* (1980). Both
reprinted and expanded in *Public Image, Private Interest: Kissinger's*

Foreign Policy Strategies in Vietnam (2002).

VOL. XXVIII, NO. 37

NATIONAL REVIEW

OCTOBER 1, 1976

| PAOLUCCI | HOLM | McGRATH | COPELAND | archy* | FUTCH |
| Page 1054 | Page 1065 | Page 1066 | Page 1073 | Page 1075 | Page 1077 |

Carter's Kissinger

America's foreign policy is increasingly shaped by a new conception of international relations, shared by the talent pool known among its members as the Community. Among them, says the author, in this highly independent reading of the diplomatic vectors, are Henry Kissinger, James Schlesinger, George Ball, Elliot Richardson, and Zbigniew Brzezinski. It was Brzezinski who, in 1973, had the prescience to spot a presidential comer named Jimmy Carter, and to fasten on him as an "educable" politician, susceptible to the Brzezinski view—Marxist-humanist-technetronic—of history, which dictates an "end-run around national sovereignty, eroding it piece by piece." *Henry Paolucci*

From the cover of *National Review*, October 1, 1976, in which the article on Carter's Brzezinski appeared.

STATE
OF THE
NATION

Volume 8, Number 1
January 1976

VOL. XXVIII, NO. 9

MARCH 19, 197

NATIONAL REVIEW

The Crime of No-Win Belligerency

Angola Finale

When Kissinger cavorts like a hawk these days pleading for a last spasm of aid to "our" side in some distant troublespot, we can be sure the cause he purports to defend is lost. He did it in the last days of Vietnam. He is doing it again as the curtain falls in Angola. His plea is invariably for insufficient aid: enough to prolong the fighting but not to avoid defeat, since defeat, by the logic of detente, is the price he has committed us to pay for Soviet-supported global peace. Kissinger had been arguing since 1957 that, if forced to choose between all-out war and passive surrender, Americans would choose the former. He therefore urged President Kennedy's advisers to forestall such a choice by pursuing a fail-safe alternative: his own limited-war strategy which, by definition, rules out both passive surrender and open-ended military escalation to avoid defeat. That has been our policy since 1961. It has cost us a protracted surrender in Vietnam, concessions of arms superiority to the enemy, and collapse of three succesive presidencies. Yet, as Mr. Moynihan acknowledges, the designers of our defeatist interventionism are still in place. They are now political desperados, caught up in an on-going situation from which there is for them no turning back. All who sense this and keep silent are accomplices.

It remains to be said that U.S. policy in Angola achieved the worst possible result The U.S. might have stayed out of Angola altogether, thus cutting its losses. Alternatively, the U.S. might have intervened with sufficient weight to forestall the MPLA victory—though this would have required adequate political preparation of U.S. public opinion. Instead the Administration secretly provided enough support to assure continuing MPLA hostility but too little to do the pro-Western side much good. It was entirely predictable that this covert aid would be discovered, and that there would follow the usual uproar. Our ineffective covert aid, in addition, made it certain that we would be implicated in the defeat of the pro-Western forces, and suffer the inevitable political damage—and, beyond that, end up in a disadvantageous position for negotiating some sort of relation with the winning MPLA faction. Already France, Britain, Italy, and other European nations are establishing diplomatic connections with the Luanda regime (and casting an eye at economic opportunities), though the Soviet influence of course remains paramount. If the tacticians in the State Department had tried to devise a game plan to achieve the worst possible result, they could not have invented a more consummate failure.

.... And when the Senate has rescued Kissinger by voting down support, one can imagine the expected confidential phone call received at the editorial offices of *National Review:* "Don't blame me, Bill. God knows how I pleaded for at least a show of fighting spirit. But what can you do with a cowardly people and an even more cowardly Congress? Your friend Whittaker Chambers was right. They don't even want to save face!"

Finally!

STATE OF THE NATION

40-05 149th Pl., Flushing, N.Y. 11354

Founded in 1969 by Thaddeus S. Dabrowski and Henry Paolucci

STATE
OF THE
NATION

Volume 7, Number 3
March 1975

Detente Power-Vacuum

*At Nuremberg, Nazi war leaders were charged with
many crimes. But scheming with the enemy to fix the
war's outcome the way criminal gamblers fix prize-
fights was not one of them. International war codes
were often ruthlessly violated in vain efforts to ward
off defeat; but always the Nazi forces, like the Viet
Cong and North Vietnamese and our own zealous
Calleys and Lavelles (not to mention Israeli and Arab
zealots of recent Middle East wars), fought to win.
Scheming not to win no matter how bravely one's
soldiers fight is something relatively new in major-
power history. The civilian policy-planners who have
staged our bloody Vietnam adventure on the pattern
of a fixed fight are thus clearly not war criminals in
the Nuremberg sense. Even with his latest plea for
U.S. aid to prolong the no-win fighting a month or
two, Kissinger hardly qualifies. What he has been
patching together with his sham-war in Vietnam, his
studiously bungled interventions in the Pakistan-India,
Greece-Turkey, Arab-Israeli conflicts, and his detentes
with Peking and Moscow, is something sui generis.
Perhaps after the feared recriminations have come and
gone, historians will conjure up an appropriate name
for it.*

The Kissinger Connection

We are saying that, like Professor Elliott, Buckley has
been used and abused by the courtier's flattery of Henry
Kissinger. In his latest book he is at pains, as we noticed, to
indicate at every turn the sort of initiative Kissinger took with
him. Perhaps he wants the record to show that he has, in
retrospect, at least a vague sense (a gentleman hesitates to have
anything more in such matters) of having been used by the
Inscrutable Henry, who will continue, it seems, to flit around
the world making anti-nationalist "deals for peace" till he
thinks our historic course has been made irreversible or until
a national-populist uprising (perhaps in the form of a blue-
collar general strike) shocks us back to sanity.

VOL. XXVIII, NO. 11
APRIL 2, 1976
NATIONAL REVIEW

Kissinger's View of History

Quite apart from the question of
its intellectual merits, his writing also raises a serious
question about the suitability, for his present position,
of a man holding the views Kissinger has so extensively
set forth.

Since 1950, an invariable quality of Kissinger's work
has been its underlying pessimism. So far, his great
hero-statesmen are *tragic* geniuses. They do what they
can to forestall disaster, they hold it at bay for a while;
but even the greatest cannot prevail, and in the end their
work goes for naught....

Kissinger's view of history explains a good deal that
might otherwise seem puzzling: his premature decision
that Portugal was lost, ... yes ... that Europe would
be Marxist inside of ten years; his deference, in the
Solzhenitsyn affair, to the sensibilities of the Kremlin;
his apparent assumption that we can offer little more
than verbal opposition to the expansion of Soviet influence; and his seeming policy of "preventive concession," as in the Panama Canal negotiations, the "open-
ings" to Castro (now so ludicrously rebuffed), and the
overly favorable terms of the grain, technology, and
other deals with the Soviets. All this is explicable only
on the settled assumption of irreversible Western decline.

Kissinger's pessimistic view of history may, in fact,
be valid. It certainly has a good deal of academic appeal.
But is it suitable for a man conducting the foreign policy
of the most powerful nation in the free world? His adver-
saries in the Kremlin, Havana, and elsewhere are not in
the least pessimistic about the fate of their own cause.
.... Why should we assign to ourselves, rather than
to the Soviets—who have plenty of internal weaknesses
—the role of decline and fall?

Finally!

STATE OF THE NATION

40-05 149th Pl., Flushing, N.Y. 11354

Founded in 1969 by Thaddeus S. Dabrowski and Henry Paolucci

5. 1964: A VINTAGE YEAR

Interest in the Conservative Party of New York State, founded by Dan Mahoney and Keiran O'Doherty in 1962 with the support of William Buckley Jr., the influential editor of National Review, escalated dramatically two years later, when NYS Republican Party leaders headed by Nelson Rockefeller, Jacob Javits, and their NYS candidate for the US Senate, incumbent Kenneth Keating, blocked the Conservative Party from carrying the Republican presidential candidate, Barry Goldwater, on their ballot. The media rushed to cover this "breaking story," what amounted to a public political quarrel that threatened a serious rift within the Republican Party and was bound to damage Republican-Conservative candidates running for public office in New York State.

When the Republican leaders proved intractable in their opposition, the Conservatives responded that they were prepared to place at the top of their ballot, not Keating, but a senatorial candidate of their own who would remind voters that the Conservative Party was backing Goldwater on the national ticket.

It was no surprise that the Conservatives had their candidate long before the convention officially opened at the end of August. An unusually large media contingent arrived in Saratoga Springs on the 31st to be present for what they knew would be a dramatic announcement. Some weeks earlier, the press had carried stories that the Conservative Party leaders had offered the nomination to columnist, playwright, former ambassador to Italy, and former member of Congress, Clare Boothe Luce — wife of *Time* publisher Henry Luce, and an enrolled Republican — and that she had accepted.

Her running as the Conservative Party candidate for the US Senate had, in fact, been broached months earlier, at the Republican National Convention in San Francisco, where Barry M. Goldwater had been chosen to head the ticket as the Party's presidential nominee. A reporter had approached Mrs. Luce to confirm her role in the upcoming campaign. Her answer was a clear signal:

> I regard Senator Keating as a personal friend and a man of real accomplishments. . . . But he has not yet announced his support for the Republican national ticket, and I believe that the New

York electorate is entitled to a Senate candidate unequivocally committed to support that ticket.

As expected, Mrs. Luce accepted the Conservative Party nomination, ready to fight for Goldwater. Conservatives saw this not only as an important battle against the liberal-minded Republican leadership in New York State but also as a fortuitous opportunity to present their platform through an intelligent and articulate candidate who had already proved herself effective in several high-level government positions and was a prominent national figure.

Within hours, the Republican leaders succeeded in getting Mrs. Luce to reverse her decision. She admitted having been pressured by the Republican leadership to bow out of the race and had done so for the sake of Party unity. She gave notice, however, that she would not support Keating unless he allowed Senator Goldwater to head the ticket of the Conservative Party. In a wire to the City Editor of The Daily News, she gave two reasons for her decision:

> First, because I have decided to concentrate all my effort in behalf of the national ticket on the Citizens for Goldwater-Miller Committee.

> And second, because certain New York Republican leaders have recently seized upon it as a means of shifting the blame for party disunity in the state from themselves to the shoulders of Sen. Goldwater and his supporters.

Division among Republicans was now a blatant reality. Conservatives were understandably concerned about this last-minute development for immediate reasons of their own. Would they be able to recruit a candidate who was at least as articulate and knowledgeable as Mrs. Luce, to fight the internecine battle that lay ahead? In a letter to Henry, one delegate later described the dismay of the rank and file conservatives attending the convention and his own personal concerns at the unhappy turn of events, especially when the candidate offered as a replacement turned out to be an unknown professor of History at Iona College, Henry Paolucci.

> I remember the after-midnight bedroom session the night before the convention, last fall, and your remarks there. We had listened and argued with others before you came in; they had not been convincing to the upstaters generally — and we were deeply

disturbed that after arrogating all the master-minding to themselves in the New York State area as to the candidacy and campaign for U.S. Senator, they had muffed the ball, leaving the Party with a last minute improvised "out." The mood was not good. . . . Finally, you were asked to speak. In the atmosphere there, it was a most difficult spot to be in. You impressed me in two ways: You had a stubborn aplomb of your own, and you made a well-stated summary of what your views were, and how you would campaign. I thought rather well of your performance. I had hoped the Party could put up someone with some prominence; you had none; in fact you were not known to any of us. The next day at the convention you did even better. . . .

Everyone was caught by surprise — myself included. The convention was just getting started, when I went into Manhattan for a dental appointment. Before leaving, I urged Henry to get us tickets (if still possible) for the main event. After all, the convention was being held in Saratoga Springs, the very place where we were spending the Summer, as we had for several years, as co-producers of summer stock musicals at the Spa Music Theater — the elegant equivalent of an off off-Broadway theater, across from the Gideon Putman Hotel (later absorbed as part of the Saratoga Springs Center for the Performing Arts). When I returned late that afternoon, I found a bevy of reporters, led by Gabe Pressman, waiting to interview me, wanting to know more about the "political unknown," who, for some reason, had the enthusiastic endorsement of Bill Buckley.

Henry registered his own initial response to the events of August 31, in a letter to Bill Buckley three months after the election. In the opening paragraph, Henry recalls (not without a touch of humor) his first reaction when approached by the Party leaders with the offer to replace Clare Boothe Luce:

When Dan Mahoney confronted me with the Party's dilemma occasioned by Ms. Luce's late withdrawal, the unanswerable monitor that governs my choices these days persuaded me, finally, that it was a matter of honor to accept the uncertain burden of the candidacy. I wasn't aware, then, that part of the burden would be a seemingly endless flow of letters, not only from well-wishers who voted for me, or who voted half-heartedly for Keating to beat awful Kennedy, but also from many who voted for Kennedy out of fear that Keating might make it, thereby making Goldwater's defeat total. My mediocre letter-writing powers were overwhelmed for a time; but I am now beginning to gain a little ground, having managed to break up the mountain of letters into a series of hills. . . .

With the nomination of a politically unknown "professor of History at Iona College," speculation and curiosity quickly escalated. The next day, the *New York Times* carried major stories, featured him on the front page as "The Scholarly Candidate," and went so far as to carry a review of the play that was being offered at the Spa Music Theater as the last production of the season — Eric Bentley's translation of *Liolà*, an early work by the Italian Nobel Laureate Luigi Pirandello (author of *Six Characters in Search of an Author*) — a somewhat unusual offering, for which Henry had written a number of original songs and lyrics.

When asked when he expected to start campaigning, Henry told reporters that he had an obligation to remain in Saratoga Springs until the play closed at the end of the week — adding, "Music is to me what touch football is to the candidate from Massachusetts." In the exchange that followed, he cited a passage from Aristotle about the effect of music, which on September 1st became the *Times* quotation of the day.

I agree with Aristotle that music is the foundation of a well-ordered life. Music tunes the heart.

In an early speech calling for statewide support of the Goldwater-Miller national ticket against the Rockefeller-Keating-Javits opposition, Henry explained in political terms what made him accept the nomination of the Conservative Party. He recalled what Mrs. Luce had said — that Mr. Keating was the only Republican candidate for the US Senate who did not support his national ticket — and emphasized what was to become a major campaign theme.

I accepted the Conservative Party's nomination for the US Senate in order to do all I could to prevent the Javits-Rockefeller-Keating clique from succeeding in their anti-Goldwater scheme. Keating has refused to support Goldwater. Rockefeller has now advised all Republican candidates for the Assembly to "turn their backs on Senator Goldwater and to support Senator Keating, the republican who is running for re-election independent of the national ticket." Keating has again and again openly appealed to anti-Goldwater voters and has made it plain that he will count every vote he receives as an anti-

Goldwater vote. And he is right in saying so. A vote for Keating is plain and simply an anti-Goldwater vote in this state, perhaps even more than a vote for the candidate from Massachusetts is anti-Goldwater.

Let me say emphatically: Goldwater supporters — whether Republican, Independent, or Democratic (and there are many nominal Democrats) — must register their disdain and contempt for the anti-Goldwater tactics of Senator Keating as well as for the Kennedy carpetbagger tactics. And they can do this best by voting for Goldwater-Miller on Row A and dropping down to Row D to vote for the only Senatorial candidate who speaks for Goldwater Conservatism.

One other strong reason for Republican opposition to Goldwater's leading the Conservative Party ticket, Henry pointed out, was that many conservatives — whatever their official party affiliation — were more than likely to vote for their candidate on Row D, if Goldwater's name was on that line, rather than vote on Row A, in which case the Conservatives would amass a considerable vote.

Adamant about not allowing Goldwater's name to appear on the Conservative Party ballot, the Republicans found themselves targets for Henry's sharp criticism. He took every occasion to embarrass them for what he considered to be their betrayal of the official Republican nominee for the Presidency. At the same time, he spoke forcefully and positively in presenting the Conservative agenda to community and political groups, at fund-raising dinners, and in interviews on the leading talk shows, turning even the most frivolous, ambiguous, and leading questions to his advantage.

The media latched on quickly when they realized they had in the Conservative Party candidate a political figure who suggested anything but the ivory tower professor or the obscure scholar immersed in research. They even collected his humorous "quips."

The *New York Times* assigned Raymond Daniell, a seasoned reporter, to accompany him on his campaign trail, something the Conservatives had not had in the previous election. Henry's in-depth analyses of issues made a strong impact on Daniell, who came to admire his intellectual honesty as well as his style in addressing audiences. He was especially struck by the fact that Henry never read from notes and could recite long passages and cite precedents from memory. Daniell's stories were thoughtful and accurate. Around the end of October, as election day drew near, he wrote what was to be a feature story for that Sunday's edition of the *Times*, an objective assessment of Henry's campaign and his impact as a speaker. It never appeared, nor did other stories he submitted that might have encouraged last minute voters to vote Row D. A fair man, Daniell was embarrassed and disappointed.

But Henry had left his mark. Reporters grudgingly admitted the rousing effect he had on audiences. Nor could they deny that he was able to hold his own under fire, in spite of their efforts to embarrass him or catch him contradicting himself. Even those who did not share his political views recognized in him a man worthy of respect and admiration. One afternoon, as we entered our apartment building on Broadway and 111th Street, we were stopped by someone who had just gone out the door, had turned around and come back in. The man identified himself as a producer on one of the major TV channels and asked: "Are you Henry Paolucci?" When Henry answered, the other came back with: "I just want to say: I wish we had more like you on our side!"

Although he could never get his opponents to agree to a debate (there never was one, not even between Kennedy and Keating), Henry was invited for interviews on the major political talk shows on television and radio. His deft manner of skirting certain topics introduced to provoke controversy and his way of recasting ambiguous or provocative questions, distinguished him and set him apart from all other candidates.

A typical exchange is this excerpt from a transcript of "Newsmakers" (CBS, September 6). The questioners were Ronald Sullivan (*New York Times*), Ed Katcher (*New York Post*), and Channel 2 News Director Joe Loughlin.

> Joe Loughlin: Mr. Paolucci, it's been said many times during the past week that you have no real chance of winning your race for United States senator from New York. Would you agree with that or not?
>
> HP: Real chance is rather a strong term.
>
> JL: Any chance?
>
> HP: Some chance, indeed.

Ed Katcher: Professor, would you accept the support from The John Birch Society or any of its members?

HP: The John Birch Society? As I understand it, the John Birch Society has so few members, especially in this state, that it could hardly be a drop in the bucket of any candidate, even a minor candidate.

Ronald Sullivan: But you wouldn't reject their support?

HP: Reject? I never ask support of groups. I would not ask for the support of Israeli-Americans or Roman Catholics. I would, therefore, not ask for support of a group like the John Birch Society. I hold —

RS: You wouldn't reject it, Mr. Paolucci?

HP: — Eisenhower's position. I do not consider accepting the support of the group. I like individuals to vote thoughtfully.

JL: Mr. Paolucci, I would like to pursue more, if I can, the basic reason as to why you are in this campaign. Are you in to win the campaign or are you in it to destroy one of the other candidates?

HP: No. no. I am definitely in his campaign to win for myself but more importantly to attract to the Goldwater-Miller national ticket those Conservatives of this state who are so resentful of the attitude of the Javits-Keating-Rockefeller group —

JL: But Professor—

HP: — that they might not vote for Goldwater and I think there are at least 100,000 voters in this state who might not vote for Goldwater if we, of Row D, the Conservative Party of this state, do not ask them to do so.

JL: You don't have to be a senatorial candidate to get people to vote for Goldwater.

HP: No, I don't think I have to be, because if we had been given what the Liberal Party has been given, namely. the right to put the national ticket on our line, then we would have a measure of how conservatives feel in this state, but if I were not running, we would have no state-wide measure of Conservative power.

JL: Is there any doubt in your mind, Professor, that the net effect of your candidacy will be to take votes away from Kenneth Keating?

HP: I don't think so.

JL: Won't that be the primary real effect of it?

HP: No, I don't think so. I believe I will attract Democratic votes and in the metropolitan area especially, Democratic votes, for Goldwater, people who would not vote Row A for anything, might vote Row A in the first slot because of my urging in this area.

RS: This seems to disagree with what some high Conservatives have told us, that you will hurt Senator Keating?

HP: I have — I don't care whether it hurts him or not. I am interested in getting Goldwater elected. I doubt that my candidacy will attract more votes from the Republicans than from the Democrats. I wish to attract as many pro-Goldwater votes as I can. I would like to give an opportunity to Democrats who are disgruntled to vote for Goldwater and also for Republicans who are fed up with this liberal acquiescence of Republicans to the one-party system we have had in this state.

EK: Professor, what, in effect, are you placing a higher premium on destroying the present Republican party than in electing Goldwater?

HP: Oh, no. I said exactly the opposite of that, exactly the opposite.

EK: Well, you could have electors on your line without any trouble, if the Conservative Party wouldn't run 58 local candidates against the Republicans.

HP: The Conservative Party means to re-establish the two-party system in this state and inasmuch as we now have in the Republican administration which opposes Goldwater, men whose liberal voting record matches and surpasses that of the Democrats, we have as our function, the same function Goldwater has nationally....

A WINS news conference (October 4) reflects the same kind of questioning, this time from Stan Brooks (Director, WINS News), Jack Smee (Senior Editor, WINS News), and Paul Parker (Reporter, WINS News).

Paul Parker: Why are you running for Senator, Professor, when the leaders of the ticket that you support, Senator Goldwater and Congressman Miller, support your Republican opponent,

Senator Kenneth Keating? How come you are defying their choice?

HP: I don't believe it can be said that the leaders of the National Ticket support Mr. Keating. They support party unity and they hope as I do that before election day Senator Keating will repent his present posture and will restore the voice of the Senator in the Republican Party to the National Ticket Campaign.

PP: Well, just a little over a week ago Senator Goldwater said outright in Albany that he supported Kenneth Keating for re-election.

HP: He also said, I hope the local Republicans put aside their horseplay. Now, I use the same phrase in my campaign, horseplay. but I refer to it as Trojan Horseplay. I believe that Senator Kenneth Keating is a Trojan Horse more dangerous to the Republican National Party than any external enemy.

PP: Well, now, but you think this Trojan Horse will change candidates in mid stream and support Mr. Goldwater?

HP: I pray that he will because this being the first time in decades that we've had a real choice on the National level, I pray that Senator Keating will stop being the lackey of Rockefeller ambition in this state.

PP: Well, you must realize that your candidacy could splinter off just enough votes to spell defeat for Senator Keating. Is this your aim? The aim of the Conservative Party in New York?

HP: The aim of the Conservative Party is to attract as many votes as possible to the Goldwater/Miller National Ticket that would not go there because of the inactivity of Keating. I believe we will attract as many Independents and Democrats as we attract Republicans to vote for Goldwater Conservatism.

PP: Let's assume that Senator Keating does change his mind in the midst of the campaign and say that he is now for Senator —

HP: I'll say, better late than never. You did a great deal of harm, you'll have to work hard to undo it.

PP: Will you pull out of the race, then?

HP: Impossible. There are still many people who don't like a turncoat. even if he turns at last to the right cause.

PP: Would you like to see Senator Keating defeated in the election?

HP: No. I'd like to see Henry Paolucci win.

PP: Well, is your candidacy then a retaliation for Keating's failure to endorse Goldwater?

HP: No. It's not a retaliation. It is, the purpose of my candidacy is to supply what the Republican candidate should have supplied, a voice for Goldwater Conservatism in New York State on the Senatorial level. It's not a retaliation. It's a positive position which should have been the Republican Senatorial Candidate's position. . . .

The letters that arrived after such TV and radio interviews were testimony to Henry's ability to hold an audience. Many viewers and listeners were surprised hearing a candidate talk as he did — "a departure from the usual political platitudes," "a breath of fresh air."

A sampling of the response of total strangers who were impressed enough to write in after such interviews, is a fair measure of Henry's public impact — especially in the light of the growing reluctance on the part of many of the liberal-minded media, to give him too much visibility at this point. Since they could not totally ignore him, especially in view of the letters that had been written to major TV programs and radio talk shows demanding equal time for the Conservative candidate, they bowed to the unavoidable and took him on as an easy target.

A flood of letters challenged the wisdom of that strategy.

> I just watched the "nonpartisan" Citizen's Union try to demolish you on "Searchlight" — like a bunch of blind bats unable to find their target. . . . When Milton started to shout and when Gabe and the mouthpiece from the *New York Post* started to stammer, I couldn't restrain myself from uncontrollable laughter. . . . If I had known you were that good at talking, I would have quit my job to campaign for you. I'll do the best I can where I work in the Radio City Post Office. (George V. Altomare, Bronx, NY)

> Perhaps you wonder whether people really listen to those all-night radio broadcasts such as that on WOR last night, in which you participated. I was doing some late night writing when I decided to turn on the radio. I found Long John Nevil boring,

switched to WOR. You were in the midst of a contention and in a few moments you came out pointedly against the U.N. By a careful marshalling of facts and reasoning from them with clarity, you made your point tellingly. I wondered who it was. . . . I have never heard a better job done in smattering the world government idea, and especially pinning its advocates on the point of the impossibility of world government without in the process destroying the ability of the various peoples of the different nations to protect those values they hold most dear. I stayed with the program to the end. (E. Hawley Bendixen, Syracuse, NY)

I wish to congratulate you on your discussion on Channel 13 TV. Your ability to clarify issues . . . was more than brilliant. (Malcolm Lay Hadden, Stratford, CT)

Last Sunday, quite by accident my wife and I tuned in to "Page One" on TV and thoroughly enjoyed your conversation with members of the "impartial" press. It was one of the best presentations we've ever seen or heard. (Robert Vale, Glen Oaks, NY)

I want to compliment you on your excellent TV performance yesterday, especially your sharp answers in stumping the "experts." (Mrs. Harry T, McMahon, White Plains, NY)

You are worthy of the office of United States Senator. You are head and shoulders above that pair running on the two major labels. (Nelson A. George, Buffalo, NY)

I heard you on the Martha Deane Program. Wonderful! Just wish you were on radio and TV more. I know that if more people heard you there would be many more votes coming your way. (Mrs. Robert W. Cleary, Brewster, NY)

I had the good fortune, while driving yesterday, to listen to your responses to the questions asked, and I wish to compliment you on your very clear understanding and the positions you took. . . . It's refreshing to have someone in your position and with your background and experience state so effectively what the average man can understand. . . . Your statements cleared the air with a lot of people who were "on the fence." (James T. Dargan, Jr., Manhattan, NY)

Thank you very much for your stand on "Searchlight." You were terrific. You hit them "right between the eyes." (Sophie Zagajeski, Staten Island, NY)

We just heard you on the Martha Deane program. . . . If the public had better judgment, no one would vote for anyone else but you. (A. Mazean, Forest Hills, NY)

Recently I listened to "Direct Line" to learn more about what you stood for. . . . Your replies to questions were clear, concise and to the point. I wish there were more like you in politics. We surely need them. (C. Beverley Benson, Hartsdale, NY)

I want to take this opportunity to express my deepest admiration for your erudite and much needed criticism of the Liberal One-Worlders as totally inept and even dangerous. (Frank S. Ahlgren, Brooklyn, NY)

I listened to the RANDY-WOR Radio Program this A.M. and want to congratulate you especially for the way you handled that character with the high-pitched voice who tried, without success, to disconcert you at all times. . . . The people of the U.S.A. should hear you more often. The manner in which you express yourself was superb. (Veronica Fleming, Brooklyn, NY)

I heard you calmly take on many of those dedicated leftists on the talk shows during these past weeks, and you were the winner, hands down. (Frances Swain, Ardsley, NY)

By now, details about the quirky "unknown professor" had spread. The image that emerged was that of a man with an extraordinary memory, a wide range of interests, extremely well-read, and with an unusual grasp of history and political philosophy. His audiences, as well as the political players around him, recognized in him the "long view" rather than the ephemeral journalistic immediacy of a "yes" or "no" answer. Those hardy enough to pose questions often forgot their initial query, shifting their attention unconsciously to whatever he had introduced as prelude to a meaningful reply. They soon discovered that he was far removed from the stereotype of the professor buried in his books; rather, they saw him as an intellectual who was also an active political realist, an ardent and effective speaker, not given to glib generalities, and with a rare facility to call up historical parallels to give current events a solid base and the weight and authority of precedents.

He never had recourse to speech writers. Always witty, but never indulging in easy rhetoric, he made full use of his learning, drawing easily from literary as well as historical sources to make his point. He shunned casual talk and was at his best when addressing an audience, large or small, on politics or philosophy or history or literature and music, for like Walter Bagehot (after Hegel and St. Augustine, his favorite writer on politics, economics, and literature) he had many interests.

A dramatic lecturer in the classroom, Henry was unforgettable as a public speaker.

By the end of the campaign the polls showed that the number of votes for the Conservative Party senatorial candidate would be much higher than predicted. Of course no one was naive enough to hope for a victory over Bobby Kennedy; but as Election Day drew near, it became obvious that Henry's name would draw many more votes than early projections and past experience had anticipated, most of which would surely have gone to Keating, had the Conservatives not put up a candidate of their own. Many had written in that they had taken his suggestion and planned to "split their vote."

With a budget that started out with $800 and never got near the kind of money spent on their campaigns by the other two candidates, Henry drew over 216,000 votes — 86.7% more than the Party drew in the 1962 election. It was a remarkable showing, under the circumstances, opening the door for Jim Buckley who, in 1968, running exclusively on the Conservative Party line for the US Senate, brought in over 1,100,000 votes and two years later went on to win the US Senate seat on the Conservative Party line with an astounding vote of over 2,200,000.

The "mountain of letters that had come in" during the campaign," which Henry was just beginning to sort out "into a series of hills," was gratifying. They were still coming in, when it was all over, all with the same positive message:

> There is no question in our minds that if sufficient financial backing was available to you, you would now be commuting to Washington D.C. (George and Harriet Rubin, Bronx, NY)

> It was a pleasure to see a hard-working and devoted man put his personal desires behind you in order to give the people of New York a real choice in this election. While Senators Javits and Keating were ignoring and denouncing the top of their own Republican ticket, you came out with your wholehearted and full support for the Goldwater-Miller ticket. . . . My mother, father,

sisters, and my brother voted for you; we thank you for giving us this opportunity. (Raymond Stefanski, Queens Village, NY)

I was one of the two hundred thousand who voted for you. I saw you on television four or five times and liked you and your style of campaigning better each time I saw and heard you. (Donald G. Gill, Manhattan, NY)

I taped your address in Carmel and your appearance on Page One and had the opportunity to play these back for others. They were effective eye-openers and [succeeded] in changing some votes. (Frederic W. Shaw, Putnam Valley, NY)

I want to thank you for running for Senator. You offered the people of New York "A choice, not an echo." (Judy Dillon, Bronx, NY)

Out-of-staters chimed in as well. One message from Baltimore, Maryland, read: "Thanks for being a Quixote."

Even more important than the immediate results of his campaign and the hopes it raised for the future of the Conservative Party was the fundamental message Henry conveyed: the need to protect our two-party system and the premise of checks and balances on which American political freedom ultimately rests.

Perhaps the most thoughtful response to his talents as a public speaker and the wider historical implications of his public statements came from someone who, after hearing Henry talk, wrote a lengthy letter to the Journal-American (October 5, 1964). In it, the writer sums up his impression: a candidate for public office who was running against all odds, not to win an election so much as to re-establish the basic principles governing our American way of life and to protect the American electorate from arbitrary and dishonest political maneuvering. The letter reports accurately what was said and gives the correct measure of the man in memorable terms.

Last night I heard an address by Dr. Henry Paolucci, professor of history and political science at Iona College and the Conservative Party's candidate for U.S. Senate. Dr. Paolucci is a man of profound knowledge and great sensitivity. But, as I listened, I became aware of something about him which I doubt he intended his audience to see but which could hardly go unnoticed by most of his listeners. Here is a man who has spent his life in a study of the world's great civilizations, who has indentified the causes of their initial expansion and acquisition of power, their virtues and their guilt, their slow dissolution into anarchy and chaos and their final destruction at the hands of the savage.

Picture then, this man, looking up from his books, to find the barbarian hordes again approaching from the East. He turned to raise the alarm, expecting to meet the united and virile voice of a proud and sovereign nation but is instead met with shouts of derision from citizens completely heedless of the horror that is at their gates, divided in their loyalties, fearful only for their own goods and properties, the sole bond uniting them, a common lust for what they think is their share of their neighbor's wealth.

I would think that a man confronted by such a sight must feel an overwhelming sense of helplessness, which, if it did not immediately break his will would in time be replaced with a strong sense of urgency and a rallying of personal courage. It was this alliance of quiet courage and compelling urgency that Dr. Paolucci could not help but convey whether he intended to or not and which raised his address to a level far above the common and maudlin speeches which we have been hearing these past weeks from the Republican and Democratic candidates for the same office.

Consider for a moment his content. Here is a man who assumed his audience couldn't be bribed. He didn't say he could do more for New York and he didn't tell us he was Israel's friend. He announced that he would not eat blintzes, nor pizzas, nor appeal in any way to any minority or ethnic group. In fact, he didn't promise anything to anybody.

Some may ask, what else could an office-seeker possibly discuss? Dr. Paolucci's audience could tell them. They heard about the importance of a government system of checks and balances, not just the horizontal safeguards at the highest level of government but about the equally vital necessity of a vertical structure from the federal government, down through the state and county, all the way to "Main Street." They were made aware of the western concept of freedom, that the only truly free man is the man who insists on accepting full responsibility for license, which can only lead to the kind of anarchy we now see in our streets.

He referred to the history of the Greek city-states, to the writings of Sophocles and Plutarch. He made them see that Man is never very far from the jungle and that when people fear to leave the safety of their own fire at night, the real object of their fear is the jungle that is creeping back into their cities. And he assured them that only a new commitment to individual responsibility could save their individual freedom and preserve the historical miracle that is Western Civilization.

In my brief lifetime, I have never heard words like these from men running for office and four years ago I never expected to. It reminds me of the Phoenix, embodiment of the Egyptian sun-god, which periodically destroys itself by fire, later rising with new life from it own ashes.

Dr. Paolucci and men like him have their work cut out for them, much as did Cicero during Rome's twilight struggle with cancerous power and its concomitant internal decay. If they succeed, I believe it will be far more than we deserve.

The writer's instinctive response to Henry's speech is an accurate description of the impact Henry had on anyone who heard him speak. Not ignoring the immediate political concerns which he addressed in many ways during the campaign, Henry gave his audiences a heightened awareness of the hard lessons of the past as they apply to the present, while impressing upon them the immediate need to protect our system of checks and balances — the essential premise that insures stability in government and protects our Democratic process and way of life.

In running for public office, Henry Paolucci had, to the best of his ability, educated his listeners in the full meaning of freedom and responsibility.

🗁 *From the Archives*

Scant information exists about the 1964 senatorial candidate put forward by the New York State Conservative Party. What follows is a collection of news stories and other relevant materials that focus on Henry Paolucci's campaign, including letters and documents from his personal files.

Clare Luce Plans To Oppose Keating As a Conservative

DAILY NEWS, THURSDAY, AUGUST 6, 1964 · 6

Washington, Aug. 5 (UPI)—Former Rep. Clare Boothe Luce has served notice on Sen. Kenneth Keating (R-N.Y.) that she plans to run against him this year on the Conservative Party ticket in New York, reliable sources said today. A Republican, she represented Connecticut's 6th District (Fairfield County) in Congress.

Her decision, if carried out, would throw the New York Senatorial race into entirely new focus, with serious implications for Keating.

Keating has said he intends to run an independent Senatorial campaign, disassociating himself from the national Goldwater-for-President effort. He has not yet formally announced his candidacy, although it is expected. The Senator declined immediate comment on the Luce development

Clare Boothe Luce
May seek Keating's seat

The New York Times

CONSERVATIVE BID GOES TO MRS. LUCE

She May Accept Offer to Run Against Keating

By EARL MAZO

Mrs. Clare Boothe Luce is seriously considering a proposal by the Conservative party that she become its nominee for the Senate seat of Senator Kenneth B. Keating.

Mrs. Luce said yesterday that candidacy well before the Conservative state nominating convention Aug. 31. The party had earlier announced in a statement that it had offered her the nomination.

Mrs. Luce, a former Republican Congressman from Connecticut and Ambassador to Italy during the Eisenhower Administration, indicated that her primary political interest was to promote the election of Senator Barry Goldwater as President.

But she indicated that she would run for Senator if her candidacy might help Senator Goldwater carry New York State.

The New York Republican party has rejected the Conservative party offer to list the Republican Presidential electors on its line on the November election ballot. Thus, in effect the Republicans have prevented the Conservatives from linking their party, officially, with Mr. Goldwater, who symbolizes conservative political ideology.

The Conservative party will formally select its Senate candidate at a state convention in Saratoga Springs on Aug. 31.

Should Mrs. Luce accept the nomination, it is generally believed she would amass a considerably bigger vote than the 141,000 gotten by David H. Jacquith, the party's candidate for Governor against Governor Rockefeller in 1962.

The bulk of that vote, according to Conservative leaders, would otherwise be Republican. Thus the Luce candidacy could injure Mr. Keating's prospects of re-election, it is said.

Mrs. Luce was elected to the House of Representatives from Connecticut in 1942. She served two terms.

Now a resident of Connecticut and Arizona, with an office in New York City, the prospect of Mrs. Luce's running in New York this year was first broached by a reporter during the Republican National Convention in San Francisco last month.

"I regard Senator Keating as a personal friend and a man of real accomplishment," she said in a statement. "But he has not yet announced his support for the Republican national ticket and I believe that the New York electorate is entitled to a Senate candidate unequivocally committed to support that ticket."

Mr. Keating, while pointedly refraining from endorsing or campaigning for Mr. Goldwater, has said he would run independently of the national ticket — if he seeks re-election again to the Senate.

Coupled with Mrs. Luce's statement yesterday was one by J. Daniel Mahoney, the Conservative state chairman, suggesting that the Republican party also consider nominating Mrs Luce for Senator in view of Mr. Keating's "reluctance to declare himself a candidate for re-election."

Because of Mrs. Luce's prominence in national politics, observers saw the fact that she would permit herself to be associated with the Conservative nomination as a boost to the prestige of that splinter party, which Fred A. Young, Republican state chairman, recently brushed off as "a political blackmail racket."

Mrs. Luce Quits Race For Senate, Aids GOP

By LESTER ABELMAN

Noting she was exercising her feminine privilege of changing her mind, Mrs. Clare Boothe Luce, in a surprise move, yesterday took herself out of the race for U. S. Senator from New York.

In an interview on the TV program, Searchlight, and in a wire to the city editor of THE NEWS, the noted playwright, former Congresswoman from Connecticut and ex-ambassador to Italy formally announced she was withdrawing her candidacy for the Conservative Party nomination for the U. S. Senate.

Mrs. Luce gave two primary reasons for her action:

"First, because I have decided to concentrate all my efforts in behalf of the national ticket on the Citizens for Goldwater-Miller Committee.

"And second, because certain New York Republican leaders have recently seized upon it as a means of shifting the blame for party disunity in the state from themselves to the shoulders of Sen. Goldwater and his supporters."

Keating to Benefit

While denying she felt any resentment toward any Republican leaders, Mrs. Luce's withdrawal statement was critical of Gov. Rockefeller and Sen. Kenneth B. Keating, now engaged in the fight of his political career in his bid for reelection. His probable Democratic opponent is Attorney General Robert F. Kennedy.

Keating, who is certain to benefit from Mrs. Luce's withdrawal, was not available for comment, but his campaign manager, former Attorney General Herbert Brownell, hailed her announcement as likely to unify New York Republicans in support of Keating.

J. Daniel Mahoney, state chairman of the Conservative Party, who appeared on the TV program with Mrs. Luce, announced four possible candidates were being considered to replace her.

The four are Kieran O'Doherty, chairman of the national affairs committee of the Conservative Party of New York State; Henry Paolucci, associate profes-

(NEWS foto by Tom Watson)
Mrs. Clare Boothe Luce, in television interview, says she will not be a candidate for U.S. Senate from New York.

sor of history and political science at Iona College, New Rochelle; David Jacquith, president of the Syracuse Board of Education, and William F. Rickenbacker, son of the aviation pioneer.

Praises Goldwater

Mahoney said any of these four will give up any other candidacy he is seeking if he receives the Senatorial nod at the Conservative Party's convention in Saratoga Springs today.

In her withdrawal statement, Mrs. Luce said that "Sen. Goldwater has consistently preached and scrupulously practiced Republican Party unity."

"Withdrawing my candidacy," she added, "should make further manifest the Goldwater spirit of party unity, which, I have been given reason to hope in the last few days, Sen. Keating will see the political wisdom of emulating.

The New York Times

PAOLUCCI NAMED BY CONSERVATIVES

Senate Nomination Made as Party Scores State G.O.P.

By RONALD SULLIVAN
Special to The New York Times

SARATOGA SPRINGS, N. Y., Aug. 31 — The Conservative party nominated Henry Paolucci, a political unknown from the faculty of Iona College, as its candidate for United States Senator today.

Mr. Paolucci's nomination followed a savage attack by Conservatives on Governor Rockefeller and Senator Kenneth B. Keating.

The session opened in the humid convention hall on the main street here less than 24 hours after Mrs. Clare Boothe Luce withdrew her candidacy for the party's Senatorial nomination.

In accepting the nomination, Mr. Paolucci, a 43-year-old associate professor of history and political science, said that the issue of civil rights in the campaign would be "unpredictable." "No one knows what the breakdown of law and order means in the North, where there has been no legal discrimination since the Civil War," he said.

Mr. Paolucci's nomination means there will be a three-man race. He will oppose Senator Keating, who was renominated today by the Republicans in New York City, and Attorney General Robert F. Kennedy, who is sure to be nominated by the Democrats and the Liberal party tomorrow.

The Conservatives entered a candidate for Senator because Mr. Keating refused to support Senator Barry Goldwater, the Republican Presidential nominee, and because the state Republican leadership refused to share G.O.P. Presidential electors with the Conservatives on the November ballot.

About 500 persons, 311 of them delegates from 41 counties, shouted and stomped at nearly every mention of the Arizona conservative. They hissed and booed every mention of Mr. Rockefeller and Mr. Keating.

The Conservatives dismissed Mr. Keating as a "left-wing traitor," termed unions "coercive," and labeled the Supreme Court "arrogant."

Pickets March Outside

Outside, in a steady downpour that turned to sunshine this afternoon, three members of the faculty of Skidmore College and about a dozen drenched students and youngsters picketed in protest against Mr. Goldwater's positions on extremism and civil rights.

Inside, the business of the convention began with the shaping of the party's platform.

Briefly, and with debate centered mainly on detail, the delegates endorsed a platform that stood "four-square on the American tradition of individual liberty, limited constitutional government, and unswerving devotion to the defense of the Republic against its enemies."

The platform calls for a sharp reduction of Federal controls and spending, an income tax cut, a curb on the spreading "plague of governmental interference," legislation to curb "monopolistic and coercive practices of trade unions," and the right to "compulsory" prayers in schools.

Opposes Review Boards

It also asks a halt to what it called the "Supreme Court's arrogant usurpations of legislative authority" and the legislative and Congressional control of apportionment. It demanded the presentation of neighborhood schools and the "strict enforcement of all laws against coercive or violent actions by individuals or groups, for the protection of the overwhelming majority of peaceful citizens of all races."

In connection with racial disorders and Negro complaints of police brutality in New York City, the platform took a strong stand against the establishment of civilian police review boards.

In its foreign section, the platform supported Mr. Goldwater's call for more manned bombers and warned that "appeasement [to the Communists] could only lead to surrender."

An amendment that would have favored giving the supreme commander of the North Atlantic Treaty Organization control over tactical nuclear weapons was put aside with a suggestion that it become part of the party's legislative program.

Keating Is Belittled

Thus, the Conservatives would not name their own slate unless it could correspond to the Republican one. And the Republicans have ruled this out. They received a ruling from the State Supreme Court over the weekend that the Conservatives could not endorse the Republican slate without Republican permission.

Mr. Jaquith also had bitter words for Senator Keating. And because of Mr. Keating's refusal to support Mr. Goldwater, Mr. Jaquith said, "We just might as well have a Democrat."

Mr. Paolucci, most Republicans believe, will draw most of his votes away from Mr. Keating, thus helping Mr. Kennedy's chances of winning.

In his acceptance speech, Mr Paolucci, standing in front of a huge photograph of Senator Goldwater, told the hot but happy delegates that most of the nation was caught "in a viselike squeeze, with street violence applied menacingly from below and with the might of the Federal Executive pressing down inexorably from above."

He declared that the Conservatives were "no fanatic group."

Most of all, he said, he wanted, like Mrs. Luce, to give Mr Goldwater a "voice in his behalf in New York."

Scholarly Candidate

Henry Paolucci

THERE may have been at some time a politician with odder qualifications and ideas about campaigning than the Conservative party's candidate for the United States Senate for New York. But diligent research fails to find one who can compare to Henry Paolucci, B.S., M.A., Ph. D., Associate Professor of History and Political Science at Iona College, New Rochelle. Item: He has no illusions about being elected. Item: He intends to kiss no babies, shake no hands, make no stump speeches. Item: His chief interest, aside from politics and teaching, is chamber music.

Item: While running for public office for the first time, and probably continuing his classes at Iona (although he's not sure about that), he may also find time to continue work on a novel and on a play about Galileo that he is writing. He has written the music for a Pirandello play "Liola" that is to be produced by the Spa Music Theater at Saratoga Springs where, during the summer, he is the co-producer.

If all this makes the 43-year-old, second-generation Italian-American sound like an intelligent, likable, schol-

Associated Press Wirephoto

No kisses for babies

(Mr. Paolucci at Convention)

arly college professor who is enjoyed by his students, then that, old friends say, is exactly what he is.

James D. Brophy, a fellow faculty member at Iona, said he would rate Dr. Paolucci among the more popular professors at the suburban Roman Catholic men's college, among both the students and the faculty.

"I just sent him a telegram saying: 'Congratulations from the first Democrat for Paolucci,'" Mr. Brophy said.

Wife Also a Teacher

Mr. Brophy collaborated with Dr. Paolucci on a book about Galileo two years ago, one of several that Dr. Paolucci has written or translated from Italian either himself or in collaboration with his wife, Anne, a teacher at City College of New York.

Dr. Paolucci was born in New York City on Feb. 4, 1921, and still lives in Manhattan, at 600 West 111th Street. His father was an immigrant cabinet maker.

He was educated in the public schools and at City College, where he took his B.B.S. degree in 1942. On graduation, he joined the Air Force and went to Italy as a bomber navigator. He had completed four combat missions when the war ended.

Dr. Paolucci stayed in Italy as an intelligence officer with an air base guard unit for several months, then returned to New York to enter Columbia under the G. I. education bill.

After taking his master's degree and a doctorate in

English at Columbia, DR. Paolucci spent two one-year periods of study abroad, first on a Columbia University traveling fellowship and then as a Fulbright scholar. He taught at City College and at Brooklyn College before joining the history and political science faculties at Iona eight years ago. Up until three years ago, he also taught night classes in Greek and Roman history at C.C.N.Y.

Friends say he has a cyclopedic mind and a pleasing style of address. He intends to do most of his campaigning through radio and television, or at large rallies.

Described as Sincere

"He's an excellent speaker," Mr. Brophy said. "I'm looking forward to hearing him expound his philosophies."

Mr. Brophy said Dr. apacci was not obtrusive with his political views, nor particularly argumentative.

"There's no question he is sincere about them, though," Mr. Brophy said.

Dr. Paolucci said yesterday at Saratoga Springs at the party convention, that he joined the party three years ago through the urging of a student at City College, Regina Kelly, who works in the conservative party headquarters in New York.

Before accepting the senatorial nomination yesterday, Dr. Paolucci had intended to run for a seat in the House of Representatives from his home 20th District, where the Democratic incumbent is Representative William Fitts Ryan.

Quotation of the Day

"I agree with Aristotle that music is the foundation of a well-ordered life. Music tunes the heart."—Henry Paolucci, Conservative party candidate for the United States Senate from New York. [40:4.]

DAILY NEWS, TUESDAY, SEPTEMBER 1, 1964 • C6 ✰

Conservatives Pick Prof for Luce Spot

(Associated Press Wirefoto)

Conservative candidate for Congress Kieran O'Doherty (l.) and state chairman J. Daniel Mahoney confer with Henry Paolucci before his name was placed in nomination as Senatorial candidate.

Saratoga Springs, Aug. 31 (AP)—The Conservative Party today nominated history professor Henry Paolucci, a political unknown, to run against Republican Sen. Kenneth B. Keating and the Democratic candidate in the slot the party had hoped Clare Boothe Luce would fill.

In the wake of Mrs. Luce's withdrawal, Conservative leaders chose Paolucci for the assignment and the party's state convention ratified their choice overwhelmingly.

Paolucci, 43, associate professor of political science at Iona College, was nominated on the first ballot with only token opposition from two other contenders. He has promised he will advocate the election of GOP Presidential nominee Barry Goldwater.

Barry's Electors Backed

At the same time the convention agreed to pursue party efforts to gain permission to endorse the same slate of Presidential electors that the Republican Party will run this fall.

This would give Goldwater two lines on the New York election ballot.

Gov. Rockefeller and other Republican leaders have refused to join forces with the Conservative Party, a splinter group formed two years ago. Conservative Party leaders said Paolucci would withdraw if the party could endorse the GOP electors.

Paolucci drew 266 votes to win the nomination over Donald Serrell of Garden City, who attracted 32 votes, and Joseph F. Joyce of the Bronx, who polled 6.

The 316 delegates plus a couple of hundred conservative partisans roared approval when the tally was announced.

Conservatives Name Paolucci For Senate Race

By DOC RIVETT
Times-Union Staff Writer

A short, stocky college professor who plans only a part-time campaign—"and I won't go anywhere without a request"—was chosen yesterday by the Conservative Party to run for the United States Senate.

The candidate, Dr. Henry Paolucci, assured the nominating convention in Saratoga Springs convention hall, "I hope to win."

But other speakers made it clear that they'd be satisfied if Dr. Paolucci could siphon off enough votes from conservatives to insure the defeat of Senator Kenneth B. Keating, the Republican incumbent.

In listing the party's future goals, after Dr. Paolucci had

Candidate Won't Barnstorm.
Page 13

been nominated, Dr. Charles G. Rice, the state vice-chairman, said "and in 1970 we're going to draw a bead on Bobby Kennedy."

Robert F. Kennedy, the U.S. attorney general, is regarded as a cinch to win the Democratic nomination today.

Henry Paolucci
TU Photo by Sheehan

Made Unanimous

Dr. Paolucci's nomination was made unanimous after a roll-call gave him an edge of 256 to 32 for Donald H. Serrell, a Garden City lawyer, and 6 for Joseph F. Joyce, of the Bronx. There were 316 delegates. A number from Erie County abstained

DAILY NEWS, TUESDAY, SEPTEMBER 1, 1964 • 10 ☆☆

Conservatives Name Prof for Clare's Spot

(UPI Telefotos)

Henry Paolucci, Iona College prof, acknowledges ovation of delegates after being chosen at Saratoga Springs convention.

Saratoga Springs, Aug. 31 (AP)—The Conservative Party today nominated political science professor Henry Paolucci, a political unknown, to run for the U.S. Senate in the slot the party had hoped Clare Boothe Luce would fill.

The action sets up a three-way race for the seat now held by Sen. Kenneth B. Keating, renominated by the state Republicans today, and U.S. Attorney General Robert F. Kennedy, certain to be nominated by New York's Democrats tomorrow.

In the wake of Mrs. Luce's withdrawal, Conservative leaders chose Paolucci for the assignment and the party's state convention ratified their choice overwhelmingly.

Paolucci, 43, associate professor of political science at Iona College, was nominated on the first ballot with only token opposition from two other contenders. He has promised he will advocate the election of GOP Presidential nominee Barry Goldwater.

Barry's Electors Backed

At the same time the convention agreed to pursue party efforts to gain permission to endorse the same slate of Presidential electors that the Republican Party will run this fall.

Gov. Rockefeller and other Republican leaders have refused to join forces with the Conservative Party, a splinter group formed two years ago. Conservative Party leaders said Pao-

Conservatives Turn
To Iona Professor

By CHARLES DUMAS

SARATOGA SPRINGS, N.Y. (AP) —Conservative Party leaders· tapped history professor Henry Paolucci for nomination today at the party's state convention to run in place of Clare Boothe Luce against Republican Sen. Kenneth B. Keating.

Mrs. Luce, a Republican, bowed out as a potential opponent of Keating' Sunday in the face of strong threats that Gov. Rockefeller's GOP state organization would withdraw support from the Republican national ticket unless she did so.

Conservative party spokesmen said that only a last-minute concession by the state GOP in a wrangle over presidential electors could prevent nomination of Paolucci, 43-year-old member of the Iona College faculty in New Rochelle, N.Y.

Mr. Paolucci, an assistant professor of history and political science at Iona College, began teaching at the school about eight years ago in the English department. He holds a B.S. degree from City College of New York and M.A. and Ph.D. degrees from Columbia University.

"Unless we have a formal statement by 1:30 p.m. from the Republican State Committee that we will permitted to run the same electors, we are going to nominate our candidate," said Kieran O'Doherty, the convention's permanent chairman.

The Conservatives want to endorse the GOP electors in order to give Sen. Barry Goldwater two lines on the New York State election ballot. President Johnson will have both the Democratic and Liberal party lines.

Rockefeller and other GOP leaders have refused, however. to join forces in any way with the Conservative Party, a splinter group that broke away from the State GOP two years ago.

Mrs. Luce, a noted author and former Congresswoman and ambassador, had said she would run against Keating if he persisted in his refusal to endorse Goldwater.

Under strong pressure from the Rockefeller organization, she announced Sunday that she was withdrawing in the interest of Republican unity.

Paolucci was chosen by a consensus of party leaders Sunday afternoon and appeared to face only token opposition in the form of Donald Serrell, a Garden City lawyer who threw his hat into the ring several weeks ago.

Between 300 and 400 delegates, chosen by the party's county committees, were expected to participate in the convention.

Paolucci had been entered as the Conservative candidate in Manhattan against Democratic Rep. William Fitz Ryan. Paolucci said he would withdraw from that race after nomination for the Senate.

Meanwhile, party leaders said they would continue their court fight to gain permission to endorse the GOP electors.

The Conservatives lost the first round Saturday when Justice Ellis J. Staley of State Supreme Court upheld the Republicans' argument — that electors had the same right as other candidates for public office to refuse any party's endorsement

Conservatives Name Paolucci For Senate; Offer Deal to GOP

By GEORGE MILLER
Gazette Reporter

SARATOGA SPRINGS — The New York Conservative party nominated a 43-year-old college professor and summer resident of this city as its candidate for the senate here yesterday.

* * *

HE IS HENRY Paolucci, a professor of history, and political science at Iona College and the City College of New York. There was no significant contest over his choice following the withdrawal from the race on Sunday of Clare Boothe Luce.

Paolucci polled 266 out of 304 votes cast, including the unanimous vote of the 10 Schenectady area delegates. Donald Serrell of Garden City got 32 votes, and Joseph F. Joyce of the Bronx, 6.

Paolucci, however, left the door open for his bowing out of the race against Kenneth Keating and Robert Kennedy.

He made it clear that the Conservative party was offering the state Republican organization this deal:

* * *

IF THE REPUBLICANS will permit the Conservative party to indorse their slate of presidential electors, the Conservative party will withdraw its candidate for the senate.

The Conservatives do not believe that Paolucci can beat Keating or Kennedy, but they assert that Paolucci can draw enough votes away from Keating to decide the election.

Thus far the Republicans have refused to permit the naming of a common slate of presidential electors. Conservatives regard this as an attempt to destroy them as a political force in the state.

The diminutive professor is five feet six inches tall and weighs 150 pounds. He is a fiery orator, however, and came highly recommended on the basis of speeches before downstate Conservative groups.

* * *

HE STRESSED a tone of "calm concern" rather than "heated rhetoric" in his acceptance speech and cited the history of the Athenian and Roman republics.

"The ancient texts cry out in warning," he declared, "that good values pushed in-

is associated with Ray Rizzo the producer.

In addition, Paolucci has written the music for a musical version of the Pirandello play, "Liola," which will be the theater's final production of the season.

The Conservative candidate said he considered himself "an investor in the economic prosperity of the tri-city area."

* * *

WHEN FIRST introduced to delegates at a morning session, Paolucci said he "hoped to win," adding:

"Civil rights is an unpredictable issue. No polls are accurate. No one can foretell what will be the effect of the breakdown of law and order in our northern cities where there has been no legal discrimination since the Civil war."

Paolucci made these remarks just before the morning session adjourned and the delegates went to lunch. As they left Convention hall they were picketed by a group of 10 persons, including two Skidmore professors, across Broadway from the hall.

The group marched throughout the lunch break in a soaking rain carrying signs reading "Support Equal Opportunity — Reject Racism," "Americans Unite Against Goldwater Extremism," "Saratoga for Keating" and "One Man — One Vote."

* * *

THE GROUP was led by an 18-year-old Harvard College sophomore from Saratoga Springs, Gregory Pilkington, a Negro.

After a few moments the group was joined by Michael Madras, 32 who was attending the convention from Yonkers. He carried a sign saying "Reds Against Goldwater."

More than 500 persons, including 311 delegates from 41 counties, attended the convention, the party's first.

Some 250 were on hand in

enforcement personnel in the "reasonable" performance of duty.

It voted down an amendment advocating giving authority to the NATO commander to employ tactical nuclear weapons against an all-out attack against NATO on the central front."

It also voted down a portion of the so-called "liberty amendment" to the U.S. Constitution. It would take the federal government out of all business activities not specifically authorized by the Constitution.

* * *

THE PLATFORM advocated "preservation of the principal of neighborhood schools, concerted action to curb the supreme court's arrogant usurpations of legislative authority," and "a total reassessment of American foreign policy" among other things.

David H. Jaquith of Syracuse, the party's 1962 gubernatorial candidate, gave the keynote address following a buffet lunch served under the vaulting arches and amid the baroque splendor of the old gambling casino in Congress park.

The delegates booed and hissed at Jaquith's references to Keating and the "so-called Republican leadership in New York." He drew a 30-second standing ovation when he declared that the party's main goal in 1964 was to assure Goldwater's election, adding, "we seem to be the only party in the state where this is the primary objective."

* * *

AS THE AFTERNOON wore on the heat and humidity drove many delegates out of the hall in search of cooler, fresher air. The overpowering effect of the weather was only reinforced when at 3:30 p.m. Katz's News room, across the street from the hall, ran out of soft drinks

Conservative Party Can Be Thorn to GOP Hopes in '66

Despite the widespread talk that Senator Goldwater's decisive defeat was a knockout blow to conservatism, the New York State Conservative Party does not seem to be in great pain over the results Tuesday.

Dr. Henry Paolucci, the Conservative candidate for the United States Senate, told newspapermen that he found "deep satisfaction in bolstering the cause of conservatism by providing voters with a choice to the liberal-dominated Republican and Democratic parties." Kieran O'Doherty, a leading spokesman for the Conservatives, calls Dr. Paolucci's showing pretty remarkable an̶d̶ ̶i̶t̶ ̶i̶s̶ ̶a̶w̶a̶r̶e̶ness among, R̶e̶p̶u̶b̶l̶i̶c̶a̶n̶s̶ that their state leadership has abandoned basic Republican principles."

EDITORIAL

* * *

THE CLASH between liberal-moderates within the Republican Party and the Conservatives seems likely to sharpen in New York State in the next two years. The Rockefeller wing of the Republican Party already is blaming the Keating defeat, the loss of the State Legislature and the fall of several key members of Congress on Senator Goldwater and the conservative bloc that backed his candidacy.

The gubernatorial campaign in 1966 will be the next major test between the moderate Republican leadership and the Conservatives in New York State. In the 1962 campaign, the Conservatives were able to reduce Governor Rockefeller's margin to 530,000 votes an accomplishment that showed they meant business itᶦ⁵ cally and that the governor did n

full public backing among voters normally Republican. His 1962 vote, substantially less than that given Senator Javits and Attorney General Lefkowitz in the same campaign, cast one of the early shadows across Governor Rockefeller's path as he tried to gain momentum for the 1964 presidential nomination.

* * *

IRONICALLY, the Goldwater defeat may strengthen New York State Conservatives as they move toward 1966. As Republican moderates-liberals in the Republican Party solidify their position, many rank and file conservatives may seek a new political home in the Conservative Party. There are signs that the Conservatives are already stronger than they were two years ago Dr. Paolucci received 203,329 votes Tuesday in the Senate race compared with the 141,877 that David H. Jaquith of Syracuse was given in the 1962 gubernatorial campaign.

* * *

THE CONSERVATIVES do not have to win to be happy. Their goal is to keep the Republican Party "honest" in its recognition of the conservative point of view They feel they are succeeding. They now are looking for new adventure, and they appear to be taking aim at Nelson Rockefeller's hopes in 1966.

All of this may be infuriating to the Republican leadership It may even be a little mean. But it is political truth that the Conservatives have within their power to make trouble and Chairman Fred Young and his associates must recognize it.

Utica Press

November 6, 1964

Prof 3rd Candidate In N.Y. Senate Race

There's a third contender for New York's Senate seat. He's Prof. Henry Paolucci, the Conservative Party's entry in the race.

The college professor has plenty to say on a variety of subjects and has, indeed, been sounding off wherever he has forum anyplace in the state. But his two rivals for the post, incumbent Kenneth Keating, Republican, and Democrat Robert Kennedy who's determined to snatch the seat from Keating, haven't even acknowledged his candidacy.

Keating and Kennedy indulge in all kinds of attacks and counter-attacks on each other, covering issues ranging from federal aid to education to the war in Vietnam.

But Paolucci is sticking close to home. While both Keating and Kennedy have brushed aside the New York City-based headache of busing children out of their neighborhood school districts to achieve better racial balance by simply opposing "long distance busing," Paolucci sounds off loudly on the subject.

* * *

"THE terrible thing," says the professor, is that some parents are being forced to seat their children, because of color, in the very school room seats from which other parents, because of color, can voluntarily remove theirs."

He has blasted both Keating and Kennedy on the issue, charging them with not doing their homework" on the subject of school busing. He said that if the other two candidates "had less money to spend on researchers and speech writers they would be better informed."

He says that the real issue in the school pairing business is not the business itself, but the discrimination the plan involves.

Paolucci, a 43-year old native Manhattanite is a

This is the last of a series of Press Spotlight articles on the U.S. Senate campaign in New York. Previous articles were on incumbent Sen. Kenneth B. Keating, Republican, and former Atty. Gen. Robert F. Kennedy, Democrat. Today's article is on the Conservative Party's candidate, Prof. Henry Paolucci.

PRESS SPOTLIGHT ON

The Senate Campaign

stocky fellow of 5 and 6 inches who weighs in at 155 pounds.

He got interested in the Conservative Party and its goals, according to an aide, through a student of his at City College.

It was back in the fall of last year when he was teaching Greek and Roman history as an associate professor at City.

A student, Regina Keily, started chatting about the party during informal discussions, after class. The result was the professor's membership in the Conservative Party.

* * *

HE GOT into the race, he explains, because of Sen. Keating's "deliberate and calculated sabotage of the Goldwater-Miller ticket."

"A vote for Paolucci," he says, "is a vote for Goldwater conservatism.

"Sen. Keating," he charges, "is the only Republican Senatorial candidate in the nation who is not supporting the Republican national ticket. How can he

expect New York Republicans to be loyal to the nation's leading practitioner of party disloyalty?"

Paolucci stepped into the race when former Ambassador Clare Booth Luce stepped out.

"The Javits-Rockefeller-Keating crowd," he says, referring to the leading liberal Republican spokesman in the state, "are not interested in this campaign, which, for the first time in God knows how long, offers the people of the United States a choice between liberalism's elaborate lie and conservatism's plain truth.

"The Albany gang," he says, "is looking for future campaigns, when — they fervently hope—Goldwater conservatism will have been defeated.

"Their hope is, I daresay, that Goldwater will go down so that in the disorder following a general Republican defeat, they may, with cunning and Rockefeller finances, manage to hold on to their positions of leadership in the state organization, and continue their rebellion against the main stream of Republican thinking around the nation."

* * *

THE candidate, although a scholar in his own right who has edited and translated several works in the field of political science, rarely engages in fancy rhetoric in his speaking appearances around the state. He states his case as simply as possible.

New York Herald Tribune   **Tuesday, September 1, 1964**

The Conservatives' Nominee

HENRY PAOLUCCI, HISTORY PROF

By James F. Clarity
Of The Herald Tribune Staff

SARATOGA SPRINGS,
N. Y.

The Conservative Party, frustrated in its desire to put Barry Goldwater at the head of its state ticket, yesterday nominated a 43-year-old college professor to run for Senate and draw votes away from incumbent Republican Sen. Kenneth B. Keating.

The first state convention in the Conservatives' two-year history nominated Henry Paolucci, an associate professor of history and political science at Iona College in New Rochelle. In accepting the Senate nomination, Mr. Paolucci said: "I want to give a voice to conservatism of the Goldwater stamp in New York. There is a great chance that we can garner pro-Goldwater votes from Republicans and disgruntied Democrats."

The 400 delegates, alternates and spectators in sweltering Convention Hall cheered and whistled enthusiastically as Mr. Paolucci spoke.

He said he would campaign "as an academican" to explain "the lessons of the history of Athens and Rome" and how those civilizations declined "when one good was pushed inordinately over another." There was wide spec-ulation among the delegates, even after Mr. Paolucci accepted the nomination, that he would withdraw from the Senate race if the Conservatives were permitted to share the Republican Presidential electoral slate for Sen. Goldwater, or if Sen. Keating were to agree to endorse the Goldwater-Miller national Republican ticket. One delegate asked that Mr. Paolucci tell the convention whether he would withdraw from the Senate candidacy under certain conditions. The delegate was ruled out of order.

NOT NOW

After his acceptance speech, he was asked the same question. Mr. Paolucci answered, "I will not think of any at this time."

The Conservatives have appealed a State Supreme Court decision that the Republicans cannot be forced to share their electoral slate and the Republican state organization, because it does not want to enhance the prestige of the Conservatives.

September 2, 1964

Dear Henry:

I am proud of you, my friend. God bless

you and our cause.

      With affectionate greetings to you both

                Wm. F. Buckley, Jr.

Professor Henry Paolucci
600 West 111th Street
New York, N. Y.

Speaks At Carmel Rally

Paolucci Pins Anti-Goldwater Label On State GOP Leaders

CARMEL—

After being escorted to the Putnam County Memorial Hall by a noisy, horn-blowing motorcade, Dr. Henry Paolucci, Conservative Party candidate for the U. S. Senate, last night, hurled stinging political darts at the Johnson administration and "Trojan horseplay" of New York's three top Republicans.

Members of the conservative Young Americans for Freedom organization heard the Iona College professor charge that Gov. Nelson Rockefeller and Sen. Jacob Javits are "working for the defeat of Sen. Goldwater."

Another Goldwater Fee

Dr. Paolucci said incumbent Sen. Kenneth Keating along with Rockefeller and Javits "needs a Goldwater d e f e a t even more than Bobby Kennedy."

If GOP standard-bearer Barry Goldwater wins the November presidential election, Dr. Paolucci said the "rascals" would be set on the road toward defeat.

Hence, he claimed, "Sen. Keating is making no effort to attract votes for Sen. Goldwater."

From New Rochelle

The fist - pounding professor predicted t h at Mr. Keating would lose the Senatorial race "but not because he was killed by us (the Conservative Party)."

Sen. Keating, said Mr. Paolucci, will have "committed political suicide."

He said the Conservative Party was not opposing anyone who had pledged support to Mr. Goldwater.

When asked if he anticipated a win for the Arizona senator in New York State, Mr. Paolucci commented, "I think he would certainly win" if Keating, Javits and Rockefeller hadn't "betrayed the Republican Party."

Turning his fire on President Johnson, the New York City-born "son of an immigrant" asked if the chief executive was "so embroiled with his intellectual courtiers that he is unable to see what is happening around him."

'Mob Violence'

While speaking on "Mob Violence and Our Chief Executive" he said he wondered if liberals actually incite mobs in the name of "social progress."

He referred to the President as "Bobby Baker's boss" and a man who is "leading the mobs."

Dr. Paolucci claimed that a great danger in America today is "the vise" of street violence below and executive p o w e r above.

He labeled this summer's violence in big city streets as "an attack on law and order."

Later he added, "Now the federal government makes a direct attack on us" by allowing dissatisfied groups to go over state jurisdiction and seek nullifying mandates from Washington.

Edging into the civil rights issue, Dr. Paolucci asserted that if the Negro wants to be treated as an equal "he must assume the responsibility of his deeds."

"Negro integration" is something in which he believes, said the professor, but there is a prior need for "integration" of the

Negro family

He said the family provides the moral cement that induces responsibility and added, "I have known integrated Negro families — but not many."

Dr. Paolucci had previously described himself as the "champion of the lowest classes."

Citing this year as one that saw "wholly unexpected triumphs for conservatism," he said the success of the movement in getting Sen. Goldwater nominated "is miraculous."

He urged those present not to "let anybody discourage you" regardless of the outcome of the November election

Paolucci Praises Barry, Assails Keating, Javits

ROME (*P*) — The Conservative party's candidate for U.S. senator launched his upstate campaign last night with praise for Sen. Barry Goldwater's opposition to medicare and a slap at New York's two Republican senators.

Harry Paolucci made his comments in a speech at a fund-raising dinner here, the first stop on a three-day swing that also will take him to Syracuse, Rochester and Buffalo.

Paolucci, a professor at Iona College, is running against Republican Kenneth B. Keating, the incumbent, and Democrat Robert F. Kennedy.

His speech was titled "medicare, public welfare and political bribery."

Referring to President Johnson as "Bobby Baker's boss in the White House," Paolucci said that the President's support of medicare had been given in "the familiar accent of the popular demogague."

The professor asserted "there's nothing of the smiling, flattering demagogue." in Goldwater's stand that medicare would be a step toward turning the Social Security system into a charity organization.

"The hard thing to say about medicare, but the true thing, is what Sen. Barry Goldwater said in voting against it," Paolucci asserted.

He noted that the five Republicans who voted with 44 Democrats when the medicare bill pased the Senate included Keating and Jacob J. Javits, New York Republicans.

JOHN CHAMBERLAIN

The role of the conservatives

For anyone who enjoys analysis for its own sake, the New York State senatorial campaign offers a most fascinating field for conjecture. With Kenneth Keating, a Republican, making a big pitch for the New York City liberal, labor and Jewish ethnic groups that turned so emphatically to the other Republican Senator, Jake Javits, in the last election, it could mean that Democratic Bobby Kennedy has been dealt a mortal wound. On the other hand, no Goldwaterite among the Irish, Polish or Italian ethnic groups that are deserting the Democrats can really go for Keating.

What I seem to sense is that the Conservative Party choice for senator, an obscure professor of history and political science at Iona College in the suburban New York town of New Rochelle, is going to run up quite a sizeable vote from upstate Republicans and big city Democrats. And it is a toss-up at the moment whether Kennedy or Keating is going to benefit more from defections to the third party man.

The obscure professor from New Rochelle is an extremely individualistic Italian-American named Henry Paolucci. Left to his own personal inclinations, Paolucci would prefer to spend his leisure time composing music for the Spa Music Theatre in Saratoga Springs. But when the Rockefeller-dominated Republican Party in New York State refused to let the Conservative Party share the official Republican Goldwater electors on its polling booth line, and when Clare Boothe Luce was persuaded to bow out as the Conservative candidate for Senator, Professor Paolucci let his sense of duty get the better of his musical instincts.

Draws from both parties

This most unlikely Conservative candidate is unusual in that he thinks, personally, he may be taking as many votes away from Kennedy as he will be taking from Ken Keating. A draw of this sort would mean that he is not a menace on balance to either of the major party candidates, other things being equal. But the question is not as simple as that.

The liberals have two candidates, Kennedy and Keating, in the field. But the conservatives have only one man, Paolucci.

Nobody knows just how the Republican conservative arithmetic will affect the Keating chances on November 3. But it is a good guess that the liberal vote could benefit Keating more than Kennedy simply because of Republican Jake Javits's hold on the New York City liberals.

Keating's cause is Javits' cause

Javits has made the Keating cause his own, which could mean a lot of ADA, Alex Rose-Liberal Party and Jewish ethnic votes in the Keating column. Meanwhile, the disoriented conservative Democrats who bulk large in Queens, Nassau and Rockland counties because of the recent population drift from Manhattan could easily have qualms about voting for either Kennedy or Keating. Who, then, is there to vote for but Henry Paolucci? And doesn't all the shuffling promise to make Bobby Kennedy the all-around loser?

Breaking the possible Paolucci vote down, the Conservative Party senatorial candidate stands to attract the "law enforcement vote" (the people who resent the fact that the New York City police force has been getting a bad press on the "police brutality" allegations). He also should get a big ethnic vote from Italians who think the old parties have done nothing to combat the stereotype that gangsters are mostly Sicilian in origin. Then there is the "institutional" conservative vote which likes the idea of having a party of its own. And, finally, there are those Democrats who have moved to the conservative-minded suburbs.

Paolucci Says Keating Sabotages Party Ticket

ROCHESTER (P) — The state's top Republicans are hoping that GOP presidential candidate Barry Goldwater will be defeated, the Conservative Party's candidate for U.S. senator said Friday night.

"The Albany Gang"

Henry Paolucci asserted that "the Albany gang" of Gov. Rockefeller and U.S. Sens. Kenneth B. Keating and Jacob K. Javits wanted a Goldwater defeat so they could, "with cunning and Rockefeller finances, manage to hold onto their positions of leadership in the state organization."

Noting that Keating had refused to endorse Goldwater, Paolucci charged Keating with "deliberate and calculated sabotage of the Goldwater - Miller ticket."

The Conservative Party nominee, continuing an Upstate campaign swing, commented in a speech prepared for delivery to the student body at the State University College at Geneseo, south of here.

Earlier, Paolucci told a news conference at Syracuse that Keating would hurt Goldwater more than Robert F. Kennedy, the Democratic nominee for U.S. senator.

The Conservative nominee said the New York GOP was running a campaign keyed to state candidates and the results would be to discourage some Republicans from voting for the full party ticket, including Goldwater.

Paolucci said Keating was "the only Republican senatorial candidate in the nation who is not supporting the Republican national ticket," and "how can he expect New York Republicans to be loyal to the nation's leading practitioner of party disloyalty?"

Paolucci noted that Keating, Rockefeller and Javits were among the Republican leaders who had refused to allow a joint slate of Republican and Conservative presidential electors pledged to Goldwater.

Senate Candidate

Paolucci Attacks State GOP Leader

CARMEL — President Lyndon B. Johnson, Governor Nelson A. Rockefeller and Senator Jacob K Javits were charged by Dr. Henry Paolucci, Conservative Party candidate for U S. Senator with being part of "the liberal establishment" which he alleges is trying to destroy the American system of government."

DR. PAOLUCCI told a rally of Young Americans For Freedom in Memorial Hall Carmel to promote the candidacy of Senator Barry M Goldwater Monday night that liberal ideas are promoting despotism in this country and the world and that freedom can only be saved through conservative principles and leadership.

The rally was attended by approximately 60 persons. Bruce Bell of Carmel, Putnam County chairman of YAF conducted the meeting. The speaker was introduced by Arthur Lyons of Mahopac, chairman of Putnam County Citizens for Goldwater and Miller.

Dr Paolucci, a professor of Roman history at Iona College, New Rochelle used illustrations from Roman and European history to support his contentions, concerning Civil rights, integration, world government and New York State and domestic and foreign politics. Dr. Paolucci is opposing U S. Senator Kenneth B Keating, the Republican incumbent and former Attorney General Robert F. Kennedy, the Democratic Liberal candidate for a seat in the U.S. Senate.

Dr. Paolucci's theme was that there is "a liberal establishment" headed by liberal intellectuals and including most of the top leaders of the Democratic and Republican parties which is promoting the rise of the lowest classes in this country in order to wipe out the middle class and thus create a despotism. The United States is also carrying on this policy throughout the world by aiding the backward nations to achieve equality with the more advanced nations, Dr. Paolucci claimed.

"THE MIDDLE GROUP throughout history has lent stability to government. When the top group, the aristocrats in the old days and today, the liberal intellectuals try to crush or eliminate this middle group tyranny results," said Dr. Paolucci.

The Conservative candidate cited instances from medieval history when the kings of countries such as France sought to break the power of the nobility by aiding the lower classes.

"What happened there was that the king sided with the common people against the nobles in every instance so that the power of the nobility was undetermined and broken. The king became a despot and the nobles became courtiers at Versailles," Dr. Paolucci said.

England was different because the middle group secured a confirmation of their rights and existence in the Magna Carta and this prevented the king from becoming a tyrant," Dr. Paolucci said.

"Barry Goldwater knows of this threat to America's freedom and he has not sang a different tune since he was nominated as some have charged. Whatever happens November 3, have faith that the conservative movement is rising and liberalism is sinking," Dr. Paolucci said.

Dr. Paolucci said in New York State that Governor Rockefeller and Senator Javits using Senator Keating as a tool have hurt Senator Goldwater's candidacy in New York State.

BE News 10/27/64

Paolucci Declares Catering to Ethnic Groups 'Insulting'

Appeals to ethnic groups were termed "insulting" by Prof. Henry Paolucci, Conservative Party candidate for the U. S. Senate, in a talk Monday evening during the Romulus Club candidates' night.

"I am proud of my Italian heritage," Prof. Paolucci said, "but I am also proud, very proud of my American citizenship and the fact that my family has integrated itself into this country.

"I feel insulted if someone says to me, they'll help get someone into the country by loosening immigration policies."

The Conservative Party candidate, a professor of history and political science at Iona College, New Rochelle, charged that both his opponents, incumbent Senator Kenneth B. Keating and Robert F. Kennedy "are playing the same game with many other so-called voting blocs."

Debate Urgently Needed

"Rest assured," he said, "that the conservative movement is here to stay, because of people like me who don't go around to Italians, to Irish and to Jews. . ."

The candidate said the nation urgently needs a debate between conservative and liberal philosophies.

DAILY NEWS, MONDAY, SEPTEMBER 7, 1964 • 6

Keating Camp Sees Union Rift Over RFK

(NEWS foto by Tom Baffer)
Conservative candidate for Senate Henry Paolucci goes over notes with wife, Anne, before television interview.

By JOSEPH McNAMARA

Sen. Kenneth B. Keating's campaign director predicted yesterday that many labor union locals will rebel against the State AFL-CIO's endorsement of his opponent, Robert F. Kennedy.

"As you know, quite a few of the big unions abstained and, I imagine, that was a silent protest."

He said, in reference to the Kennedy boyish elan, that "we'll match Sen. Keating on handsomeness against his opponent."

Face Bears Witness

Brownell then said Keating's face "shows the great service over the years he has rendered to the people of New York State."

Keating is 64 years old, Kennedy, 38.

Keating himself returned to New York for a speech at a Greek - American organization after a succesful tour of the Catskill Mountain resorts over the weekend.

He attended services in the 154-year-old Monticello Presbyterian Church. His glad mitting tour included hotels, swimming pools, night clubs and village streets. He said many people had represented themselves to him as Democrats who vouched they would vote for him because of the carpetbagger tag he had pinned to Kennedy.

Assails Keating on Buses

Meanwhile, others slapped at the Republican slate of Barry Goldwater-William Miller.

Roy Wilkins, executive secretary of the NAACP, said election of Goldwater could bring on a police state.

Henry Paolucci, Conservative Party candidate for U.S. Senator, described Keating as "a kindly old man" swayed by public opinion polls.

On radio's Newsmakers program, he charged that Keating had given no thought to compulsory school busing before announcing Saturday that he was opposed to it.

Remapping, Civil Rights Criticized By Paolucci

By **BRUCE F. LOWITT**

"Reapportionment strikes against the basic structure of the constitution."

So spoke Dr. Henry Paolucci, associate professor of history and political science at Iona College and former unsuccessful Conservative Party candidate for the New York State Senate, as he addressed a gathering of about 50 persons at the Port Chester YMCA last night. His appearance was arranged by the American Speakers Bureau.

In his one-hour speech, entitled "The Revolutionary Character of Reapportionment", Dr. Paolucci said that it would "destroy the self-respect of the middle classes," and charged that both the current reapportionment and civil rights movements "are policies in and of themselves and not in the national interest."

"Suppose," he said, "that under the proposed one-man, one-vote system, we had three men living in one small apartment in the city and one man who owned 1,000 acres of farm land and they each had an equal vote, and it was proposed that farmers pay all the taxes.

"Well, naturally, the farmer would lose in a vote and pretty soon he'd decide it would be better to move into the city.

"But then one of the three guys from the apartment comes out says, 'Since you can't afford to keep producing on the farm, we'll pay you not to grow any-thing'.'' Dr. Paolucci said making reference to federal farm subsidy programs.

He said that the "liberals" way of government is one in which "the few do the dispensing of money and the many, dependent on those few, do the spending. This," he siad. "is what the communists have been breaking their backs for years trying to accomplish."

Dr .Paolucci stated. that the ruling party can only justify its power when it is held with the consent of the minority, in any situation "and the only way Lyndon Baines Johnson can justify his power is by the consent, not of the 68 per cent who voted for him, but of the minority who voted for Barry Goldwater."

He charged that "liberals who are pushing reapportionment are doing so with the knowledge that they will break the peoples' morale and destroy the checks and balances of our government."

In answer to a question concerning his opinion of the John Birch Society, Dr. Paolucci stated he was not a member of the organization. He also said that, speaking as an individual, rather than as a spokesman or member of the Conservative Party, he sees the society "as a group now doing the most daring work in the area of the right wing."

The World of Henry Paolucci

BY TY

The Conservative Party of Rockland - that last outpost, for the disgruntled, disenchanted, and rejected political animal - can boast of a windfall.

Certainly not an organization for the erudite political thinker, our local Conservative group can exult over, not one, but two genuine intellectual candidates, which may have put quite a strain on the cerebral gifts of its political rank and file.

This windfall includes two doctors; one a man of science, and the other, a man of the liberal arts.

To Dr. Patrick, the scientist, goes the accolade of a skilled rhetorician and angry young letter-writer in the editorial pages of our local newspapers.

But the real prize is a young professor teaching political science at a local college, whose entry into U.S. Senatorial race came through the Claire Luce surrender.

To Henry Paolucci, Ph. D in English, composer of sentimental music, and above all a devotee of Aristotle's principle that "music is the foundation of a well-ordered life", goes the hope of a minority dedicated to Goldwaterism.

But Dr. Paolucci's music doesn't seem to have the proper swing, nor will he emerge as a political Pied Piper, since a dismal result is forecast.

Like most Conservatives, he is invariably drawn to antiquity for reference material, but the art of reference is highly developed and sophisticated in his case.

Greek city-states, Sophocles, Plutarch, St. Thomas, St. Augustine, Dante, and even Hegel on Tragedy, are part of the world of Henry Paolucci.

And it is through all this wisdom and knowledge that the Conservative Candidate for Senator comes to the bizarre conclusion that Goldwaterism is the hope for America.

With the graves of these philosophers shaking at this thought, the professor glibly pursues the charge that, "Liberalism is an elaborate lie on the verge of exposing the emptiness and vanity at its heart".

When pressed on the more specific question of the plight of the poor and meek in spirit and what seemed like a capitalist economy as being too formidable for these rejected humans - Dr. Paolucci replies that "nobody is poor in this country"!

Compared to the average condition of the world, "we are all rich," he states.

This lyrical image depicted by our scholar may very well be the answer to the people of Appalachia, who have but to look at the rest of the world and then thank God and Aristotle for the better life.

Since poverty in America is now being referred to as the third largest killer of humans, music seems hardly the medicine for the weak and underfed.

Pursuing the question of these poor dependents, Dr. Paolucci goes on to say that "no dependent of the state should have a right to vote, and that dependents belong in social hospitals"

This columnist became perplexed at what appeared to be a benevolent form of euthanasia, so the good doctor was prodded on this point without much success

But to his followers in Rockland, there is very little that is perplexing.

For Dr. Paolucci, there is an image of hope to those who see the barbarian hordes approaching from the east.

Very little was said about the south, and one can assume that the liberals must be responsible for pushing civil rights legislation too quickly.

However the case, Henry Paolucci, a Dante scholar, must certainly be aware of a canto in the "Inferno" which treats of sinners who are fortune tellers, of the future (like our Conservative Party predicting the end).

The punishment for these unfortunates is to have their heads turned backwards on their bodies and to be compelled to walk backwards through all eternity, their eyes blinded with tears. Those who sought to penetrate the future cannot even see in front of themselves.

Our Conservative Party- apparently- is able to achieve this condition on earth in our time.

Let us be thankful that it is not for all eternity

THESE DAYS:

N.Y. Conservatives Stand to Gain

By JOHN CHAMBERLAIN

FOR ANYONE who enjoys analysis for its own sake, the New York State senatorial campaign offers a most fascinating field for conjecture. With Kenneth Keating, a Republican, making a big pitch for the New York City liberal, labor and Jewish groups that turned so emphatically to the other Republican Senator, Jacob' Javits, in the last election, it could mean that Democratic Bobby Kennedy has been dealt a mortal wound. On the other hand, no Goldwaterite among the Irish, Polish or Italian ethnic groups that are deserting the Democrats can really go for Keating.

CHAMBERLAIN

What I seem to sense is that the Conservative Party choice for Senator, an obscure professor of history and political science at Iona College in New Rochelle, is going to run up quite a sizeable vote from upstate Republicans and big city Democrats. And it is a toss-up at the moment whether Kennedy or Keating is going to benefit more from defections to the third party man.

The obscure professor from New Rochelle is an extremely individualistic Italian-American named Henry Paolucci.

This most unlikely Conservative candidate is unusual in that he thinks, personally, he may be taking as many votes away from Kennedy as he will be taking from Keating. A draw of this sort would mean that he is not a menace on balance to either of the major party candidates, other things being equal.

But the question is not as simple as that. The liberals have two candidates, Kennedy and Keating.

But the conservatives have only one man, Paolucci. Now, some Republican conservatives are going to stick with Keating because he bears the traditional Republican label. Others are going to stay with him because they fear the re-emergence of a "Kennedy dynasty." Paolucci, on the other hand, will get Republican conservatives who want to chastise the Rockefeller Republicans for not putting out any real effort for Goldwater.

✳   ✳   ✳

NOBODY KNOWS just how the Republican conservative arithmetic will affect the Keating chances on Nov. 3. But it is a good guess that the liberal vote could benefit Keating more than Kennedy. simply because of Republican Javits' hold on the New York City liberals. Javits has made the Keating cause his own, which could mean a lot of ADA and Liberal Party votes in the Keating column.

Meanwhile, the disoriented conservative Democrats who bulk large in Queens, Nassau and Reckland counties because of the recent population drift from Manhattan could easily have qualms about voting for either Kennedy or Keating. Who, then, is there to vote for but Paolucci? And doesn't all the shuffling promise to make Kennedy the all-around loser?

Breaking the possible Paolucci vote down, the Conservative Party senatorial candidate stands to attract the "law enforcement vote" (the people who resent the fact that New York police have gotten a bad press on the "police brutality" allegations).

He also should get a big vote from Italians who think the old parties have done nothing to combat the stereotype that gangsters are mostly Sicilian in origin. Then there is the "institutional" conservative vote which likes the idea of having a party of its own. And, finally, there are those Democrats who have moved to the conservative-minded suburbs.

Against all this there is the incalculable attraction of the Kennedy name, which could draw votes away from Keating among Republicans who consider the Kennedys conservative enough. It's all a nice tangle. My only certainty is that Paolucci will do very well for himself in absolute voting terms. The little Conservative Party could come out of the election stronger than ever.

New York World-Telegram

Paolucci: Goldwater Betrayed

Associated Press

ROCHESTER, N. Y., Sept. 19—The Conservative party's nominee for U. S. Senator says "the Javits-Rockefeller-K e a ting crowd" wants Republican Presidential candidate Barry Goldwater to lose

That group of Republicans hopes that, through a Goldwater defeat, they could, "with cunning and Rockefeller finances, manage to hold onto their positions of leadership in the state organization," Henry Paolucci declared last night.

Paolucci was referring to Gov. Rockefeller and United States Sens. Kenneth B. Keating and Jacob K. Javits.

He said Keating, who has refused to indorse Goldwater, was guilty of "deliberate and calculated sabotage of the Goldwater-Miller ticket. How can he expect New York Republicans to be loyal to the nation's leading practitioner of party disloyalty?"

Paolucci noted, in a speech to students at the State University College at Geneseo, that Keating, Rockefeller and Javits were among Republican leaders who had refused to allow a joint slate of Republican Conservative Presidential electors pledged to Goldwater.

Conservatives Ready To Sacrifice Paolucci

SARATOGA SPRINGS, N.Y. (AP) — New York State Conservatives had a U.S. Senate candidate in the field today, but remained frustrated in attaining their main objective—having Sen. Barry Goldwater head their ticket in the November election.

The Conservative Party is prepared to withdraw its Senate candidate — history professor Henry Paolucci — if the Republican Party permits Conservatives to endorse GOP presidential electors committed to Goldwater.

Clinging to fading hopes that Republicans would permit such a move, the Conservative Party Monday authorized its state committee to remove Paolucci's name from the ballot, if the GOP consents.

Paolucci, a political unknown, was nominated by the Conservative Party convention Monday to oppose Sen. Kenneth B. Keating in the slot the party had hoped Clare Boothe Luce would fill.

Paolucci, 43, a member of the Iona College faculty, was nominated on the first ballot with only token opposition from two other aspirants.

As for a Conservative line on the ballot for Goldwater. Gov. Rockefeller and other GOP leaders have refused to join forces with the Conservative Party.

The issue is being fought out in the courts.

The Conservative Party, composed mostly of dissident Republicans, was formed two years ago in opposition to what it considers the too liberal policies of Rockefeller and other GOP leaders.

Manhattan lawyer Kieran O'Doherty, a Conservative leader, said that, if the Republicans remain adamant on the ballot question, the Conservative leadership would ask party members to vote for Goldwater on the Republican row.

Any move to take Paolucci out of the race must be accomplished by Sept. 9, the deadline for withdrawal by candidates for public office in New York State.

Paolucci Addresses Packed Auditorium

Before an overflow crowd of some seven hundred supporters and listeners in Doorley Auditorium last Tuesday, Dr. Henry Paolucci, Conservative candidate for Senator of New York and Professor of History at Iona, delivered a report on the reasons of his candidacy and his own observations of the election as a whole.

After a brief introduction by Jim Reid, President of the Conservative Club which, with the Special Events Committee of the Student Council under Richard Biondi, had sponsored the affair, Dr. Paolucci was greeted with an enthusiastic demonstration by his supporters. Their spirit spread to the entire audience and Dr. Paolucci became the object of continuous cheering and whistling. He then began speaking after the first demonstration had lasted for about five minutes.

Picturing himself as more of an academician for the Conservative philosophy than a political candidate, Dr. Paolucci stated that he was actually doing the same thing he has been doing for the past two years, but under different auspices, i.e., speaking in support of Conservatism. In his consideration of this movement, he viewed the candidacy of Senator Goldwater as a turning point of American history as it forces Americans to re-examine the relationship of the individual to the community, and to discover exactly where the sources of authority are to be discovered.

In relation to the Goldwater policy, Dr. Paolucci saw no calm and rational debate between its tenets and the tenets of liberalism. Rather it has been Goldwater's "affiliation" with the Birch Society which the Liberal Democrats have seized as one of the fundamental issues of the campaign. These people, he pointed out don't want a serious debate because it would involve the process of thinking ("And they haven't thought a serious thought for three decades") and would probably upset their comfortable complacency. In the race for Senator of New York, he observed a perfect example of this form of diversion on the part of the Liberal Democrats, aided substantially by the Republicans. The so-called Liberal Republicans under Rockefeller, Javits and Keating have attempted to create a picture of the "true" Republican and have succeeded only in destroying party unity and in creating a "Liberal" Ken Keating.

Iona's history professor did admit that the Liberal tradition had been of some service, serving as a system of checks and balances on the excesses of the government. This was, however, before the government became almost totally libral in its conception of the role of the individual in society. "Thus we have liberal intellectuals who dismiss Goldwater as mentally unfit, and when questioned as to the fitness of the President, refuse to answer and claim 'that's another matter.' The liberal of today is merely an academician who has become a 'courtier', writing papers of position, with absolutely no cri-

(Continued on Page Two)

Dr. Henry Paolucci talks with a group of students at UB

On Reapportionment

Paolucci Critical of Keating Stand

By RAY HERMAN

Dr. Henry Paolucci, the Conservative Party's senatorial candidate, charged here Monday that one of his election opponents, Republican Sen. Kenneth B. Keating, bolted the state's GOP by his recent position on legislative reapportionment.

The candidate, a 43-year-old associate professor of history and political science at Iona College in New Rochelle, said that Keating "voted to scuttle" the Dirksen reapportionment bill which would have stayed the Federal Court order requiring a new election of the New York State Legislature in 1965.

In his second visit to this area since his nomination Aug. 31, Dr. Paolucci, who accepted the nomination after Clare Boothe Luce declined to run, addressed about 100 State University at Buffalo students at Norton Union on the campus.

He spoke earlier in the day at Salamanca.

Paolucci's other senatorial foe is Democrat Robert F. Kennedy. Paolucci and other Conservatives are extremely unhappy with Keating because the GOP incumbent has pointedly refused to endorse Republican presidential candidate Barry Goldwater.

On the question of reapportionment, Paolucci charged that Keating is now "following in the footsteps" of GOP Sen. Jacob K. Javits of New York City "in an effort to get Javits' swing vote in New York City."

He observed that it's actually the GOP position on both the state and national level to delay "hasty reapportionment" and that this position has been adopted by such New York GOP notables as Lt. Gov. Malcolm Wilson.

He noted that Wilson had supported a resolution which called upon Congress to enact legislation barring federal courts from interfering with apportionment of state legislatures for at least four years.

The court ordered reapportionment of state legislative boundaries for next year and an election with the new boundary lines in 1965 in the wake of a U. S. Supreme Court decision that this state's formula for legislative apportionment was unconstitutional. The net effect of the order is that the state legislators will have to run this year, next year and in 1966, a normal election year for them.

Paolucci was honored at a reception Monday night given by the Citizens for Paolucci at Rollek's Wishing Well Restaurant, 2431 Broadway, Sloan. However, a New York City engagement today forced him to cancel an afternoon appearance today at Rosary Hill College. The State University talk Monday afternoon was sponsored by the Students for Goldwater-Miller at the university

—PRESS PHOTOS BY JOHN BOLAS.

Prof. Paolucci Expounds . . .

Matthew Arnold, Mr. Paolucci also seemed to be hammering at these arguments:

ONE — The high-tax, welfare-state policies and programs of the Johnson administration, although inspired by "humanitarian" motives, are lessening the importance of the father as head of the family and are destroying the middle class, historically the bulwark against violent revolution.

TWO—The Democratic administration and liberal Republicans, by assigning any control over U. S. destiny to the UN, are yielding up American sovereignty to an organization in which "emerging nations unequipped for self-government" have much voting strength.

THREE—Negro equality should not be achieved by using federal marshals in the South to "push whites down," but by the more difficult process of Negroes raising themselves to the w h i t e level, chiefly through repairing their family structures, historically weakened during the slavery epoch.

FOUR—Giving anything to rioters in the streets is like "throwing a growling dog a bone. When the dog is done, he wants more."

FIVE—The Johnson administration, seeking "co-existence" with a "growling" Khrushchev, "threw him Cuba like a bone."

SIX—The only way to co-exist with the Russian leader is to be as tough and as dedicated as he is; to say, as Khrushchev has said, that we will go to war if necessary and win the war.

Mr. Paolucci said it is not true that Conservatives want to "push the ship of state to the right."

"We want to push it straight ahead," he said, "but we have to steer it to the right to do that, because it has veered so far to the left."

The Conservative nominee charged newspapers with being unfair in covering his campaign

The New York Times, he said assigned a "former hatchet man on Huey Long" to cover him daily, but pulled off the reporter as soon as the reporter stopped putting nasty digs in his copy.

NOTING that his meeting last night was sparsely attended and covered by newsmen, the nominee said he sometimes speaks to crowds of 500 with no reporters present and no mention in the newspapers.

He said the Conservative "movement" has a broad base of support, chiefly among "nice people, middle-class people who can't always attend political rallies because they can't afford baby-sitters."

At a Suffolk County rally, he said, he w a s introduced by Archibald Roosevelt, nephew of the late Theodore Roosevelt, to a large crowd ranging from "the highest level of society to the most vulgar truck driver."

He told his audience that the Conservative movement is more than just a Goldwater cult, "it is a movement," a patriotic force.

"IF GOLDWATER d o e s n ' t live up to my principles," he said, "he will lose my support, but the movement will go on.

"Numbers don't count. A Conservative is worth 10 liberals. If Goldwater is beaten, I will be worth 100 liberals and I'll be ready to do anything that is necessary."

He warned that a Johnson victory would put "world government ADA Humphrey only a heart-beat away from the White House" and accused the Democrat-liberal Republican alliance of being soft on criminals, excused for their acts "because they are not responsible."

LE NOSTRE COMUNITA'

Personalità alla ribalta

IL PROGRESSO ITALO-AMERICANO — Martedì 9 Luglio 1974

Docente festeggiato

Il dott. Henry Paolucci, docente di scienze politiche alla St. John's University, è stato festeggiato di recente ad iniziativa del "Conservative Party" di Flushing, N.Y. nella villa Bianca, Northern Blvd., Queens, N.Y.

Il dott. Paolucci è vice-presidente del Partito Conservatore di New York, così come presidente del "Walter Bagehot Research Council on National Sovereignty". E' anche redattore ed editore di "State of the Nations".

Ha pubblicato, tra l'altro, libri ed articoli su Galileo, Cesare Beccaria, Hegel, Sant'Agostino e Macchiavelli, oltre ad articoli spesso albergati nella "Op Ed Page" del New York Times. E' anche editorialista del periodico italiano "Il Borghese".

Il dott. Paolucci è membro della commissione del "Center for the Study of the Presidency". Di recente ha partecipato a un dibattito sulla crisi del Watergate insieme con Ramsey Clark, ex Procuratore Generale degli Stati Uniti, e Jacqueline Wexler, rettore magnifico dell'Hunter College.

E' nato a New York ed è titolare di diplomi di laurea del City College e della Columbia

Henry Paolucci

University. Nel 1948-49 è stato inviato in Europa della Columbia University e nel 1951 è stato ancora in Europa con una borsa di studio Fulbright.

Il banchetto celebrativo è stato organizzato da Jesse Cromer; tra gli ospiti d'onore erano l'on. Mario Biaggi, il sen. Frank Padavan, l'on. Vincent Nicolosi e Lucile De George.

THE NEW YORK TIMES, MONDAY, OCTOBER 5,

Two Conservatives Bitterly Attack G.O.P. Rivals

Paolucci Calls for Boycott of Keating as 'Turncoat'

Two Conservative candidates made bitter attacks yesterday on their Republican rivals, Senator Kenneth B. Keating and Representative John V. Lindsay.

Henry Paolucci, an associate professor of history and political science at Iona College, New Rochelle, who is running as a Conservative for the Senate, denounced Mr. Keating as a "trojan horse" and a "turncoat." He argued that voters should boycott the Senate contest rather than vote for the Republican candidate.

Kieran O'Doherty, Conservative opponent of Representative Lindsay in the 17th Congressional District, accused the Congressman of being a member of a "small band of renegades" who continually cross party lines to support the Johnson Administration's legislative program.

Dr. Paolucci was interviewed on WABC-TV's "Page One" program and on WINS radio. Mr. Keating was not present. Mr. O'Doherty made his attack on answering questions on WNBC-TV's "Direct Line" program, in the presence of Mr. Lindsay and his Democratic opponent in Manhattan's so-called Silk Stocking District, Mrs. Eleanor Clark French.

Representative Lindsay re-

Associated Press

Henry Paolucci

plied that Mr. O'Doherty was out to destroy the Republican party. Declaring that he acted "independently" when the good of the country or his district demanded it, Mr. Lindsay said he had voted according to principle and had never put party regularity above principle.

Mrs. French supported Mr. O'Doherty's view. Senator Barry Goldwater, the Republican party's Presidential nominee, is the issue, she declared, adding that if Mr. Lindsay could not support

O'Doherty Includes Lindsay in 'Band of Renegades'

Senator Goldwater he ought to get out of the Republican party.

Dr. Paolucci denied that his nomination was a "Stop Keating" move. "Oh, not a bit," he said.

"It's a move," he said, "to get for the Goldwater-Miller national ticket as many votes as possible in this state." He said he hoped to attract to the Goldwater-Miller ticket "at least 100,000 votes that would not otherwise be drawn to that ticket and could well make the difference for Goldwater-Miller in carrying the state or losing it."

Dr. Paolucci said the Conservative aim was to get in New York "a conservative Republican party."

"We work at it two ways, Goldwater on the national level calling for unity, and we in the local level reminding this party which has submitted to liberal domination that it ought not to do that," he declared.

The college teacher said that in recent issues the overwhelming majority of the Republicans in the Senate voted with Senator Goldwater but Senators Keating, Jacob K. Javits and three others voted against them. He did not name the others.

"I think it's clear that these people are the ones who are preventing us from having a distinct choice nationally," he asserted. "That's my objective."

Conservative Party Candidate Backs GOP Districting Fight

Prof. Henry Paolucci, Conservative Party candidate for U.S. senator, warmly endorsed here last night the court fight undertaken by two Republican state senators—John H. Hughes and Lawrence M. Rulison— to challenge the recent Federal Court deision requiring all state lawmakers to run for election three times in three years.

A U.S. Supreme Court decision mandated that the legislative apportionment system in this state be changed to give more representation to the New York City area and less to Upstate. A three-man Federal Court panel in this state, implementing the decision, has devised a system whereby all state legislators must run for election this fall, again next fall, and the following fall.

Paolucci spoke last night in the Midtown Plaza auditorium. During the Conservative Party rally held there, Paolucci sharply criticized U.S. state senators—Kenneth B. Keating, the Republican incumbent, for "helping to scuttle the Senate bill, proposed by Senate Minority Leader Everett Dirksen, which would have stayed the "hurry up" Federal Court order until Jan. 1, 1966, thus mandating a two-year term for the state legislators elected this fall."

Paolucci stated that Keating "jointed six other so-called Republicans, including New York's Jacob Javits, in supporting the Mansfield substitute for the Dirksen bill. This was the margin of victory for the Manfield biff, which passed the Senate 44-38."

"Almost every Upstate Republican candidate for the state Legislature is centering his campaign on this reapportionment issue, following the leadership of Senators Hughes and Rulison," Paolucci concluded. "It is a sorry fact that Kenneth Keating, an upstate Republican himself, has abandoned his party on this vital issue in hot pursuit of New York City votes."

Keating, Kennedy and Paolucci Locked in Three-Cornered Race

BY STAN COHEN

With political campaigns in their last six weeks, the West Side promises to become a focal point of the tough Senatorial scramble.

Robert F. Kennedy has already been here and promises to return. Senator Keating, who has been stumping on the Lower East Side, is preparing to train his biggest guns on this traditionally Democratic section. And the Conservative Party candidate, Prof. Henry Paolucci, resides on the West Side, at 600 W. 111 St.

The race promises to be one of the most unusual, centered upon the candidacy of Barry Goldwater. Senator Keating, the Republican incumbent, is running independent of the national ticket but has refused to come out in opposition to Goldwater.

Dr. Paolucci, on the other hand, has given full endorsement to the GOP leader and his views although he has not been a registered Republican for ten years and twice was enrolled in the Democratic Party since that time.

Paolucci Hits Hard In Goldwater Cause

By WALTER MURPHY
Of the World-Telegram Staff

No kissing babies and no street corner handshaking for Dr. Henry Paolucci, Conservative Party candidate for Senator.

Paolucci, an associate professor of history and political science at Iona College in New Rochelle, is a man who wastes no time on electioneering tradition. He is out to sell a product — Sen. Barry M. G o l d w a t e r —and he doesn't think cooing and grinning is the way to do it.

Podium for Arena

His political arena is the podium, from which he extols conservatism with the soothing assurance of a classroom instructor while lambasting "the Liberal establishment" with the biting humor of a standup comedian.

The result is that Paolucci, a political unknown before getting the nomination, is winning the hearts of rightwing audiences.

Last night the podium was in Staten Island, where the 43-year-old professor kept 500 persons attending a Richmond County Conservative rally alternately cheering and guffawing. He praised Goldwater and he mimicked President Johnson, and the crowd loved it.

Not a Spokesman

Acknowledging that he has not received any public support from the Republican standard bearer and claiming that he would reject such support in the interest of Republican party unity, he said:

"I am not an authorized spokesman for Goldwater. am a volunteer for Goldwater. I don't ask him to indorse me. I indorse him."

He accused Republican Sen. Kenneth Keating, whom he refers to as "the poor old man," of betraying party unity and making it necessary for the Conservative party to put its own candidate in the Senate race.

But the short, chunky professor said he is not trying to undercut Keating, only to win votes for Goldwater. Sen. Keating has refused to indorse Goldwater.

"I expect to attract at least 100,000 votes for Goldwater that he would not get if I wasn't running," he says.

Campaign's Daily

Paolucci, who edits and translates philosophic works and composes music in his spare time, has been campaigning "every single day since Aug. 12," while keeping up with his classroom duties three days a week.

His only other campaign experience was in 1961, when he campaigned for Comptroller Arthur Levitt in his primary fight against Mayor Robert F. Wagner. He headed a group of Conservatives for Levitt in his Morningside Heights neighborhood.

The Candid Candidate

IT WOULD require quite a bit of optimism by his supporters to imagine that Dr. Henry Paolucci, the Conservative party candidate for Senate, poses a grave challenge to either Sen. Keating or Robert Kennedy.

Yet one has to give Dr. Paolucci a high mark for candor and credit for a refreshing sort of political naivete.

FOR INSTANCE, on his way to Rome, N.Y., where he was to be principal speaker at a testimonial for the comptroller of Oneida County, Dr. Paolucci dropped this comment: "I can't say much about him at a testimonial dinner because I never set eyes on him before."

As for naivete, he was talking during the flight upstate about his astonishment at reports that Republicans were prepared to spend more than a million dollars on Sen. Keating's campaign.

"WELL," he said, "I've got $800 and I guess more will be coming in as the campaign progresses. But we have lots of dedicated and loyal friends who will work hard as volunteers."

Question: Can a candidate with $800 and this sort of casual candor ever make good in politics?

UNFORTUNATELY, this isn't the election to answer that question. To get an answer, one would need to pit Dr. Paolucci against another candidate with $800 and no candor.

Paolucci Challenge

Henry Paolucci, Conservative candidate for U. S. Senator, last night challenged his major party rivals—Sen. Kenneth B. Keating, Republican, and Robert F. Kennedy, Democrat—to debate the school busing issue.

Speaking at the New Era Club, 197 E. Broadway, Paolucci called his opponents "ignorant" of the facts in the school row.

"The terrible thing is that some parents are being forced to seat their children, because of color, in the very school room seats from which other parents, because of color, can voluntarily remove theirs," Paolucci said. "Never have we had a more flagrant abuse of civil rights, with the children the direct victims."

DAILY ◧ NEWS
NEW YORK'S PICTURE NEWSPAPER ●

SEPT. 26, 1964

(NEWS foto by Tom Baffer)
Conservative Senatorial candidate Henry Paolucci (left) shakes hands with Attorney General Lefkowitz at 234 W. 109th St.

Paolucci to Rockefeller:
Switch to Goldwater

. . . and the Conservative Party candidate for U.S. senator and his wife are greeted by sign bearing well-wishers.

Times-Union Staff Photos by Higgins

By DOC RIVETT
Times-Union Staff Writer

The other candidate for U.S. senator—the unpublicized Henry Paolucci of the Conservative Party—made a flying trip into the Albany area last night to urge a united effort on behalf of Senator Barry Goldwater by all who "prefer Conservatism's plain truths to Liberalism's elaborate lie."

Professor Paolucci, who teaches political science at Iona College in New Rochelle, was greeted at Albany County Airport by about a dozen sign-bearing local party members. There were about as many peo-

le in the television crews that covered his arrival.

In his talk to a dinner sponsored by the Schenectady County Conservative Club at the Jamaica Inn, Professor Paolucci struck to the themes he has expressed in other formal campaign talks.

Bid to Rockefeller

But in an interview, he expressed the "fervent hope" that Governor Rockefeller would 'change his mind, and undo the damage he has done, by coming out in support of Senator Goldwater" Friday when the Arizonian speaks in Albany.

Dr. Paolucci, in answering a question, condemned Senator

Kenneth B. Keating's charges last weekend that Robert F Kennedy, the Democratic candidate, had aided Nazis in arranging the sale of General Aniline.

"I hope it is the last such vilifying outburst we have in the campaign," said Dr. Paolucci. "I feel Keating owes Kennedy an apology on this score. It was too obvious a thrust for ethnic votes. It was an almost desparate gesture. I think it will backfire; it has backfired."

Ordinarily an intensely serious man, Dr. Paolucci showed a sign of humor when asked he would prefer if it were strictly a contest between Keating and Kennedy. "Kennedy—Keating; Keating—Kennedy. They're getting to be so much alike," he

said, "that I can hardly remember which one comes from
Massachusetts."

The professorial Dr. Paolucci
writes all his own material, he
said, and sometimes delivers
his text to party headquarters
personally.

As a result of one campaign
swing through the Western part
of the state and from appearances in New York City, Dr.
Paolucci said he had detected
two primary issues in the campaign.

Upstate, he said, the big issue
is reapportionment. He expressed a fear that insistence
on giving only one vote to a
person who holds "great lands
for the public benefit" while
giving the same weight to a
vote of a person "who lives
with six others in a single
room" is dangerous.

It would result, Dr. Paolucci
explained, in driving people off
the land with dire results "as
happened in ancient Rome."

In New York City, Professor
Paolucci said, the overriding
issue is "compulsory busing for
integration." He is against
that too. "It never has been
the American way to force
people to mix," he said in rejecting a charge that the might
be appealing to the so-called
white backlash.

At the same time he con-
tended that pairing of schools
was put into effect "for no
other purpose than to attract
the organized Negro vote. I
think it insults the Negro and
he should reject it."

Dr. Paolucci and his wife,
Anne, flew into Albany as regular passengers on a regular
Mohawk Airlines flight from
New York. On a previous trip
they had been forced to take
separate seats but this time
were able to sit together. 'A
man was very nice and changed
seats so we could be together,"
Mrs. Paolucci explained.

Both of them had put in a
full day teaching — Mrs. Paolucci is an English professor at
City College — before starting
their campaign trip.

Henry Paolucci steps
from a plane last night
at Albany Airport . . .

The New York Times

SEPTEMBER 6, 1964.

Paolucci Urges Rivals to Debate Major Issues of Their Campaign

By RAYMOND DANIELL

The Conservative candidate for the United States Senate opened his campaign here yesterday with a challenge to his Republican and Democratic rivals to debate with him some of the principal stands they have taken.

Henry Paoluci, who was thrown into the breach when Clare Boothe Luce withdrew an earlier statement that she was available for the Conservative nomination, said he would like to discuss publicly the issue of civil rights with Robert F Kennedy, the Democratic candidate

Similarly, he said, in an interview at his home, 600 West 111th Street, he would like to cross verbal swords with Senator Kenneth B. Keating on the issue of party loyalty and support for the Republican Presidential ticket of Senator Barry Goldwater and Representative William E. Miller. Senator Keating has withheld support from the national ticket.

"It would be pathetic in this state to have a campaign in which no Senatorial candidate spoke for Goldwater," said Mr. Palucci.

Interrupting himself now and then to quote from volumes in his book-hned study, Mr. Palucci undertook to outline his political philosophy. He believes, he said, that the liberal Democratic Administration in Washington is out of joint with the times.

"The country is in a state of mental paralysis," he said, "with all the politicians but Goldwater terrified of polls indicating that truth-telling might cost votes."

Federal aid for the unemployed and needy, he said, was good in the Depression years but crash programs for the relief of poverty in these prosperous times undermine the moral fiber and tend toward a levelling downward instead of upward.

Paolucci accusa 4 capi del GOP di ambiguita'

Il professore Henry Paolucci, candidato del Partito Conservatore al Senato degli Stati Uniti ha accusato Nelson Rockefeller, Jacob Javits, Kenneth Keating e John Lindsay per il loro "rifiuto unico e senza precedenti di annunciare come voteranno nelle elezioni presidenziali di martedí prossimo" durante un pranzo organizzato sotto il patrocinio del Dutchess Conservative Party e tenuto al Poughkeepsie Inn di Poughkeepsie, New York.

"Il Governatore Rockefeller ha spiegato Paolucci - annuncio nel 1960 che avrebbe votato per Richard Nixon. Ora, invece, egli ha scoperto che un simile annuncio nel 1964 violerebbe i suoi principii. Ma non si tratta, evidentemente, di una questione di principio. Il desiderio di Rockefeller è soltanto quello di arrecare il massimo danno alla lista Goldwater-Miller, rispettando nel contempo la consegna verbale di sostenere quella lista. Javits, Keating e Lindsay, d'altra parte, hanno apertamente proclamato le loro intenzioni di sabotare la lista Goldwater-Miller, ma essi sottraggono alle logiche conseguenze di tale inganno nel disperato tentativo di conservare qualche pretesa di essere considerati repubblicani. La segretezza del voto - ha concluso Paolucci - è una tradizione che gli americani custodiscono gelosamente, ma non è stata mai richiesta a coloro che rappresentano la leadership politica".

Prof. Paolucci Urges Support For Goldwater

Professor Henry Paolucci, n tionally known Associate Profe sor of History at Iona Colleg New Rochelle, New York, an a supporter of the late Presiden Kennedy, last night urged bo rough Democrats to back t h GOP standard bearer in Tues day's presidential election.

"As a former Democrat, I an proud to urge support of the presidential candidacy of Sena tor Barry Goldwater, "Prof. Pao lucci said· "He represents the real Americanism and the prin ciples of freedom and nationa honor which used to characterize the Democratic Party.

"Under the influence of hyper liberals like Hubert Humphrey," Prof· Paolucci continued, "un fortunately, the Democratic Par ty I once knew and supported, no longer exists."

Prof· Paolucci called f o r a Goldwater win to reverse the trend towards bigger government and more taxes and regulations "piled on our backs for the bene nt of special interests and pres sure groups here and abroad."

"I cannot help but feel," Prof. Paolucci said, " that the public has grown tired of wheeling and dealing, in the tradition of Bobby Baker and Billy Sol Estes, between clubhouse politicians in Washington and elements of big business and big labor."

A frequent speaker of human rights, Prof. Paolucci has writ ten several works in the field of political science, and has edit ed and translated the works of Hegal, Machiavelli and Galileo, He is a contributor to the Ency clopedia Americana and the conservative weekly, National Review.

The Knickerbocker News Photo

CONSERVATIVE COMMENT—Henry Paolucci, Conservative Party candidate for the U. S. Senate, addresses Conservatives and Conservative Republicans at Jamaica Inn, Route 7, Colonie. Mrs. Paolucci listens.

Paolucci Opens Albany Visit With Kennedy-Keating Quip

THE KNICKERBOCKER NEWS

PAGE ONE ** SECTION C

Thursday, September 24, 1964

★ ★ ★

Prof. Henry Paolucci, the Conservative Party candidate for U. S. Senate says he has trouble telling his two opponents apart.

"Kennedy-Keating or Keating-Kennedy. They're getting to be so much alike that I can hardly remember which one comes from Massachusetts."

Dr. Paolucci, a professor of political science at Iona College, made the comment last night on his campaign tour of the Albany area.

15 at Airport

About 15 Conservative Party members welcomed him and

his wife (an English professor at City College of New York at the airport.

Dr. Paolucci said he's not unhappy because he's not attracting teenagers or large crowds on his tours. "I think Bobby ought to get a television program like the Beatles when this campaign is over," he quipped. He then added: "I shudder to think about what I'd do if I had teenagers wanting to pull me apart like Dionysian revelers.

The Conservative Party candidate, at a rally attended by 150 at the Jamaica Inn in Colonie, called for continued support of Senator Goldwater for president.

Elect Goldwater

"One of my main purposes in undertaking this campaign is to give as forceful a voice as possible to Goldwater conservatism on the senatorial level of the election campaign in this state . . . The ultimate object is to put Goldwater in the White House — everything else is subordinate to that."

Dr. Paolucci told his applauding audience: "We of the Conservative Party will feel that we have accomplished a large part of our preliminary object in this campaign if the Republican state leadership will demonstrate equal diction to the Republican national ticket, if it will urge all Republicans, as well as independents and disgruntled Democrats to join in support of the Goldwater-Mil ticket"

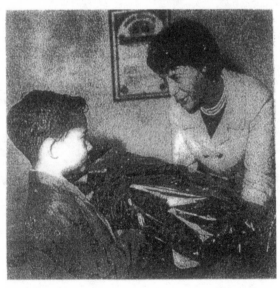

CONSERVATIVES CONFER. J. Daniel Mahoney of Manhas-
set, left, state Conservative Party chairman, talks last night
with Dr. Henry Paolucci, the party's U. S. Senate candidate,
at the party's annual dinner-dance in Port Washington.

Paolucci's Humor

Henry Paolucci, the Conservative Party candidate for U. S. Senate, anticipates a fascinating moment in politics when Governor Rockefeller introduces Senator Goldwater at the State Office Building tomorrow.

Mr. Paolucci said in Colonie last night:

"It'll be worth anything to see Rocky's face when he introduces him on Friday. What's he going to say? It'll be a priceless show—and it's free."

In a half-hour speech rich with humor and aphorisms, Mr. Paolucci also had these other observations:

"Kennedy platform! I wasn't aware he had a platform."

"Kennedy-Keating. Keating-Kennedy. It's getting so I can't tell which one is from Massachusetts."

"I don't believe a man should go to Congress in order to get handouts for his state."

"I hope when Goldwater gets here Rockefeller will tell him he has repented and Ken Keating has repented and they'll do all they can to help Barry Goldwater win this state."

"Scholars always do make a living with books years later, though they are silent on issues at the time they are crucial."

"Political demagoguery works this way. You take a majority, divide it into minorities, and say to each minority, 'Seek your own. We're on your side. We'll help you.' "

"The federal government has become the handout headquarters for political bribery. The great danger is its seductive appeal—a man feels like a fool to give up his handout."

"Getting elected for most people in this country is a fulltime occupation and they don't have time for anything else— for getting any knowledge."

THESE DAYS:

N.Y. Conservatives Stand to Gain

By JOHN CHAMBERLAIN

FOR ANYONE who enjoys analysis for its own sake, the New York State senatorial campaign offers a most fascinating field for conjecture. With Kenneth Keating, a Republican, making a big pitch for the New York City liberal, labor and Jewish groups that turned so emphatically to the other Republican Senator, Jacob Javits, in the last election, it could mean that Democratic Bobby Kennedy has been dealt a mortal wound. On the other hand, no Goldwaterite among the Irish, Polish or Italian ethnic groups that are deserting the Democrats can really go for Keating.

What I seem to sense is that the Conservative Party choice for Senator, an obscure professor of history and political science at Iona College in New Rochelle, is going to run up quite a sizeable vote from

CHAMBERLAIN

upstate Republicans and big city Democrats. And it is a toss-up at the moment whether Kennedy or Keating is going to benefit more from defections to the third party man.

The obscure professor from New Rochelle is an extremely individualistic Italian-American named Henry Paolucci.

This most unlikely Conservative candidate is unusual in that he thinks, personally, he may be taking as many votes away from Kennedy as he will be taking from Keating. A draw of this sort would mean that he is not a menace on balance to either of the major party candidates, other things being equal.

But the question is not as simple as that. The liberals have two candidates, Kennedy and Keating. But the conservatives have only one man, Paolucci.

Now, some Republican conservatives are going to stick with Keating because he bears the traditional Republican label. Others are going to stay with him because they fear the re-emergence of a "Kennedy dynasty." Paolucci, on the other hand, will get Republican conservatives who want to chastise the Rockefeller Republicans for not putting out any real effort for Goldwater.

* * *

NOBODY KNOWS just how the Republican conservative arithmetic will affect the Keating chances on Nov. 3. But it is a good guess that the liberal vote could benefit Keating more than Kennedy, simply because of Republican Javits' hold on the New York City liberals. Javits has made the Keating cause his own, which could mean a lot of ADA and Liberal Party votes in the Keating column.

Meanwhile, the disoriented conservative Democrats who bulk large in Queens, Nassau and Rockland counties because of the recent population drift from Manhattan could easily have qualms about voting for either Kennedy or Keating. Who, then, is there to vote for but Paolucci? And doesn't all the shuffling promise to make Kennedy the all-around loser?

Breaking the possible Paolucci vote down, the Conservative Party senatorial candidate stands to attract the "law enforcement vote" (the people who resent the fact that New York police have gotten a bad press on the "police brutality" allegations).

He also should get a big vote from Italians who think the old parties have done nothing to combat the stereotype that gangsters are mostly Sicilian in origin. Then there is the "institutional" conservative vote which likes the idea of having a party of its own. And, finally, there are those Democrats who have moved to the conservative-minded suburbs.

Against all this there is the incalculable attraction of the Kennedy name, which could draw votes away from Keating among Republicans who consider the Kennedys conservative enough. It's all a nice tangle. My only certainty is that Paolucci will do very well for himself in absolute voting terms. The little Conservative Party could come out of the election stronger than ever.

Buffalo Evening News,
September 19, 1964, p.7.

The Country Needs Truly Meaningful Two-Party System

By HENRY PAOLUCCI
Conservative Candidate
For U.S. Senate

I am pleased and grateful for this opportunity to express my views concerning the issues in this campaign to the readers of The Civil Service Leader. The most serious issue in this campaign, so far as New York State is concerned, is the restoration of a meaningful two party system in the Empire State.

I am wholeheartedly committed to the Republican national ticket of Barry Goldwater and William Miller, and I am the only senatorial candidate in this campaign who supports that ticket. My primary motive in accepting the Conservative Party nomination for the United States Senate was to provide a voice, in New York State, for Goldwater conservatism.

Neither of my opponents in this race is supporting the Goldwater-Miller ticket. It is not surprising that the Democratic candidate has taken this position, but the Republican candidate's position is absolutely unique. He is the only Republican Senate candidate in the nation who is not supporting the Republican ticket.

State GOP Seeks Goldwater Defeat, Paolucci Asserts

ROCHESTER, Sept. 19 (AP) — The Conservative Party's nominee for U. S. Senator says "the Javits-Rockefeller-Keating crowd" wants Republican presidential candidate Barry Goldwater to lose.

That group of Republicans hopes that, through a Goldwater defeat, they could, "with cunning and Rockefeller finances, manage to hold onto their positions of leadership in the state organization," Henry Paolucci declared Friday night.

"The Javits-Rockefeller-Keating crowd are not interested in this campaign, which, for the first time in God knows how long, offers the people of the United States a choice between liberalism's elaborate lie and conservatisms' plain truth," Mr. Paolucci said.

He said Senator Keating, who has refused to endorse Senator Goldwater, was guilty of "deliberate and calculated sabotage of the Goldwater-Miller ticket."

Senator Keating was "the only Republican senatorial candidate in the nation who is not supporting the Republican national ticket," Mr. Paolucci said. "How can he expect New York Republicans to be loyal to the nation's leading practitioner of party disloyalty?"

NATIONAL REVIEW

A JOURNAL OF FACT AND OPINION

For Senator from New York

W. H. VON DREELE

In 1961, Americans for Constitutional Action awarded Senator Kenneth Keating their Distinguished Service Award. Recently, Americans for Democratic Action awarded him an 88 per cent "right" voting record in ‸e Senate. Were they talking about ‸e same man? Yes indeed. For the question Keating routinely asks himself come November 3rd is not What do I believe? It ‸is, rather, What do they want to hear? Then he tells them.

This year, he's been telling them with a vigor which stems from vast financial resources. And Thomas E. Dewey is helping, and Herbert Brownell has returned, and Rockefeller is going full throttle. The bus ads, the TV and radio spots, the "Democrats for Keating" fronts shoot up like toadstools. Senator Jacob Javits is out stumping for Keating with an intensity which suggests that a loss to Democratic challenger Robert F. Kennedy would be decisive. Which it would. Their fright has been summed up baldly by columnists Evans and Novak: "Without a Republican base in Albany, chances for the Republican Liberals to dethrone the Goldwaterites at the 1968 convention would decline."

All of which makes glorious reading for New York conservatives, be ‸iey Smith Democrats or mainstream Republicans. This year, they have a senatorial candidate, too. He is Professor Henry Paolucci, and he is traveling about the state on a sched-ule so interspersed with half-hour TV interviews that the unwary mistake him for the high-priced spreads. But only for a moment. For Mr. Paolucci has been trumpeting a Conservative Party choice whose echoes are bouncing off the walls of both Democratic and Republican headquarters. And his choices are spiced with that·most rare of political condiments, candor.

Forced School Bussing

Consider the candor of the three candidates on forced public school bussing. In New York City, an "open enrollment" policy permits voluntary student transfers from one school to another—with the sole proviso that applicants are either Negro or Puerto Rican. Also in New York City, a "pairing" policy forces, by law, the bussing of selected students from their neighborhood schools to schools sometimes miles away, to obtain better racial balance.

Parents caught in this squeeze have been in a permanent state of outrage. What do the candidates offer? Kennedy is strictly hands-off. Keating touches both bases: he is 1) "opposed to compulsory bussing of children long distances from their neighborhoods," but 2) "as everyone knows, I am a strong advocate of racial integration in the schools." Only Paolucci goes to the issue's core. "The terrible thing is that some parents are being forced to seat their children, because of color, in the very school seats from which other parents, because of color, can voluntarily remove theirs. Never have we had a more flagrant abuse of civil rights, with the children the direct victims."

Paolucci s stand is not a campaign maneuver. It is settled Conservative Party doctrine. The Party has fought for the neighborhood school with parents' groups in the courts, in the superintendent's office, and at City Hall. Professor Paolucci says he is "proud to be the candidate of the only political party in New York State which has taken an unequivocal position in favor of the neighborhood school."

There's another vital issue knocking about, but it's not perfumed for voter excitement. It is called "reapportionment." In a recent case, the U. S. Supreme Court willed that both upper and lower houses of state legislatures must be based on population. "One man, one vote" was the way the Chief Justice phrased it, recalling similar statements from various developing African nations. This decision makes all states the creatures of their population centers. Unless overturned by the states themselves through a constitutional amendment,

Illinois will be Cook County; Hudson and Essex will dominate New Jersey, while New York will submit to its southern population mass. What say the candidates?

Kennedy goes all the way with the Court. Keating, as usual, yaws wildly around the buoy. While in Congress he voted against all efforts to curb the Court; while on the hustings he's for a weighted upper house. Henry Paolucci, alone, was livid from the start. He supported Justice Harlan, who said that the Court's action "amounts to nothing less than an exercise of the amending power by this court." He supports a constitutional amendment, now, to withdraw federal jurisdiction over the apportionment of state legislatures. "Unless the court is checked," he says, "this all-out assault on our rural areas will precipitate the decline of our republican form of government."

Finally, who's supporting Barry Goldwater for President? Not Kennedy, naturally. Not Kenneth Keating. (His "never" in a *Herald Tribune* story shocked party regulars.) That leaves Henry Paolucci.

NOVEMBER 3, 1964   967

THERE'S ALWAYS PAOLUCCI

Cries of "chicken chicken!" have been rocketing back and forth between Sen. Keating and Robert F. Kennedy, who wants the voters to make him Sen. Kennedy and retire Keating. The screaming has been about proposed TV debates, which apparently will never happen.

There is nothing to keep the voters from concluding that Kennedy and Keating are mortally afraid to meet each other in debate—and nothing to keep any qualified voter from casting a ballot for Henry Paolucci, the Conservative candidate.

Paolucci Raps Keating On Busing Stand

Henry Paolucci, Conservative Party candidate for U.S. Senator, described Sen. Kenneth B Keating yesterday as "a kindly old man" swayed by public opinion polls.

Mr. Paolucci, associate professor of history and political science at Iona College in New Rochelle, said he had entered the race to win and that he had "some chance, indeed" of doing so.

If he fails, he was asked would he prefer to see the election of Sen Keating or Robert F Kennedy, the Democratic candidate?

I don t know," he said, "I don t know which is the lesser of two evils "

Mr Paolucci made the comments during an interview on WCBS-TV's Newsmakers" and in the studio afterward

He contended that Sen Keating had given "no thought" to compulsory school busing before announcing on Saturday that he was opposed to it.

Instead, Mr. Paolucci said, the Senator had determined from public opinion polls that he would gain votes by voicing opposition and then took that stand

Mr Paolucci made these other points on the program:

⊄He would not ask the support of any group including the John Birch Society, whose votes would be "only a drop in the bucket

⊄There is a crisis in the governmental system of checks and balances with an effort by President Johnson to gain a concentration of power

⊄He agrees with Sen. Goldwater s opposition to the nuclear test ban treaty and his proposal to give battlefield commanders the right to use nuclear weapons without consulting the President

⊄If he had been in the Senate, he would have voted against the Civil Rights Bill because Federal moves in that area would "inevitably segregate people in their hearts "

"I don't care whether (my campaign) hurts (Sen Keating) or not—I want to attract as many Goldwater votes as I can," he said.

Mr Paolucci said there had been no legal discrimination" against Negroes in the U S since the Civil War.

The Civil Rights Law, he said, was a Democratic effort to win Negro votes

He blamed the opposition of Southerners to integration on Northerners who had 'abused" the people of the South in repeatedly calling them guilty. This, he said,

New York
Journal American
TUESDAY, NOVEMBER 10, 1964

If you are a conservative, and are looking for a hopeful sign, you will take great heart from what happened in New York State, where the Conservative Party's candidate for Senator, Henry Paolucci, got 203,369 votes, a high-water mark for his party.

* * *

WHAT ALL THIS MEANS, in terms of New York politics, is that the Rockefeller Republicans must reckon with a small but potent "leverage" group whose vote or endorsement might make or break a GOP candidate for almost any important state office.

* * *

By JOHN CHAMBERLAIN

New York World-Telegram
The Sun

The Conservative party weathered the nationwide rebuke to conservatism by scoring more than 200,000 votes for its unknown Senate candidate and providing the victory margin for GOP Assemblymen Fred Preller in Queens and Edward Amann in Staten Island.

* * *

NOVEMBER 4, 1964

Buffalo Evening News,
September 19, 1964, p.7.

The Country Needs Truly Meaningful Two-Party System

By HENRY PAOLUCCI
Conservative Candidate
For U.S. Senate

I am pleased and grateful for this opportunity to express my views concerning the issues in this campaign to the readers of The Civil Service Leader. The most serious issue in this campaign, so far as New York State is concerned, is the restoration of a meaningful two party system in the Empire State.

I am wholeheartedly committed to the Republican national ticket of Barry Goldwater and William Miller, and I am the only senatorial candidate in this campaign who supports that ticket. My primary motive in accepting the Conservative Party nomination for the United States Senate was to provide a voice, in New York State, for Goldwater conservatism.

Neither of my opponents in this race is supporting the Goldwater-Miller ticket. It is not surprising that the Democratic candidate has taken this position, but the Republican candidate's position is absolutely unique. He is the only Republican Senate candidate in the nation who is not supporting the Republican ticket.

State GOP Seeks Goldwater Defeat, Paolucci Asserts

ROCHESTER, Sept. 19 (*AP*) — The Conservative Party's nominee for U. S. Senator says "the Javits-Rockefeller-Keating crowd" wants Republican presidential candidate Barry Goldwater to lose.

That group of Republicans hopes that, through a Goldwater defeat, they could, "with cunning and Rockefeller finances, manage to hold onto their positions of leadership in the state organization," Henry Paolucci declared Friday night.

"The Javits-Rockefeller-Keating crowd are not interested in this campaign, which, for the first time in God knows how long, offers the people of the United States a choice between liberalism's elaborate lie and conservatisms' plain truth," Mr. Paolucci said.

He said Senator Keating, who has refused to endorse Senator Goldwater, was guilty of "deliberate and calculated sabotage of the Goldwater-Miller ticket."

Senator Keating was "the only Republican senatorial candidate in the nation who is not supporting the Republican national ticket," Mr. Paolucci said. "How can he expect New York Republicans to be loyal to the nation's leading practitioner of party disloyalty?"

Paolucci raps creeping liberalism in GOP

By DON DeMAIO

GOSHEN

Dr. Henry Paolucci, the Conservative Party's candidate for U.S. senator in the last election, warned Wednesday against creeping liberalism in the Republican Pary, which, he said, could destroy the two-party system.

More and more Republicans are becoming liberal Democrats, he said. He laughed at a reference by Orange County Conservative Party Chairman Thomas Moore that a coalition party loosely refered to as the "Rockycrats" were collaborating on a Republican mayoral candidate for New York City, and a Democratic candidate for governor.

Gives figures

"It's like this," he said. "If the Democrats can win 60 per cent of the vote and the Republicans only 40 per cent, the Republicans must try to win the other 11 per cent. If you abandon the 40 per cent to try for the liberal 60 per cent, you are disenfranchising the 40 per cent. That middle percentile is what connects the two extremes.

"Don't try to pull everyone into one class," he warned. "This is communistic."

Making an impromptu speech at the Goshen Inn, Paolucci said that too many Republicans are trying to get the Negro vote, the elderly vote, the Jewish vote, etc., and are becoming liberal Democrats to do it.

"I don't relish the idea of conservatives seeking a national third party " he said in answer to a member of the audience. "This creates factionalism. Blocks begin to organize and create a menace with an organized vote. These are blocks like the Ku Klux Klan and the National Association for the Advancement of Colored People (NAACP)."

The political science professor at Iona College said he thought the Conservative Party's function was to balance a wobbly ship. With the Republicans going to the side of the Democrats, he said, it is up to the Conservatives to balance out the two-party system.

Republicans, he added, are now saying that they are in the middle. "Middle of what?" he questioned. "There are no rightists How does one go to the middle of the left. There is no such thing."

Paolucci thought the best thing was for Conservatives to leave the ranks of the Republican Party and join in one movement.

"If we number 400,000" he noted, "then we can pull the Republican Party back in line."

In answer to one Republican in the audience, he said: Conservative Republicans should take a leave of absence with this thought -- I'll be back. . . and I'll take my 400,000 friends with me."

He ripped apart President

Johnson's plan for a Great Society, saying the President's statement that one-fifth of all Americans are poor makes no sense.

"Poor in respect to whom?" he asked. "You could say that one-third of America is poor or one-half, depending on what is being used as a standard.

"One-third of the Americans," he added, "are not poor when compared to the other 2 billion people in the world."

He described the conservative movement as one which is gaining force. In 1962, he said, Goldwater would have only received 17 million votes. In 1964, he got 27 million.

Opposes labels

"New York Republicans are deluding themselves," he said, "if they think they can win with guys like (Sen. Jacob K.) Javits."

No doubt the two parties could be totally liberal and conservative, he said, but should they have the names? "I'd like to see that preserved," he added. "I don't like the names because the Democratic Party is actually the Conservative Party. They have been in power for 40 years and they don't want to change the status quo. It's too easy to be wishy-washy."

Concerning presidential candidate Barry Goldwater, Paolucci said he wasn't elected because he said he would do things like send the Marines into Viet Nam.

"And see what President Johnson is doing?" he noted. "But President Johnson was forced to become an advertising salesman during the campaign with a smooth voice and nice talk.

"Goldwater wouldn't have had to send in the Marines because the enemy was afraid of him. Instead, the President promised not to extend the war and the enemy took advantage of his promise."

VALLEY STREAM MAIL AND GIBSON HERALD THURSDAY, OCTOBER 1 1964

Know Your Candidate

The Conservative Viewpoint:
Prof. Henry Paolucci and Mason Hampton sound off.   Exclusive to Maileader Publications
by Norman Jay

Paolucci

I visited with Professor Henry Paolucci, Conservative Candidate for the Senate. I was amazed to find this very vocal conservative living in a highly-integrated section close to Columbia University.

Differences

My first question was . . . "Professor, what do you consider the main areas of difference between you and your opponent?"

"I'm glad you used the singular in asking me about the difference with my opponent, because although I have two opponents, Keating, and the Candidate from Massachusetts, they are from my point of view, identical . . . both of them appealing to the same kind of voter — the Liberal voter — the anti-Goldwater voter! The basic difference between my opponent "Tweedle-dee" and "Twedle-dum" and "me" is that I provide what neither of them provides . . . "A voice for Goldwater Conservatism in New York State!"

Planks

Professor, if you are elected to the Senate, what would you consider to be your three most important planks?

"I don't like to use the word "planks", Norman, because I don't regard myself as coming forward as a politician. I have, all my mature life, since the end of World War II. been an ardent anti-Communist and I would make the re-straint of COMMUNIST AGGRESSIVE IMPERIALISM, which threatens to bury us and has already swallowed-up almost two-thirds of the world; a restraint of Communism would be my primary object as a spokesman for the people of New York in the United States Senate."

"The second most significant thing that I would give myself to would be removing the causes of the disorders in the streets of our great cities. The streets of our great cities, now, look like I never imagined they would look! But I know long ago that they would look like this as I observed the triumphant liberals in our country pressing what was once — a good in the thirties' — to such an extreme that it has unleashed the wildest appetites conceivable in large sectors of our population."

"The third one would be one having to do not so much with the present generation, which is so endangered by the Communist Imperialism abroad and by 'street riots at home' but would have to do with posterity; to pass on to successive generations the system of government which our forefathers established for us! It's a system of checks and balances maintained by the two-party system. I believe that the two-party system is in great danger because of the one-sided triumph of liberalism in the past three or four decades, and most especially in New York State, where the Liberal Party, the third party; (the Conservative Party is the fourth party not the third party) . . . where the Liberal Party has succeeded in so manipulating the other

Conservative candidate for the U.S. Senate from the State of New York, Professor Henry Paolucci, is shown here with his wife, Anne, in their apartment at 600 West 111th Street, New York City. They are both Doctors of Philosophy; Paolucci teaches Political Science at Iona College in New Rochelle.

two parties that it has made one of them so that you can hardly distinguish which is the more liberal, Keating or Kennedy. The restoration of the genuine two-party system, by imposing some penalty on one or the other of the two parties for being too much like its nominal opposite is the function of the Conservative Party in the State of New York, and I will make that the third chief interest of my work as a Senator, if I am elected."

National Election

Professor, do you believe the national election this year will materially affect your chances; and if so, in what way?

"I should reverse the question. When I agreed to be the candidate for the Senate in the Conservative Party, my object was to enhance the chances of the national ticket of the Republican Party. My chief object in taking up this campaign is to fulfill what Clare Booth Luce said her chief object would be if she took it, mainly, to give a voice to Goldwater Conservatism on the Senate level in the current election. I believe, however, that if the Conservative Party could have had the name of Goldwater-Miller on its ticket, although it is likely that it would not have put up a Senatorial Candidate, the Conservative Party line on the ticket might have received well over a million votes in New York State.

"Conservatism"

Professor, do you believe that there is a trend toward 'Conservatism in America' today?

"Astute political observers of past generations have remarked that very frequently great movements well up in

the people that are only dimly reflected in the newspaper, which usually lags in its sentiments a generation behind, and is, therefore, less capable than it thinks itself to be, of catching on to what's going on. Two years ago, it would have been absolutely unthinkable —the most ardent conservatives in New York State laughed when they referred to the possibility of Goldwater being a Presidential Candidate — yet he is here!!"

"Many people think . . . "Well, suppose he was defeated — that would prove that the majority of the American people are opposed to conservatism." Oh No! It would prove that from about 2% of the population, three or four years ago, they have become, whatever percentage of the population Goldwater gets, which on any graph will be a steep upgrade. Conservatism is the one force in this country that can save it! . . . that has the guts to save it! . . . . the realism to save it! . . . and if it doesn't make it now it will make it tomorrow!!

Label

Professor, I would ask, at this point . . "how do you label yourself?"

"Right at this moment, Norman, as a consequence of a conversation I had with a very noble person this afternoon, I am tempted to call myself the policeman's candidate."

Why??

Professor, I don't know what you mean by "the policeman's candidate." I would have known what you meant if you said you were conservative. Would you mind going a little further in your last statement and explain yourself?

"I meant, simply, that while I am, indeed, the Conservative Party Candidate for the Senate, I was certainly impressed, today, with the gravity of the problem confronting our law enforcing authorities throughout the country and particularly in great states like New York, with great cities. The attack on the police that has taken place in our time I regard as the greatest danger to the continuance of our orderly society, and for that reason I've given this a great deal of thought."

Problems

Professor, what do you believe are the three most pressing problems facing the voters of this State today?

"The most obvious problem facing the voter, here, in New York State, is to make a choice that is meaningful with his vote! There are the habitual distinctions between Republican and Democrat which tempt voters just simply to run right along one line."

"In this election, the problem is tha the two major parties, which should b the two opinions of the American elec torate, have become identical in thei platforms, in what they espouse. Botl Keating and Kennedy (candidate fo Massachusetts and New York) appea to the same kind of voter . . . the ADA sympathizing liberal — anti-Goldwate voter! The problem now is to make the Democratic system, which calls fo the restraint of the majority, meaning ful again! I think the only way thos independent voters who like to put restraint on the majority can do so i by voting Conservative in the Senato ial race.

More

Professor, I think you've just mad a fine political speech about the Part What I am after is you. What do yo think are the three most pressing prol lems facing the voters of this State t day?

Paolucci Campaigns Unnoticed, Stressing His Belief in 'a Choice'

By RAYMOND DANIELL

Special to The New York Times

ROCHESTER, Sept. 18—Henry Paolucci passed through Syracuse and this city today almost unobserved.

But wherever he could, the full-time professor and part-time politician made it clear that his prime aim in the United States Senate campaign was "to give voice to Goldwater conservatism in this state."

Dr. Paolucci, the Conservative party candidate, said he did not care if his campaign hurt the incumbent Senator, Kenneth B. Keating.

The principal opponent of Mr. Keating, a Republican, is Robert F. Kennedy, the Democratic nominee.

Finds No Choice

In one question-and-answe session after another Dr. Paolucci said that he was seeking to give the voters of New York a choice between liberal and conservative philosophy that he believed the candidacies of Senator Keating and Mr. Kennedy precluded.

In one interview he said that it seemed to him that Senator Keating, Mr. Kennedy, President Johnson and Senator Hubert H. Humphrey were "all running on the same ticket." He repeatedly urged all supporters of conservatives to vote for Senator Barry Goldwater and

Representative William E. Miller to preserve the two-party system in New York.

The Conservatives, whose endorsement of the Republican slate of electors was rejected by the Republican State Committee, have no electors of their own on the ballot.

Even without them Dr. Paolucci, who teaches at Iona College, New Rochelle, said he thought he might be able to deliver 100,000 voters to the Goldwater-Miller ticket. Had the Republican State Committee been willing to permit the Conservatives to endorse their slate of electors Dr. Paolucci said he might have been able to deliver at least 900,000 votes to the head of the Republican ticket.

Counting on Volunteers

Short of funds and with a sketchy organization, the Conservatives, said Mr. Paolucci, were counting on their dedicated core of volunteers" to spread the message of Goldwater conservatism and to help save the country from committing political suicide by drifting into acceptance of dependence on handouts from smiling demagogues in Washington."

One of the dedicated supporters of the Conservatives in Syracuse turned out to be Carl Schultz, an insurance company executive. Mr. Schultz has been promoting the cause of conservatism by distributing books of the American Opinion Library in the Onondaga Hotel in Syracuse.

Letters to the Editor

Conservatives and Keating

To the Herald Tribune:

Your editorial, "Sen. Keating vs. the Opportunists," was extreme in its denunciation of my nomination as the Conservative party candidate for United States Senator.

The Conservative decision to oppose Sen. Keating is premised mainly upon his voting record, which is rated at 88 per cent by the liberal Americans for Democratic Action (compared to a 94 per cent rating for Sen. Humphrey). The Conservative party stood ready to forego its compelling case against Sen. Keating if the New York Republican leaders would have permitted their Presidential electors to accept Conservative endorsement, in the same manner in which the Democratic Presidential candidate always runs on both the Democratic and Liberal lines.

If, as they profess, they sought to further the Goldwater cause, New York's Republican leaders would have found the Conservative party ready and willing to co-operate constructively.

The refusal of the New York Republican state leadership to allow Sen Goldwater to run on two lines calls into question their professed support of the national ticket. Their ardent endorsement of Sen. Keating, the only Republican Senatorial candidate in the nation who refuses to support that ticket, reinforces the doubt.

HENRY PAOLUCCI,
Conservative party candidate for the United States Senate.
New York

New York Herald Tribune
September 9, 1964

THE NEW YORK TIMES, MONDAY, NOVEMBER

#	Office	A Republican	B Democratic	C Liberal	D Conservative	E Socialist Labor	F Socialist Worker
1	ELECTORS OF PRESIDENT AND VICE-PRESIDENT — Vote once	Barry M. Goldwater / William E. Miller	Lyndon B. Johnson / Hubert H. Humphrey	Lyndon B. Johnson / Hubert H. Humphrey	Henry Paolucci	Eric Hass / Henning A. Blomen	Clifton DeBerry / Edward Shaw
2	UNITED STATES SENATOR — Vote for one	Kenneth B. Keating	Robert F. Kennedy	Robert F. Kennedy	Kenneth J. Mullane	John Emanuel	Richard Garza
3	JUSTICES OF THE SUPREME COURT 1st JUDICIAL DISTRICT — Vote for five	Abraham D. Levy	Charles G. Tierney	Edward R. Dudley	Constantine G. Cannoliori		
4		Nicholas Tsoucalas	Edward R. Dudley	George Starke	James S. Phair		
5		George Starke	Darwin W. Telesford	Max Bloom	John G. Keenan		
6		Samuel M. Gold	Samuel M. Gold	Samuel M. Gold	Belle V. Dodd		
7		Matthew M. Levy	Matthew M. Levy	Matthew M. Levy			
8	JUDGES OF THE CIVIL COURT OF THE CITY OF NEW YORK — Vote for three	Frank Gioell	Joseph R. Marro	Joseph R. Marro			
9		Harold Baer	Harold Baer	Harold Baer			
10		Harry B. Frank	Harry B. Frank	Harry B. Frank			
11	REPRESENTATIVE IN CONGRESS 17th DISTRICT — Vote for one	John V. Lindsay	Eleanor Clark French	Eleanor Clark French	Kieran O'Doherty		
12	STATE SENATOR 24th DISTRICT — Vote for one	William F. Larkin	Paul P. Rooban	Leon Becker			
13	MEMBER OF ASSEMBLY 6th DISTRICT — Vote for one	Paul J. Curran	C. Joseph Hallinan, Jr.	Bernard Sack			

TER'S CHOICE: This is how voting machines in New York State will look tomorrow. Candidates, other than those for President and Vice President, vary according to judicial, Assembly and other divisions—list is for 1st Judicial District, 17th Congressional District and 6th Assembly District.

TIMES 11/4/64 Associated Press

TWO FOR THE CONSERVATIVES: Dr. Henry Paolucci, Conservative party candidate for the Senate in New York, with Mrs. Paolucci at polling place in the city.

Canvass Shows Conservatives Rivaled Liberals in City Vote

By EARL MAZO

An official canvass of the New York City vote, certified yesterday by the Board of Elections, showed the two-year-old Conservative party had polled as well in major contests on Nov. 3 as the Liberal party, which was founded 20 years ago.

The formal tally also disclosed that the total vote cast for President Johnson and Senator Barry Goldwater in the five boroughs was 97,058 below that of the Kennedy-Nixon election four years ago, despite a substantial increase in the number of eligible voters since 1960.

The Board of Elections re-

NATIONAL REVIEW

A JOURNAL OF FACT AND OPINION

● The Conservative Party of New York, even though Gov. Rockefeller had denied it the right to endorse Goldwater and Miller, roared out of the election in great shape. Against the wonderful 142,000 votes Mr. David Jaquith got on the gubernatorial line in .1962, it racked up 200,000 votes this year for Prof. Henry Paolucci, running for the Senate against Robert Kennedy and Kenneth Keating. The 200,000 is the more astonishing because each voter had to 1) overcome the temptation to bypass the Conservative Party solely in order to decelerate Kennedy by supporting Keating, and 2) take the trouble to pick off the Paolucci lever pretty far away from home territory on the voting machine. Meanwhile, the entrenched Liberal Party, hoping for 600,000, got only 250,000 votes, even though it had President Johnson at the top of its ticket. It's not beyond possibility that the Conservative vote will some day surpass the Liberal. Even before that day, the Conservative Party will have richly earned the applause of New York conservatives of both parties.

NOVEMBER 17, 1964

Paolucci Gets 4%
of City's Vote

By Ralf Chapman

Of the Herald Tribune Staff

Henry Paolucci, Conservative candidate for the U.C. Senate, never had a chance to win but, with 80 per cent of yesterday's ballots tabulated, his total was 160,000, a new high for the party.

Polls had predicted that he would get 4 per cent of the New York City vote and they proved to be almost exactly right. Upstate his support was somewhat less.

He had said during the campaign that he did not expect to win unless Sen. Goldwater carried the state. He conceded defeat one hour and 10 minutes after the polls closed at 9 p. m.

"My candidacy will have served, I think, to encourage more and more conservative-minded persons from every walk of life . . . to come forward as candidates; and they will . . . revitalize American politics, driving the political opportunists and hacks from the field."

Kieran O'Doherty, one of the founders of the party and its candidate for Congress from the East Side 17th District, was even more confident of the party's future when he conceded.

"The Conservative party has made definite inroads in Republican liberalism in this area and will give the Rockefeller-Javits-Lindsay bloc good reason to reconsider their tactics of turning their backs on Republicans to woo Democratic liberals," he said.

The two-year-old Conservative party has sought to become to the Republicans what the Liberal party is to the Democrats—the potential balance of power in an election.

But there's a difference. Most of the Conservative votes have come at the expense of the Republicans; the Liberal votes usually go to the aid of the Democrats.

And for that reason, the Democrats court the Liberals, while the Republicans have ignored the Conservatives.

The Liberals, for example, shared Presidential electors in yesterday's voting, insuring that President Johnson would get the combined Democratic-Liberal vote, plus two lines on the ballot. Republican leaders turned down a similar proposition from the Conservatives, who were anxious to help Sen Goldwater.

MRS. LUCE

The Conservatives, who had turned cool toward Son Keating because of his "increasingly liberal" voting record, retaliated with the word that Mrs. Clare Boothe Luce former Ambassador to Italy and wife of Henry Luce, of Time, Inc, would be their candidate to oppose Mr. Keating.

There was speculation that Mrs. Luce's candidasy might

share its electors.

As a result, the Conservatives, most of whom came to Saratoga expecting to nominate Clare Boothe Luce for the Senate, left for home without Sen. Goldwater on their ticket and with a Senatorial candidate few of them know much about.

Mrs. Luce withdrew her name from consideration for the nomination Sunday in order, she said, to help unify the Republican campaign for Mr. Goldwater in New York. She had said she might run against Mr. Keating because of his refusal to support Mr. Goldwater. The Conservative leadership decision to run a candidate against Mr. Keating and the Democratic Senatorial candidate, was also based on opposition to Mr. Keating's non-support of the Goldwater ticket.

UNANIMOUS

Mr. Paolucci lives with his wife, the former Anne Attura, a professor of English Literature at CCNY, at 600 W. 111th St. in Manhattan.

The candidate is short, swarthy, has close cropped black hair, and speaks in the professorial tones of the classroom. He has contributed numerous articles to the National Review, a Conservative weekly magazine, and has edited and translated works of Hegal, Machiavelli and Galileo. He said he was a registered Democrat several years ago, but quit that party when he found he disagreed with its positions on most issues.

Mr. Paolucci's nomination was made unanimous after he received 266 of the 304 delegate votes cast. Donald H. Serrell, a Garden City, L. I. attorney, received 32 votes, and Joseph Joyce, Conservative candidate for Congress in the Bronx, received six.

Mr. Paolucci's Senate nomination makes it necessary for him to withdraw his candidacy for Congress on the Upper West Side, where he was opposing Rep. William Fitts Ryan.

Mr. Jaquith drew rousing cheers from the conventioneers when, in his keynote speech, referring to Sen. Keating's refusal to support Mr. Goldwater, he said, "If this is good Republicanism, we might just as well have a Democrat."

PAOLUCCI UNABLE TO ACT LIKE LOSER

Conservative Says He Hasn't 'Sad Bone in Body'

Times 11/4/64

By RAYMOND DANIELL

"Look sad," ordered a photographer of Henry Paolucci last night as returns on a television screen showed that he and Senator Barry Goldwater had been buried under an avalanche of Democratic votes.

The Conservative party Senatorial candidate, who is associate professor of history and political science at Iona College in New Rochelle, and who dabbles in music and the theater, refused even in defeat to put on an act.

"If you want a grin," he said, "I'll give you one, but I haven't a sad bone in my body. You're a conspirator trying to influence public opinion."

Earlier, another photographer had asked him to pose in front of a blackboard showing the results. Dr. Paolucci beckoned him into the office at 141 East 44th Street, from which Daniel Mahoney, state chairman of the party, directed his campaign. The candidate pointed at a television set and said: "That's our bulletin board, and it cost almost as much as my campaign."

"Take out a handkerchief and mop your eyes," demanded the photographer. "You lost, didn't you?"

In the three-room suite of offices that serves as the Conservative party's headquarters, about a dozen persons had been watching the tidal wave of Democratic votes sweep away their hopes for a Republican victory in the nation.

At 9 P.M. Dr. Paolucci and his wife arrived at the offices just in time to hear the first New York State returns. Soon afterward, the little group had the only chance of the evening to applaud: A projection showed that Dr. Paolucci appeared to have won 3 per cent of the vote against Robert F. Kennedy and Senator Kenneth B. Keating. Later figures showed he got about 2.4 per cent.

The scholarly candidate, who conducted much of his campaign as though he were lecturing a college class, had never expected even to come near winning. But at 10:10 P.M. he conformed with one political tradition—that of a beaten candidate—by conceding.

He had prepared a formal statement and had had it typed. While he was waiting for Mr. Mahoney to approve it, Dr. Paolucci said he had no plans for a vacation.

Philosophical as usual, he said he found satisfaction in bolstering the cause of conservatism by providing the voters with a choice to what he terms the liberal-dominated Republican and Democratic parties. That, he explained, was his only motive.

"Because of defections of liberal Republicans to the Democratic slate," he said, "the vote for Goldwater must be taken as the hard core of conservatism in the Republican party."

In his formal statement, Dr. Paolucci said that the important question was whether the "total vote for Goldwater represents a rise or a decline for political conservatism." He concluded that the results definitely showed a rise, and he modestly claimed some credit.

"My candidacy," he said, "particularly will have served, I think, to encourage more and more conservative - minded persons from every walk of life—doctors, dentists, teachers like myself, scientists, accountants farmers, journalists, businessmen as well as lawyers to come forward as candidates.

New York

Journal American

Forgotten Man ... Not Paolucci

By JAMES L. KILGALLEN

He doesn't regard himself as "the forgotten man" in the race for the U.S. Senate.

So says Henry Paolucci, the Conservative Party candidate, who is opposing Robert F. Kennedy (Dem.) and Sen. Kenneth B. Keating (Rep.) in the hectic New York state campaign.

"I'm running a frank, honest campaign," Dr. Paolucci declared in an interview at his home, 600 W 111th st., Upper Manhattan.

"I dont kiss any babies. I don't go around shaking hands with strangers. I don't have loud speakers blaring my arrival at places where I am to speak. I talk seriously with serious people.

"My objective is to give voice on a senatorial level to Goldwater conservatism."

SCHOLARLY CANDIDATE

Dr. Paolucci, 43, is a scholary candidate. A native of New York City, he is an associate professor of history and political science at Iona College in New Rochelle. He holds the degrees of B.S. M.A., and Ph.D.

Discussing his unique way of campaigning, he said:

"I'm not slighting the unpleasant issues, such as street riots, inflationary costs of Federal welfare program, experimentation with our children and the continuing menace of Communist international imperialism."

He added: "I'm not going to flatter ethnic groups. But that is not to say I'm not proud of my Ialian-American status."

Dr. Paolucci, who is running for public office for the first time, is a second-generation Italian-American, born Feb. 4, 1921, in 152nd st. near Cortland ave, the Bronx.

He recently made a four-day tour of northwest New York, visiting Utica, Rome, Syracuse, Geneseo, Rochester and Buffalo. He also makes TV and radio appearances.

"I only go to places where am invited," Dr. Paolucci said. "Rallies and fund-raising dinners are arranged, at which never less than 500 or 600 persons attend.

"We also have many coffee hour meetings in homes of dedicated conservatives. Affairs usually draw 70 persons.

"I'm fighting for a cause—conservatism. With Tweedledee Kennedy and Tweedledum Keating appealing for anti-Goldwater votes, my candidacy is necessary."

Refuting the idea that he is "the forgotten man" in the Senatorial race, he asserted:

"I was unknown. But I'm becoming better known every day."

Journal-American, October 16.1964.

THE KNICKERBOCKER NEWS

No. 28–Vol. 59   Albany. N. Y.   Wednesday, September 9. 1964   Price Ten Cents

At the Theater

Candidate Turns Composer

By EDWARD SWIETNICKI

THE Conservative Party candidate for U. S. senator from New York is winning himself some votes this week as a star of sorts at the Spa Music Theater.

Theater officials are staging Luigi Pirandello's comedy "Liola" and Prof. Henry Paolucci is composer of the music for the unique presentation of this sprightly Boccaccio-like tale. "Liola" never before has been performed in America and Raymond Rizzo, Spa producer, plans on taking his "American premier presentation" offBroadway this fall. That's why history is also being made this week at the Spa Music Theater.

Mr. Paolucci relaxed last night from the political campaign trail (his opponents for the U. S. Senate post are Democrat Robert F. Kennedy and the Republican incumbent Kenneth Keating) to watch the Spa's opening night American premiere of "Liola" and listen to the music he composed to highlight the three-act play.

He looked pleased. At the end Mr. Paolucci said, "With a little more work here and there and with some more songs we'll be ready (for off-Broadway)."

What is "Liola" all about? Why is it worth a visit to the Spa Music Theater this week to share in something radically off the beaten path?

The play's Italian playwright is fascinated by the stage and its illusions of reality and make-believe. His serious play "Six Characters in Search of an Author" is a minor classic. George Bernard Shaw called Pirandello the most original playwright of the century.

Pirandello uses 'Liola" to continue his fascination with reality and illusion. This is the story: Uncle Simone. a Sicilian landowner, is old and unhappy because his young wife has not produced any children for him. At the same time, his niece Tuzza is unhappy because she has let the Village Romeo. Liola, have his way. She is pregnant. Tuzza and her mother put their heads together. They tell Simone he is the father of the child. Simone is very happy. Now he can tell everyone in the village that he. Simone. is the father of a child. What does it matter if it is not so? So long as everyone believes so.

But Simone's young wife is now unhappy, Liola, too, becomes indignant. So Liola and the young wife come together. Liola naturally suggests a rather obvious way for the young

wife to solve the whole problem. Mina, the young wife consents. She soon gives Simone the happy news that she is pregnant with Simone's child. If Simone knows he is not the father of this child, too, what does it matter? He feels he is. Everyone pretends he is and "justice" triumphs in a humorous sort of way for all concerned.

Pirandello's jewel-like lines sparkle and glitter. Examples: "Home is where the children are." "The hen that runs about comes home good and stout." and If a grape is too high, leave it and don't say it is too sour.

Mr. Paolucci's "Liola's Song" is excellent and there is a curt rhythm to his background for the scene of women gossiping as they shell almonds. A lilting tarantella in the concluding act and a gay snatch of song from several children's dance scenes recur. Some of the songs, however are not fully developed.

Liola" is not for everyone. There is a roughness to the production and; some may find it hard to enjoy the comed because of its indelicate theme.

Producer Tony Rizzo. however, is aware of all this and is asking audience members to share in the problems of a "preview" presentation with written comment about the play.

Last night's audience reaction was mostly enthusiastic One spectator wrote: . . . You should be complimented for trying something new . . . Another onlooker, however wrote: "With all due respect to the cast—Ugh!"

SPA MUSIC THEATRE

LIOLA

SPA MUSIC THEATRE

RAYMOND RIZZO

presents

LIOLA

By

LUIGI PIRANDELLO

Translation by   *Music by*

ERIC BENTLEY   HENRY PAOLUCCI

with

PAUL ANTONY   EARL HENRY   CAROLYN CHRISMAN

and

| Anna Pugliese | Lena Spencer | Carol Trigg | Paula Leake | Anne Bishop |

Directed by   *Musical Director*

RAYMOND RIZZO   ALLAN LEWIS

Settings by   *Costumes*   *Lighting by*

HOLLY HAAS   JO IPPOLITO   THOMAS MUNN

THE ENTIRE PRODUCTION UNDER THE PERSONAL SUPERVISION OF MR. RIZZO

She Wears Campaign Well

Mrs. Henry Paolucci
. . . the magic word is organization

By KAY FISH

How does the wife of a contender for the U.S. Senate from New York manage a full-time career and campaigning?

"The magic word is organization," replied Anne Paolucci, the attractive and genial wife of Dr. Henry Paolucci, Conservative candidate, who with his wife spent a typical whirl-wind day campaigning in Rochester yesterday.

Mrs. Paolucci was interviewed at the Sheraton Hotel.

She is an articulate person, easy to talk to, and one who seems to exude a sincere, quiet friendliness.

"I enjoy the exhilaration of meeting people and the exchange of ideas. We've met so many nice people, calm people, concerned people," she said of her few weeks in the political spotlight.

✽   ✽   ✽

FOR MRS. PAOLUCCI, as well as her husband, those days on the political circuit must be shared with days facing students in a college classroom. Dr. Paolucci is professor of history and political science at Iona College in New Rochelle.

His wife, who received her doctorate at Columbia University, is a teacher of Shakespeare at City College in New York. She also is a poet and author of several articles, some on Greek and Italian drama.

In commemoration of the 400th anniversary of Shakespeare, she has edited a paperback entitled "Shakespeare Encomium" that will appear on bookstands next week. The latter word in the title, she explained, means "in praise of." The booklet contains her own essay, as well as those of students and other faculty members.

She shares, with her husband, a great many academic interests. We read many books. "Our four-room apartment in 111th Street, New York City, is bursting at the seams with books."

They also translate books. And summers, in recent ears, they have combined their talents and efforts in

music and drama by participating in producing presentations at the Spa Music Theater in Saratoga Springs.

*   *   *

THE PAOLUCCIS met at Columbia University and were
    married in 1949 at St. Martin of Tours Church in the
Bronx, across the street from the home in which Anne
grew up. Both were the children of Italian immigrants.
Both studied in this country on Fulbright scholarshhips.

    Mrs. Paolucci's father, the late Joseph Attura, served
as an American volunteer in France in World War I in the
same division. with. Archibald Roosevelt (Teddy Roosevelt's son). Her father died when she was 4½ from the
effects of gas poisoning contacted in the war. Her mother
then returned to Italy with the family. They came back to
the states when Anne was eight. Mrs. Attura still lives in
the Bronx her daughter said.

    Mrs. Paolucci has accompanied her husband on all of
his campaign tours to date. Last evening, they attended a
rally in this city, following an appearance at St. John
Fisher College.

    Today, they are back in their respective classrooms.

6. PRESERVING THE LEGACY

Goldwater's defeat in 1964 was a blow to conservatism nationally, but the Conservative Party of New York State came out of that campaign with a sense of accomplishment, encouraged by the unexpectedly large vote for their U.S. senatorial candidate, who led the ticket. With minimum funds at his disposal, Paolucci had managed to draw almost twice as many votes as the Party had attained in 1962, had gained new followers with every appearance, and had inspired fellow conservatives with high hopes for the future.

Immediately following the election, he joined the other leaders in the Party in denouncing Representative John V. Lindsay, a liberal Republican, part of the Rockefeller-Javits axis, who was entering the 1965 New York City mayoralty race. Their efforts against Lindsay intensified when Bill Buckley entered the race as the Conservative Party candidate. Henry put all his campaign talents to work for Buckley, helping to bring in 13.4% of the vote for the Conservative Party's illustrious candidate. Lindsay defeated the city Comptroller, Democrat Abraham D. Beame, and went on for two more terms. Beame won the election in 1973. Bill Buckley never tried again for public office; but as the leading spokesman for conservatism, he added to the intense response the Party had received in 1964 and helped prepare the way for Jim Buckley's more than a million votes solely on the Conservative line, in his first bid for the U.S Senate in 1968.

In a letter written to Henry a few weeks after the 1968 election, Jim Buckley thanked him for his backing. "Without the kind of moral and financial support which you have given," he wrote, "the tremendous victory achieved by the Conservative Party this year would not have been possible."

And it was a victory. . . . One out of six New York voters, more than 1,100, 000 of them, voted Conservative. . . . This massive endorsement of conservative principles will not be lost on professional politicians in this State or in Washington. Every major network and newspaper has conceded that the Conservative Party has now consolidated a position of tremendous importance.

Losing a major election with such a spectacular showing, the Conservative Party gained new stature in the political arena; and in 1970, Jim Buckley made a second bid for the Senate seat. The incumbent, Charles E. Goodell, had been appointed by Governor Nelson Rockefeller in 1968 to fill the vacancy caused by the death of Bobby Kennedy. In 1970 he ran for his first full term. His Democratic opponent was Richard Ottinger.

The Goodell people ran an ad shortly before election day — a voice over graphics — assuring New York voters that they had a real choice in that year's senatorial race:

> Congressman Richard Ottinger, the Democratic candidate, who has sponsored two pieces of legislation in six years in the House. Republican Senator Charles Goodell, who has sponsored forty-four major pieces of legislation in twenty-two months in the Senate. Conservative nominee, James L. Buckley, who has an economic plan for the nineteenth century. Those are your choices on election day: the light weight, the heavy weight, and the dead weight.

The "dead weight" won.

Henry basked in the victory, proud of his Party and what it had been able to do. As a Vice Chairman, he was now much in demand for advice, talks, consultation, and often called upon by county leaders to settle in-house disputes. Party members who had never heard of him before 1964 were now enthusiastic followers.

The political life energized him. He never refused the demands made on him by his fellow conservatives; he was always there if they needed him, ready to listen, willing to take time to resolve what to some may have seemed like petty disputes.

Serious differences arose as well. Henry took the lead in supporting the Democratic contender for the New York mayoralty in 1973, against the Party founders, and convinced the five county leaders to endorse Representative Mario Biaggi. In 1974, Dan Mahoney and Kieran O'Doherty were once again faced with a difficult situation — a "possibly fatal setback" as the *Times* reported it — when Henry, together with a large number of Party members, refused to endorse Governor Malcolm Wilson for his first full term. In 1958, Wilson had been instrumental in getting Nelson Rockefeller, at the time a political novice, elected Governor of New York. Wilson himself was elected Lieutenant Governor, a position he retained for the next fifteen years. He became Governor when Rockefeller resigned in 1973. His background as part of the Rockefeller team for over a decade made many Conservatives uneasy, in spite of his describing himself as an "an economic conservative" and, as a Roman Catholic, an adamant opponent of legalized abortion.

A majority of the Conservative state committee voted to endorse Wilson. But others had chosen to support a conservative from upstate New York, David Bullard. Having received 40% of the state committee's votes, Bullard's name would automatically appear on the primary ballot, unless he removed it by a certain date. Confronted by what many conservatives saw as peremptory decision-making at the very top, Henry allowed his own name to be placed with Bullard's on the primary ballot as Lieutenant Governor. "All of which," the *Times* wrote, "makes some Conservatives suspect that Professor Paolucci would like to be the party leader."

Nothing could have been further from Henry's mind. He had no intention of taking over the Party leadership. His role was to do precisely what he had done on many occasions in the past: remind the leadership that there were many voices within the Party and that a strategic and more democratic approach in reaching decisions was essential for Party unity and harmony. It was Henry in fact who eventually convinced David Bullard to withdraw his name, as he himself had done, and thus avoid a battle in the primaries.

In spite of this continuing political activity and a sabbatical which he used to accept an invitation from the Chinese Information Service to visit Taiwan (a trip which he extended to include the Middle East), he never compromised on what was his top priority, his major role, what superseded all else: his life as a teacher. The classroom was his true forum; students, his ideal audience.

His primary goal had not changed. His task still was to open up the world of knowledge for the young people who registered for his courses, to train them to use their mental faculties correctly, instilling in them a desire to protect those values that had made our nation great. Of paramount importance was approaching a subject through its historical development, avoiding the misleading contemporary attraction to preach the fads and abstract notions of the day. In citing authors from a wide variety of sources, he also made his students culturally literate.

His main subjects came to rest in the history of political thought, where current events were interpreted as part of a continuity that instilled a respect for all that came before. Indirectly, he trained potential law students in the power of logic and educated those who planned to enter government service in the strategic control of power. In his own ease of expression, no matter how controversial or difficult the subject, he also provided his students with a model rhetoric for dealing with opposing views. He urged respect for what they disagreed with, as well as the need to master the arguments of the opposition in order to deal with them accurately and effectively.

In the late 60s and early 70s, he assumed a major role in the practical business of replacing the Ph.D. in the Department of Government and Politics as St. John's with a Doctor of Arts — a practical move that created an inter-departmental degree that included courses in history, sociology, and psychology. New courses were also designed, especially in subjects that attracted pre-law students.

Researching new subjects and writing continued to occupy him outside the classroom, but he also found time to play the piano, compose songs and lyrics, and write hundreds of pages of fiction. He found time also for colleagues who came to him for help in writing their articles and books. He would read carefully, offer detailed suggestions, make corrections, often rewrote entire passages to make a point more effectively. If one questioned him about the wisdom of using his precious time to correct the work of others, he dismissed such a remark by saying that in doing so he learned things he would otherwise never have come to know. Somehow, in this busy world of his, he also found time to indulge his own intellectual curiosity, leaving behind hundreds of notes on cards and scraps of paper.

In the midst of old and new obligations, he continued to produce *State of the Nation* every month, and spent hours on articles for *Review of National Literatures,* the major publication of Council on National Literatures, for which he had been asked to serve as Chief Researcher and Featured Contributor.

In March 1980, he accepted an invitation from the

United States Information Agency to represent the U.S. at a conference in Rome. The other American participant was Nathan Glazer.

In 1988 St. John's had honored him with their Outstanding Faculty Achievement Award. In 1992, the Board of Trustees honored him with the title of Professor Emeritus.

It was the year of the Columbus quincentennial.

Henry had been at work since 1986 assembling new material to mark the 500th anniversary of Europe's entry into the "New World." It was a difficult time, when many, including professors who should have known better than to use the podium as a soapbox, threatened to destroy the celebration, undermining its historical importance. In all the turmoil of those days, Henry upheld the premise that the realities of conquest cannot and should not be judged with the empty rhetoric and unrealistic standards of both the naive idealist and partisan minorities provoked into resurrecting old grievances long-since settled. Henry's rich contribution to the Columbus archives was a reminder that history should be studied objectively, events of the past interpreted within the parameters of standards and beliefs of the time, not judged according to current arbitrary or personal ideologies.

In 1991 he wrote the musical score for *Cipango!*, a videoplay about the ironies of the Columbus story. The video was picked up by commercial distributors in New York and Texas and was chosen as an official project of the Christopher Columbus Quincentennial Jubilee Commission set up by President Reagan.

In 1992, the first of four volumes he prepared for the quincentennial — *Columbus, America, and the World* — appeared as part of CNL's major annual series, *Review of National Literatures*. Carefully assembled, the *Columbus* issue contained scholarly and controversial articles, as well as unusual comparisons — among the most striking:

> (John Gillespie) "Paul Claudel's *Christopher Columbus* and Japanese Noh Plays";
> (O. Carlos Stoetzer) "The Myth of Discovery: Edmundo O'Gorman's Perspective";
> (Dino Bigongiari) "Dante's Ulysses and Columbus."
> (Frank D. Grande and Henry Paolucci) "American Foundations of Columbus Scholarship."

He co-authored the introductory essay, "Columbus and the Idea of America," where he deals with many of the doubts that still surface about Columbus and the discovery. He quotes an eminent scholar on the "precursors" of Columbus — not only claims by the Scandinavians and the Irish, but other

> vigorously defended claims by the Dutch, Chinese, Polynesians, Phoenicians, Romans, Arabs, Turks, Hindoos, Basques, Welch, French, Polish, Germans, Japanese, and Portuguese. . . .So many that the question is less "Who discovered America?" than "Who didn't?"

He cites an ancient Roman, who speculated about what might lie beyond the vast oceans.

> And, as any book that deals even superficially with the discovery of America is apt to remind us, it was the Roman playwright Seneca — a native of Spain (d. 65 A.D.) — who included in his tragedy *Medea* the prophetic lines:
>
> > *There will come a time, after many years have lapsed,*
> > *Cycles of time when Ocean will loosen the chain of things*
> > *And a vast land will be revealed,*
> > *And Tiphys shall explore new worlds,*
> > *Nor shall Thule remain ultimate on earth.*

Conjectures abound. What is indisputable however is that Columbus was the first to set foot on this huge land mass and write home about it. His letter to Queen Isabella, announcing the "discovery," is (as one historian reminds us) the first document of American history.

In dismissing the claims of Italian-Americans, that the twelfth day of October is their special holiday, he reminds everyone that history demands a different reading and that the date should be celebrated as a national or, more accurately, a continental holiday, not an ethnic one.

> In the United States, a general consensus has emerged that the 12th day of the 10th month of each year is to be marked on the calendar as a distinctively Italian-American celebration. For the quincentenary celebration that consensus must be at least temporarily set aside, and the Italian-Americans must themselves take on the lead in stressing the global significance of the day.
>
> It belongs, first of all, to the Americas as a whole, extending from the northernmost tip of the North American continent — where

it almost touches the eastern extreme of the vast European/Asian landmass — down to the southernmost reaches of Tierra del Fuego, beyond the famous Strait of Magellan.

He parallels the first journey of Columbus to that of the American astronauts to the moon, but reminds his readers that the advanced technology for the moon landing had been developed over many years. The trajectory was known and mapped; the outcome predictable. He explained that unlike the carefully monitored journey of the astronauts, Columbus faced an unchartered ocean, nothing to go by except his skills as a navigator and his courage in facing a journey that even the most experienced sailors of the day, the Portuguese, did not dare attempt.

He contributed to the quincentenary also in CNL's second annual series, *CNL World Report*, with articles in *Selected Papers on Columbus and His Time*, and *Modern Views on Columbus and His Time.*

His major project in this area was motivated by the quincentenary but took several years of research and writing to accomplish. It involved extensive study of the massive work of Justin Winsor, the first librarian of Harvard University and co-founder of the American Historical Association, whose eight thick volumes, *Narrative and Critical History of America* were published between 1884 and 1889. In it, Winsor brought together articles by the leading scholars of the time and covered every aspect of America's early development. In his book *The European Discovery of America,* S. E. Morison, who wrote extensively on the many voyages of Columbus into the North Atlantic and the Mediterranean, as well as his exploratory voyages into the southern waters of the Atlantic, referred to Winsor's series as "an irreplaceable work," his own books merely a "supplement" to Winsor's.

It was Morison's praise that led Henry to Winsor. Ignoring the hostility and criticism that challenged all efforts to commemorate the anniversary, including the activities projected by the national commission set up by President Reagan, Henry spent that time and the several years that followed extracting from Winsor's volumes passages about the native populations and early explorations and arranging these for easy access into three volumes for the CNL series, *Review of National Literatures.* He titled the volumes:

Native American Antiquities and Linguistics (1995),
Cultures of the Aztecs, Mayas, and Incas (1996),
Early Spanish, French, and English Encounters with the
  American Indians (1997).

The project, completed two years before his death, is further testimony to Henry's scrupulous commitment as a scholar and historian to preserve materials on the origins of the nations that emerged from the European "discoveries," nations that rose to assert their own distinct identities and cultures within Indo-Spanish America, Portuguese America (Brazil), English America (the United States), and Anglo-French America (Canada).

His basic premise throughout was that history cannot be rewritten to suit personal beliefs or current social, religious, and political views. For him, it must always be a continuum that preserves the past, a legacy to be respected and preserved, for it has shaped in one way or another all subsequent generations.

The four volumes were distributed, as they came out, to over six hundred libraries in the United States, Canada and other countries of the world, as part of the arrangement that had been worked out with CNL some years earlier.

In 2004, the annual Henry Paolucci /Walter Bagehot Book Award was established in Henry's memory at the Intercollegiate Studies Institute, located in Wilmington, Delaware. Although the award guidelines, in accordance with Henry's primary interest in foreign policy and the nation-state system, favor submissions in those areas, other subjects — law, the Constitution, and subjects in the humanities — are not excluded, especially if they have been ignored in the past. The first book award in 2004 was *Prosperity and Plunder: European Catholic Monasteries in the Age of Revolution, 1650-1815* — a unique historical account of how the European monasteries of that period fared, a book chosen from over a hundred submissions. The author was Professor Derek Beales of Cambridge University; the publisher, Cambridge University Press. The 2011 Award went to Professor Pauline Maier (William R. Kenan Jr. Professor of American History at MIT) for her excellent study of a little known period in our history: *Ratification, The People Debate the Constitution, 1787-1788.* In between, the Award has gone to books in a variety of different areas, books that are unique or tackle a subject in an unusual way, or take on an important controversial topic with discretion and historical precision. The list includes:

The Renaissance Perfected: Architecture, Spectacle and Tourism in Fascist Italy by O. Medina Lasansky (2005);

Executive Secrets: Covert Action and the Presidency by William J. Dougherty (2006);

A History of the English-Speaking People Since 1902 by Andrew Roberts (2007);

A Secular Age by Charles Taylor (2008);

Last Judicial Duty, Philip Hamburger (2009);

Advice to War Presidents by Angelo M. Codevilla (2010).

Ironic coincidence: Henry's files recently turned up a copy of a letter dated August 18, 1972 written by William Y. Elliott (Kissinger's former mentor at Harvard) to Kenneth Cribb, Jr., when Mr. Cribb was Eastern-Southern Director of ISI activities, explaining an emergency that made it impossible for him to speak at ISI. He suggests two other names: Vladimir Relsky Dubnic, a Woodrow Wilson Professor at the University of Virginia, and Whittle Johnson, also a Woodrow Wilson Professor at the University of Virginia.

And still another professor who might do as well or better, . . . is Professor Henry Paolucci, whose *State of the Nation* newsletter and many published works mark him even higher than the usual professorial level. . . .

One wonders what a meeting between Mr. Cribb and Henry Paolucci might have brought about at that time. . . .

A prominent conservative supporter of ISI is Lew Lehrman, an investment banker, historian, author of several books — two on Abraham Lincoln. In 1982, with Henry's support and encouragement, he ran against Mario Cuomo in the race for governor of the State of New York and lost the race by a narrow margin. In 2005, he established at ISI the American Studies Center, which sponsors Summer Seminars at Princeton University.

ISI has proved to be the ideal place for the Henry Paolucci /Walter Bagehot Book Award. It has also aided in the distribution of books by Henry issued through GHP between 1999 and 2008 and has publicized them on their website.

The following are excerpts from an early unfinished draft by Henry Paolucci for a projected article on the Conservative Party and conservatism generally (ca 1970).

The number of votes cast for me in the senatorial race of 1964 provides an unambiguous measure of the rate of growth of the Conservative movement in this state since the Party was founded in 1962.

Despite the fact that State Republicans leaders refused to share Goldwater electors with us for the express purpose of holding down our vote, Goldwater Conservatives deliberately split their tickets to vote on our line. Compared with the 116,000 votes cast for the Conservative senatorial candidate in 1962, our 212,216 showing in 1964 represents roughly an 86% rise in the state-wide vote.

The vote-buying experts, the puppet-masters of our liberal establishment, who manipulated their demagogic victory by appealing to the meanest hopes and fears of a TV-saturated society, ought to temper their rejoicing long enough to weigh the significance of the conservative rise in New York State. If they are at all alert, they will realize that, so far from representing a repudiation of conservatism, the 1964 national election has served to define, to measure precisely, the unadulterated mounting strength of conservatism.

The Democratic-Liberal victory, gained by the treacherous collaboration of so-called Republicans like Rockefeller, Javits, Keating, Casey, and Kuchel, who have urged their supporters to split their tickets, assures us that every vote registered for Goldwater nationally must count as a genuinely conservative vote, no chaff mixed with the wheat.

The important question is therefore this: Does the total vote for Goldwater represent a rise or a decline for political conservatism?. . . .

It is no coincidence that New York is declining under the stewardship of a governor who doesn't care about his job and who is insensitive to the suffering his policies are inflicting on the middle class, on senior citizens, on all New Yorkers. If we replace Hugh Carey with a governor who cares about New Yorkers, we can once again look forward to living in safety and prosperity.

New York (like many states) bestows its governors with enormous executive powers. Therefore, an activist governor will have an immediate impact on the economy, the criminal justice system, and government waste. A conservative governor with a clear agenda can effect a conservative revolution by the sheer force of his convictions.

The prospects of electing a truly conservative governor fortunately are better than ever. The Conservative Party is privileged to have several worthy candidates seeking its support. These candidates have established records of public service and they are men who will continue to serve the needs of the people of New York.

Foremost among them is Lewis E. Lehrman. Along with establishing a distinguished record of achievement in business and public service, Lew Lehrman has the ingredients it will take to elect him the next governor of New York. As his campaign swings into full gear, the people of this state will clearly see that he has the administrative skills to govern effectively. He will work to implement his conservative solutions to New York's economic and crime problems.

On numerous occasions I have witnessed Lew Lehrman successfully communicate his vision of New York's future in a manner that wins the approval of his audiences. He appears to be more substantive than the average politician. He projects the image of a public servant who wishes to use his God-given talents to improve the conditions of his fellow New Yorkers. And I am pleased to report, this image is the real Lew Lehrman.

[*Lehrman ran against Mario Cuomo in 1982, losing the election by a very narrow margin.*]

Our Party's first aim is to break the hold of Liberals on both major parties by pulling the votes of conservative Republicans away from the liberal Republicans.

But our appeal proved strong with the Democrats, which means we helped to elect not defeat Liberal Republicans like Rockefeller and Lindsay particularly.

But Conservative Republicans saw the advantage: they could get Democratic conservative votes on our line.

We have attained balance of power in the State Assembly.

The only way to beat Liberal Republicans like Lindsay or Rockefeller is to endorse Democrats. That is usually impossible. It almost happened in New York City in 1969, when Procaccino turned us down and split 58% of the vote with John Marchi.

On the gubernatorial level it is never possible.

In 1966, when we won Row C, Democrats lost because of the Liberals and we ran candidates. This year the ideal situation is Jim Buckley *vs* Goodell and Ottinger.

Since 1962, the conservative movement has advanced in strength at a considerable rate, and now that a regrouping of conservative Democrats with conservative Republicans has begun to take place, in northern urban areas as well as in the South, there is bound to be an acceleration forward for our conservative movement.

My candidacy particularly will have served, I think, to encourage more and more conservative-minded persons from every walk of life, to come forward as candidates; and they will, as leaders of the middle classes, of the intermediate groups which stabilize society, revitalize American politics, driving the political opportunists and hacks from the field. I think there will be an end to campaigns like the one waged by Kennedy and Keating in [the 1964] election.

Conservatives must now work actively to reconstitute and strengthen all intermediary groups in our country, between the chief executive and the isolated mass of individuals at the bottom. These include the federal legislature, state governments, labor and industrial organizations, all groups who share the common national purpose, who feel about this country the way the publishers of the *New York Times* feel about their newspaper: very conservatively, I assure you. Here is what James Reston said in his eulogy of Orvil Dryfoos: "They" (referring to Ochs, old Sulzberger, and Dryfoos [Sulzberger's son-in-law])

> saw a newspaper as Edmund Burke saw a nation, not only as a partnership of the living, but as a partnership "between those who are living, those who are dead, and those who are to be born."

Writers like Reston and his publishers at the *New York Times* give their newspaper the kind of allegiance political conservatives believe a nation deserves. For it is the nation that makes possible the existence of the *New York Times* and all other intermediary groups, including the NAACP, the unions, the manufacturers associations, the universities, etc. . . .

There is the danger of this kind of liberal thinking affecting the highest level of government, encouraging the chief executive to put a vise-like squeeze on intermediary groups. When the highest political office joins with the lower classes to level everything in between, a great nation suffers and will eventually collapse, as history has taught us. . . .

Barry Goldwater complained eloquently against the "partisanship of one branch of government, the executive, versus the popular representation of another branch, the legislative." He rightly urges the

> restoration of the balance between executive and legislative powers so that national policy can be truly national, truly bipartisan, truly believable to friend and foe.

Conservatives must also prepare for government. I don't mean vying for office, which is somewhat simpler, but to prepare for governing while out of office as though they were in office. To set up an alternate executive branch of the government dedicated to the formulation of an executive program based on the conservative principles of continued national sovereignty and prepared to realize that program effectively starting from the very day that public decides to transfer executive leadership to a conservative. . . .

Krushchev said in a speech:

> Some gentlemen will now start chattering that Krushchev is threatening someone. No, Krushchev is not threatening but making a realistic prediction. If you fail to understand realities, if you fail to create conditions for agreement on disarmament, that means that there will be an arms race. And any arms race will, in the last analysis, lead to a military showdown. If war starts, many of those who are sitting here will be found missing.

This speech of Krushchev is a far cry from Stevenson's "to save our collective skins." The new weapons that are supposed to make such a vast difference simply mean that now all of us, not just a privileged minority with military skills, can make the old aristocratic choice — for we are all, all equally in danger. As Barry Goldwater replied to those who say that conservatives like himself are war-mongers who talk tough because they are safe on the sidelines:

> The term is absurd. No one is safe on the sidelines today. No one in this audience is safe on the sidelines. There are no sidelines.

There is no escaping the heroic choice today. Krushchev says the Russians have made it: they will not serve. Merely to co-exist with such a people, we in America must not less boldly make the same choice: we will not serve. It is a choice that has nothing to do with weapons, large or small. It is the same kind of choice the Northmen or Norman English sailors had to make confronting the waves of the Atlantic. And sailors long before them have had to make the same choice. At sea, waves can overwhelm a ship like an atomic bomb overwhelms a city. You know the story: it's very ancient. Inexperienced soldiers, called upon by duty to board a ship and proceed to the rescue of a beleaguered contingent, saw the sea churning up in a violent storm and so they cried out: if we dare to sail, we will surely die. Their commander returned them to safety with the words: To sail is necessary, to live is not necessary — *Navigare necesse est, vivere non est necesse.* The Italian trading cities took it up in the late middle ages; the Hanseatic League later took it up, inscribing the words over the port of Lubeck; when the English defeated the Hanseatic League Armada in 1588, they took it up — to sail is necessary, to live is not necessary. And so Britannia ruled the waves. Much of that spirit passed into this country. And it is still here, still here to be picked up and lived by if we wish. Negroes are daily picking it up: though their professed defiance of oppressors, backed by federal troops, has a comic side, the obverse of the tragic.

Fear is not, cannot be a national policy! Fear means that fearless Castro can have his way. Fear means that our allies cannot rely on us. Fear means that the spiritual leaders of Christianity must look to their own defenses as they did in the 6th century, when Roman strength of will had utterly failed. Fear means that we cannot guarantee any kind of order, not at home, not abroad, whensoever we are confronted by fearless men. Fear means an end of the American ideal of the melting-pot, an end to the life we have always said is worth living — which is, let us not forget, precisely the life we can live, howsoever brief it may be, between the moment we cease to be afraid of dying and the moment we die.

What can conservatives do about this crisis in the national will that imperils national survival, that will leave us either ludicrously disarmed in indecision or more a menace to our friends than to our enemies in some wild outburst of meaningless action? We are mortal. Everyone alive 250 years ago is now dead, every one. And everyone alive now will be dead, eventually, with or without nuclear war. Perhaps when death threatens to strike you may run, I may run; but let's not run now, let's not tremble now.

This much is clear to me. Love of country, which is the essence of conservatism, is rising irrepressibly all around us, animating the minds of people, despite thirty years of liberal international domination of our society and its schools. And this love of country is bound, I assure you, to triumph over the cheap demagoguery of our liberal establishment, which in this election gained a last Pyrrhic victory.

☞ *From the Archives*

LIBERA UNIVERSITA' INTERNAZIONALE DEGLI STUDI SOCIALI
(D. P. R. 5 - 5 - 1966, n. 436 e D. P. R. 31 - 5 - 1967, n. 482)

00198 ROMA
Viale Pola. 12
Tel. (06) 84.10.51

Convegno

" UNA SOCIETA' IN TRANSIZIONE: GLI STATI UNITI DAL ___ ..o AD OGGI

Roma, 27, 28 Marzo 1980

iovedì 27 Marzo 1980

ore 9, 30   Saluto del Rettore dell' Università, Prof. Rosario Romeo.

LA DIFFUSIONE DEL POTERE POLITICO

ore 9, 45   Relatore   Henry Paolucci, docente di scienze politiche nella St John University
" Tra la Casa Bianca e il Campidoglio lo spostamento de centro del potere dopo Franklin D Roosevelt"

ore 10 30   Correlatore   Francesco D'Onofrio, ordinario di diritto costituzionale ita liano e comparato nella Facoltà di Scienze politiche dell'Ist tuto Universitario Orientale di Napoli.

Program for Rome conference sponsored by the US Information Agency, March 27-29, 1980, where Henry was invited to speak on : "A Society in Transition. The United States, 1945 to the Present."

Chinese Information Service
An Agency of the Government of the Republic of China
159 Lexington Avenue, New York, N.Y. 10016 • Telephone: (212) 725-4950 • Cable Address: CHINFORMS

May 3, 1974

Prof. Henry Paolucci
Graduate Division
Dept of Government & Politics
St. John's University
Grand Central & Utopia Parkway
Jamaica, N.Y. 11439

Dear Prof. Paolucci:

It gives me great pleasure to extend to you a cordial invitation for you to visit the Republic of China for two weeks at any time convenient to your schedule.

The Government Information Office, our home office in Taipei, will arrange an itinerary according to your wishes. We will provide you with a roundtrip, economy class ticket between New York and Taipei, and take care of your accommodation and local transportation in Taiwan.

If you desire, you can extend the trip to other parts of Asia, or even come back by way of the Middle East and Europe, paying the small difference yourself. Please have your travel agent contact Mr. Raymong Leung of this office to work out the details.

After we met last time, I had been away a good part of April, first on a consultation trip to Taipei and then accompanying Dr. Fredrick Chien, director general of the Government Information Office, on his speaking tour across the United States. He is now back in Taipei and looking forward to meeting you when you arrive.

Please convey my gratitude to your wife for sending me the complete set of Review of National Literatures.

With best wishes,

Sincerely yours,

I-cheng Loh
Minister for Information,
Chinese Embassy,
Washington, D.C., and
Director,
Chinese Information Service

ICL/el

Washington • Suite 552, National Press Building, Washington, D.C. 20004
Los Angeles • 3440 Wilshire Boulevard, Suite 918, Los Angeles, Calif. 90010

**Invitation by the Chinese Information Service
for Henry to visit the Repnblic of China.**

INTERCOLLEGIATE STUDIES INSTITUTE
F. M. KIRBY CAMPUS

To better ensure the continuity of the Intercollegiate Studies Institute and its mission, loyal ISI supporters established the F. M. Kirby Campus as the Institute's national headquarters. The main building was constructed for the Worth family in 1937 and is situated on twenty-three acres in Wilmington, Delaware. It was renovated into a modern, efficient office space in 1995, for which ISI received a Historic Preservation Award in 1997.

Top (left to right): **Jeff Nelson (Executive Vice President, ISI); Dr. Frank D. Grande (President, Griffon House Publications); Professor Derek Beales, Cambridge University (winner of the first Henry Paolucci/Walter Bagehot Book Award, 2004); Dr. Anne Paolucci; Jeff Cain (Vice President, ISI); NYS Senator Serphin R. Maltese.** *Bottom:* **Professor Beales signing his award-winning book.**

INTERCOLLEGIATE STUDIES INSTITUTE

Please join ISI for the 2011

HENRY PAOLUCCI/WALTER BAGEHOT BOOK AWARD

featuring a lecture by award winner

PAULINE MAIER

author of *Ratification* and the William R. Kenan Jr. Professor of
American History, Massachusetts Institute of Technology

Thursday, November 3, 5:30 P.M.
Reception will follow.

University and Whist Club
805 North Broom Street
Wilmington, DE 19806

RSVP at http://Paolucci.isi.org
or by calling Sandy August at (302) 524-6106

ABOUT THE AUTHOR

COMM. ANNE ATTURA PAOLUCCI, PH.D.

Born in Rome, Italy, Anne Paolucci settled with her family in New York at the age of eight. She attended public school in New York City, Barnard College, and Columbia University, where she won the first Woodbridge Honorary Fellowship in the Department of English and Comparative Literature for her Ph.D. dissertation on Dante and Spenser. She spent a year as a Fulbright Scholar at the University of Rome and later returned to Italy for two years as a Fulbright Lecturer in American Drama at the University of Naples. While in Naples, she saw her first full-length play, *The Shot Season*, produced under the auspices of the American Embassy with the participation of NATO actors. The play was later staged in showcase production at the Cubiculo in New York, under the direction of Maurice Edwards and produced by Nicholas John Stathis. During her stay in Naples, she also produced and directed Edward Albee's *The Zoo Story*.

In 1979, Dr. Paolucci was a guest of the Australian National University's Research Centre (Canberra) for several months. She also visited Yugoslavia twice at the invitation of that government and lectured extensively in those countries as well as in Canada, England, Italy, Austria, and the United States. She taught at the City College of New York (CUNY) before joining the faculty of St John's University in New York as its first University Research Professor.

A prolific writer on Renaissance drama, dramatic theory, Hegelian aesthetics, Spenser, Dante, Machiavelli, Pirandello, Albee and the Theater of the Absurd, and classical and Shakespearean tragedy, Dr. Paolucci also translated major works from Italian and French. Her translation of Machiavelli's *Mandragola* has gone through forty printings, and more recently her *Selected Poems of Giacomo Leopardi* was singled out for recognition by the Italian Ministry of Foreign Affairs and was awarded a cash prize.

She wrote what has become the classic work on Albee's early plays, *From Tension to Tonic: The Plays of Edward Albee* (1972). In 2010 she published a second book on Albee—*Edward*

Albee: The Later Plays. In connection with the publication of this study, Dr. Paolucci lectured at The Players. Mr. Albee was in attendance and gave high praise to her work.

Dr. Paolucci also became known for her work on Pirandello's plays and fiction. *Pirandello's Theater: The Recovery of the Modern Stage for Dramatic Art* was published in 1974, and as president of the Pirandello Society of America for seventeen years, she brought the work of the Italian Nobel laureate to the attention of academics and theater people universally.

Dr. Paolucci's awards include an honorary degree from Lehman College (CUNY), the knighthood of "Commendatore" from the Italian Republic, and the national Elena Cornaro Award of the Order Sons of Italy in America (OSIA). In 1986, President Ronald Reagan appointed her to the Council on the Humanities, where she continued to serve under the administration of Presidents George H. W. Bush and Bill Clinton. In 1996, Governor George Pataki chose her to serve on the board of trustees of CUNY, the second largest university system in the United States, and in 1997, Dr. Paolucci was named chairwoman of the board, a position from which she resigned in 1999 to devote all her time to writing and publishing. In 2008 she received the Lifetime Achievement Award and Gold Medal of the New York State Senate as well as recognition by the New York City Council.

As founder and president of the Council on National Literatures (CNL), Dr. Paolucci served as editor of both its prestigious annual *Review of National Literatures* (1970–2001) and *CNL/World Report* (1976–2001). In 2000 she established the CNL/Anne and Henry Paolucci International Conference Center in New York. After that, she published a number of new books by her husband, Dr. Henry Paolucci, as well as reprints of his work. In recent years, she also published three mystery novels, a book of short stories, and her last book, *Henry Paolucci: A Conservative Voice for All Seasons*.

In 2004, Dr. Paolucci set up at the Intercollegiate Studies Institute (ISI) the annual Henry Paolucci/Walter Bagehot Book Award in honor of her husband and the British economist after whom Professor Henry Paolucci named his Walter Bagehot Research Council on National Sovereignty. In addition to her support for ISI's work, she was the major benefactor of Christ the King Regional High School in Middle Village, New York.

Dr. Paolucci passed away on July 15, 2012, after a short illness and a long and illustrious career. She is survived by her niece Azar Attura; her dear friends Dolores Frank Cohen and Barney Cohen, Clara Sarrocco, Constance and Serphin Maltese, and Diego Lodico; her nieces and nephew, Clare Kretzman, Barbara O'Brien, Joan Lovler, and Joseph Attura (children of her deceased brother, George); and Ian and Shannon Robinson, son and daughter-in-law of her late niece Shirin Haidari (daughter of her deceased sister, Sylvia Attura). Dr. Paolucci's husband, Henry, predeceased her in 1999.